MULTICULTURAL EDUCATION SERIES

James A. Banks, Series Editor

(continued)

Unsettling Settler-Colonial Education

THE TRANSFORMATIONAL INDIGENOUS PRAXIS MODEL

Cornel Pewewardy, Anna Lees,
and Robin Zape-tah-hol-ah Minthorn,
EDITORS

FOREWORD BY Tiffany S. Lee

AFTERWORD BY Michael Yellow Bird

TEACHERS COLLEGE PRESS

TEACHERS COLLEGE | COLUMBIA UNIVERSITY

NEW YORK AND LONDON

Published by Teachers College Press,® 1234 Amsterdam Avenue, New York, NY 10027

Copyright © 2022 by Teachers College, Columbia University

Front cover art and design by Ryan Red Corn.

Library of Congress Cataloging-in-Publication Data is available at loc.gov

ISBN 978-0-8077-6680-4 (paper)
ISBN 978-0-8077-6681-1 (hardcover)
ISBN 978-0-8077-8095-4 (ebook)

Printed on acid-free paper
Manufactured in the United States of America

Contents

PART III: HIGHER EDUCATION

PART IV: EDUCATIONAL LEADERSHIP

Series Foreword

Gloria Ladson-Billings (2006) maintains that educators need to rethink the "achievement gap" idea and focus on the structural and systematic factors in schools that impede the academic achievement of Indigenous and minoritized students. This can best be done, she argues, by focusing on the educational debt that the nation owes to marginalized people of color. The nation owes an enormous debt to Indigenous groups because of forced assimilation and deculturalization in boarding schools (Lomawaima, 1994; Spring, 2022) and the erasure of Indigenous cultures, beliefs, and practices that has occurred egregiously throughout U.S. history. The abuses that Indigenous youth experienced at boarding schools in both the United States and Canada were poignantly revealed by the recent uncovering of unmarked graves on the grounds of several of these schools (Austen & Bilefsky, 2021; Blakemore, 2021; Chung, 2021). Indigenous scholar Tsianina Lomawaima (2000) maintains that "the history of American Indian education can be summarized in three words: 'battle for power'" (p. 2). Indigenous groups, throughout their history in the United States, have resisted cultural erasure and tried to educate their youth in ways that would sustain their cultures, languages, and values. This has been an uphill and strenuous battle because the schooling of Native peoples in the United States has often reflected the sentiments of Captain Richard Henry Pratt, an army officer who founded the Carlisle Indian Industrial School in 1879, the first Indian boarding school in the United States. Pratt's quote, "Kill the Indian in him, and save the man," is infamous. Brayboy and Lomawaima (2018) describe the systematic deculturalization that occurred in Indian boarding schools:

> Colonial federal schools devastated Indigenous children and their communities. Long hair was cut, children were scrubbed with kerosene to kill lice, "home clothes" were locked away in trunks, and government-issue uniforms remade Indian bodies and identities. (p. 85)

This engaging, informative, and unique book is a collection of essays by Native American scholars and educators who describe ways that Indigenous cultures, values, perspectives, and knowledge can be reclaimed and institutionalized within schools, colleges, and universities. The authors of these essays are visionaries and transformative educators but are also clear-eyed and realistic. They point out, for example, that Indigenous Tribal groups have varying cultures and values; consequently, it is essential that culturally responsive and culturally sustaining educational strategies reflect the cultural nuances and characteristics of particular groups. The contributors to this book also realize how challenging it will be to incorporate Indigenous knowledge and values into a school curriculum that is dominated by Anglocentric versions of history and knowledge that marginalize and erase the experiences and values of Indigenous peoples. The angry, organized, and sustained attacks that took place in 2021 by mobilized conservative and parent groups against efforts to teach versions of American history that accurately describe institutionalized racism in the United States are an indication of how difficult it is to implement a transformative curriculum in the nation's schools. These attacks on teaching about race in the schools were mobilized by false claims that critical race theory was being taught in the schools (Lòpez et al., 2021; Wallace-Wells, 2021). As Charles M. Blow (2021) points out, this false claim was effective because it evoked fear among white parents.

Cornel Pewewardy (Pewewardy et al., 2018), the lead editor of this book, adapted ideas developed by James A. Banks (1989) and Michael Yellow Bird (1998) to devise the Transformational Indigenous Praxis Model (TIPM) that the contributors to this book have used to frame their conceptual work and practice (see Figure I.1 in the Introduction, p. 4). The four dimensions that comprise the TIPM are adapted from the four curriculum approaches that I developed when working with classroom teachers to help them move their teaching about diverse cultures from low-level curriculum approaches such as "heroes and holidays," which were widespread when I first published this conceptual framework in *Multicultural Leader* in 1988 (Banks, 1988/1989), to transformative and social action approaches, which focus on high-level thinking and student civic engagement. The four curriculum approaches I conceptualized are (Banks, 1989, p. 192):

> Level 1, the *Contributions Approach*, which focuses on heroes, holidays, and discrete cultural elements.
> Level 2, the *Additive Approach*, which consists of content, themes, and perspectives that are added to the curriculum without changing its overall structure.
> Level 3, the *Transformative Approach*, in which the structure of the curriculum is changed to enable students to view concepts, issues, events, and themes from the perspectives of diverse ethnic and cultural groups.
> Level 4, the *Social Action Approach*, in which students make decisions on important issues and take actions to help solve them after they have participated in a decision-making process that includes collecting and analyzing data using the scientific method (Banks et al., 1999).

My conceptualization of the four approaches focuses on curriculum; in Pewewardy's adaptation of the four approaches, which are called "dimensions" in the TIPM, the focus is broadened to deal with holistic school reform.

This book describes innovative principles and guidelines that can be used to transform education for Indigenous students and is a timely and significant contribution to the Multicultural Education Series. The major purpose of the Multicultural Education Series is to provide preservice educators, practicing educators, graduate students, scholars, and policymakers with an interrelated and comprehensive set of books that summarizes and analyzes important research, theory, and practice related to the education of ethnic, racial, cultural, and linguistic groups in the United States and the education of mainstream students about diversity. The dimensions of multicultural education, developed by Banks (2004) and described in the *Handbook of Research on Multicultural Education* and in the *Encyclopedia of Diversity in Education* (Banks, 2012), provide the conceptual framework for the development of the publications in the Series. The dimensions are *content integration*, the *knowledge construction process*, *prejudice reduction*, *equity pedagogy*, and an *empowering institutional culture and social structure*. The books in the Multicultural Education Series provide research, theoretical, and practical knowledge about the behaviors and learning characteristics of students of color (Conchas & Vigil, 2012; Lee, 2007), language minority students (Gándara & Hopkins, 2010; Valdés, 2001; Valdés et al., 2011), low-income students (Cookson, 2013; Gorski, 2018), other minoritized population groups, such as students who speak different varieties of English (Charity Hudley & Mallinson, 2011), and LGBTQ2S youth (Mayo, 2022).

Structural and institutional racism is a significant factor that causes the forced assimilation and deculturation that Indigenous groups experience in the United States. A number of books in the Multicultural Education Series focus on *institutional and structural racism* and ways to reduce it in educational institutions. The significance of these books increased when the national reckoning with racism intensified after George Floyd, a Black man in Minneapolis, was killed by a police officer on May 25, 2020. These books include Özlem Sensoy and Robin DiAngelo (2017), *Is Everyone Really Equal? An Introduction to Key Concepts in Social Justice Education* (2nd ed.); Gary Howard (2016), *We Can't Teach What Do Don't Know: White Teachers, Multiracial Schools* (3rd ed.); Jabari Mahiri (2017), *Deconstructing Race: Multicultural Education Beyond the Color-Bind*; Zeus Leonardo (2013), *Race Frameworks: A Multidimensional Theory of Racism and Education*; and Daniel Solórzano and Lindsay Pérez Huber (2020), *Racial Microaggressions: Using Critical Race Theory in Education to Recognize and Respond to Everyday Racism*.

This is the third book in the Multicultural Education Series that focuses on the education of Native American students—the other two are *"To Remain an Indian": Lessons in Democracy from a Century of Native American Education* by K. Tsianina Lomawaima and Teresa L. McCarty (2006) and *Indian Education for all: Decolonizing Indigenous Education in Public Schools* by John P. Hopkins (2020). These interrelated and reinforcing books provide insightful analyses of the problems of educating Indigenous groups in the United States and describe visionary interventions for school reform.

Incorporating Native values, perspectives, knowledge, and insights into the curricula of the nation's schools, colleges, and universities will not only enhance the academic achievement of Indigenous students but will also enrich the lives and schooling experiences of mainstream students, students from other marginalized groups, and the nation as a whole. Jack Forbes (1973), the eminent Native American scholar, argued that American values such as capitalism, individualism, and little respect for other living beings have resulted in rapid global warming, income inequality, and many other challenges. Forbes maintained that the incorporation of some of the traditional values of Indigenous peoples, such as living in harmony with nature, valuing collectivity, and having a spiritual link with all living creatures, would decrease some of the nation's problems. Writes Forbes (1973), "One of the reasons why the White society is proceeding so rapidly in the direction of its own destruction is that the accumulated wisdom of 20,000 years of living on this land called America has been consciously excluded from schools and colleges" (p. 202). I am pleased to welcome this book to the Multicultural Education Series because the Indigenous voices and perspectives it contains will enrich and enlighten its readers about ways to reform schools, colleges, and universities so that they will become more effective for Native American and all other students.

—James A. Banks

REFERENCES

Austen, I., & Bilefsky, D. (2021, July 30). Hundreds more unmarked graves found at former residential school in Canada. *The New York Times.* https://www.nytimes.com/2021/06/24/world/canada/indigenous-children-graves-saskatchewan-canada.html

Banks, J. A. (1989). Approaches to multicultural curriculum reform. *Trotter Review, 3*(3), Article 5. https://scholarworks.umb.edu/trotter_review/vol3/iss3/5 (Reprinted from *Multicultural Leader, 1*(2), 1–2, 1988)

Banks, J. A. (1989). Integrating the curriculum with ethnic content: Approaches and guidelines. In J. A. Banks & C. A. M. Banks (Eds.), *Multicultural education: Issues and perspectives* (pp. 189–207). Allyn and Bacon.

Banks, J. A. (2004). Multicultural education: Historical development, dimensions, and practice. In J. A. Banks & C. A. M. Banks (Eds.). *Handbook of research on multicultural education* (2nd ed., pp. 3–29). Jossey-Bass.

Banks, J. A. (Ed.). (2009). *The Routledge international companion to multicultural education.* Routledge.

Banks, J. A. (2012). Multicultural education: Dimensions of. In J. A. Banks (Ed.), *Encyclopedia of diversity in education* (Vol. 3, pp. 1538–1547). SAGE Publications.

Banks, J. A., Banks, C. A. M., & Clegg, A. A., Jr. (1999). *Teaching strategies for the social studies: Decision-making and citizen action* (5th ed.). Addison-Wesley.

Blakemore, E. (2021, July 9). A century of trauma at U. S. boarding schools for Native American children. *National Geographic.* https://www.nationalgeographic.com/history/article/a-century-of-trauma-at-boarding-schools-for-native-american-children-in-the-united-states

Blow, C. (2021, Nov. 3). White racial anxiety strikes again. *The New York Times.* https://www.nytimes.com/2021/11/03/opinion/youngkin-virginia-race.html

Brayboy, B. M. J., & Lomawaima, K. T. (2018). Why don't more Indians do better in school? The battle between U. S. schooling & American Indian/Alaska Native education. *Daedalus, 147*(2), 82–94. https://direct.mit.edu/daed/article/147/2/82/27223/Why-Don-t-More-Indians-Do-Better-in-School-The

Charity Hudley, A. H., & Mallinson, C. (2011). *Understanding language variation in U. S. schools.* Teachers College Press.

Chung, C. (2021). Researchers identify dozens of Native students who died at Nebraska school. *The New York Times.* https://www.nytimes.com/2021/11/17/us/native-american-boarding-school-deaths-nebraska.html

Conchas, G. Q., & Vigil, J. D. (2012). *Streetsmart schoolsmart: Urban poverty and the education of adolescent boys.* Teachers College Press.

Cookson, P. W., Jr. (2013). *Class rules: Exposing inequality in American high schools.* Teachers College Press.

Forbes, J. D. (1973). Teaching Native American values and cultures. In J. A. Banks (Ed.), *Teaching ethnic studies: Concepts and strategies* (pp. 200–225). National Council for the Social Studies.

Gándara, P., & Hopkins, M. (Eds.). (2010). *Forbidden language: English language learners and restrictive language policies.* Teachers College Press.

Gorski, P. C. (2018). *Reaching and teaching students in poverty: Strategies for erasing the opportunity gap* (2nd ed.). Teachers College Press.

Hopkins, J. P. (2020). *Indian education for all: Decolonizing Indigenous education.* Teachers College Press.

Howard, G. (2016). *We can't teach what we don't know: White teachers, multiracial schools* (3rd ed.). Teachers College Press.

Ladson-Billings, G. (2006). From the achievement gap to the education debt: Understanding achievement in U. S. schools. *Educational Researcher, 35*(7), 3–12.

Lee, C. D. (2007). *Culture, literacy, and learning: Taking bloom in the midst of the whirlwind.* Teachers College Press.

Leonardo, Z. (2013). *Race frameworks: A multicultural theory of racism and education.* Teachers College Press.

Lomawaima, K. T. (1994). *They called it Prairie Light: The story of Chilocco Indian School.* University of Nebraska Press.

Lomawaima, K. T. (2000).Tribal sovereigns: Reframing research in American Indian education. *Harvard Educational Review, 70*(1), 1–23.

Lomawaima, K. T., & McCarty, T. L. (2006). *"To remain an Indian:" Lessons in democracy from a century of Native American education.* Teachers College Press.

Lòpez, F., Molnar, A., Johnson, R., Patterson, A., Ward, L., & Kumashiro, K. (2021, September). *Understanding the attacks on critical race theory.* School of Education, University of Colorado Boulder, National Policy Center. https://nepc.colorado.edu/sites/default/files/publications/PM%20Lopez%20CRT_0.pdf

Mahiri, J. (2017). *Deconstructing race: Multicultural education beyond the color-bind.* Teachers College Press.

Mayo, C. (2014). *LGBTQ youth and education: Policies and practices.* Teachers College Press.

Pewewardy, C. D., Lees, A., & Clark-Shim, H. (2018). The Transformational Indigenous Praxis Model: Stages for developing critical consciousness in Indigenous education. *Wičazo Ša Review, 33*(1), 38–69. https://doi.org/10.5749/wicazosareview.33.1.0038

Sensoy, O., & DiAngelo, R. (2017). *Is everyone really equal? An introduction to key concepts in social justice education* (2nd ed.). Teachers College Press.

Solórzano, D., & Pérez Huber, L. (2020). *Racial microaggressions: Using critical race theory to respond to everyday racism.* Teachers College Press.

Spring, J. (2022). *Deculturalization and the struggle for equality: A brief history of the education of dominated cultures in the United States* (9th ed.). Routledge.

Valdés, G. (2001). *Learning and not learning English: Latino Students in American schools.* Teachers College Press.

Valdés, G., Capitelli, S., & Alvarez, L. (2011). *Latino children learning English: Steps in the journey.* Teachers College Press.

Wallace-Wells, B. (2021, June 18). How a conservative activist invented the conflict over critical race theory. *The New Yorker.* https://www.newyorker.com/news/annals-of-inquiry/how-a-conservative-activist-invented-the-conflict-over-critical-race-theory

Yellow Bird, M. (1998). *A model of the effects of colonialism.* Office for the Study of Indigenous Social and Cultural Justice. https://www.scribd.com/document/38980647/A-Model-of-the-Effects-of-Colonialism-Dr-Michael-Yellow-Bird

Foreword

Tiffany S. Lee (Diné and Lakota)

I am Dibé Łizhiní (Blacksheep Diné) and born for Naałaní (Lakota). I am from To niłts'ílí (crystal clear water), known as Crystal, New Mexico, on the Navajo Nation. I am also from Pine Ridge, South Dakota. I am a professor and the chair of Native American Studies at the University of New Mexico, the land of the Tiwa. I have recently been engaged with a team on a research project to learn from Indigenous language immersion schools. These schools have been established for 10 years or more, some for more than 30 years. Their students arrive to school primarily speaking English and then are immersed in their Indigenous language in all facets of the school day, from the classroom, to recess, to lunch, and even after-school care.

We immediately felt the passion for language revitalization when we entered the schools and began to talk with school leaders, teachers, families, and students. The Akwesasne Freedom School, one school we collaborate with in the upper Northeast among the Mohawk (the school has given us permission to name them in this foreword), was born out of the struggle to prevent the assimilationist and oppressive western schooling structures from continuing to take hold of Akwesasne community's children. Parents refused to send their children to the domineering state-sponsored schools. Threatened by the school system that they would be jailed if they did not enroll their children in the public schools, the parents stood strong and created their own school, holding classes in their own homes, barns, and other spaces until they could construct a small building.

Forty years later, this school has become a renowned language immersion school and is an excellent illustration of the Transformative Indigenous Praxis Model (TIPM; Pewewardy et al., 2018) because of its impact on the students, families, and community.

The story I share next from the school illuminates TIPM's Dimension 4, *cultural and social justice action*, by centering the Indigenous community's values for relationships, children's gifts, and community consciousness and building. The school community's work throughout the year embodies this dimension, and this is merely one example of many. Elvera Sargent, a long-term leader of the school, described a ceremony performed at the beginning and end of each school year called the receiving and releasing ceremony. The receiving ceremony occurs on the first day of school, when teachers receive their students from parents. At this time, Elvera shared that the parent describes their child's gifts to the teacher. On the last day of school, the teacher releases the child back to the parent, noting what the teacher did to foster the child's gifts. "The teacher might say, 'I did my best,'" Elvera stated, and then suggest how the child's gifts might be used to contribute to the community. For example, "If they like to sing, maybe they can be a [ceremonial] singer." This is part of "citizenship education," Elvera noted. "It's building our Mohawk nation" (interview, October 9, 2019). The receiving and releasing events completely transform the schooling experience by placing and expressing the responsibility of the school in reciprocal and relational trust between the parent, child, and teacher. The parent has entrusted the child's gifts to the teacher for nearly a year in the child's life. In receiving and releasing the child from and to the parent, the teacher takes responsibility for that relational trust—a concept not found in the state-sponsored schooling experience. Elvera also referenced the wider community- and nation-building goals that resonate with an understood responsibility to cultural continuance through relational accountability.

I begin with this story because TIPM, as demonstrated in this book, builds upon our story knowledge and story work as Indigenous peoples. The story, like this book, enacts the true purpose of Indigenous education—to create human beings who contribute to their communities. The book wave-jumps in each chapter's deep reflections to create transformative possibilities for our futures, and each scholar provides a contribution that gives back to the community. It represents Indigenous innovation in the academy of scholarly publishing. I am humbled to be asked to write the foreword for a forward-thinking book with a comprehensive approach from Indigenous scholars and scholars of Indigenous education. The editors state in their introduction that "we engage insurgent research to actualize decolonization through radical reform" (p. 1), and they put forth TIPM to inspire critical consciousness and Indigenize our educational systems in the midst of constant fluctuation and resistance to decolonization. TIPM's progressive dimensions for educators who start from contributions and move on to additive, transformative, and finally cultural and social justice action remind me of Yellow Bird's stages of critical thinking (Wilson & Yellow Bird, 2005) and illustrate tangible pathways to critical consciousness for educators.

The book is organized holistically to address issues that affect and impact children from many facets of education—in school and community, teacher education, higher education, and educational leadership. The work represented here is especially important in the face of several state legislatures' challenges to teaching related theories such as critical race theory (CRT). These actions come from a serious lack of understanding of the theory and its antiracist, transformative purpose. Reactionary public fears fueled by ignorant social media and uninformed policymakers will overshadow any progress toward racial understanding and embolden the intolerance and violence we still face as Indigenous peoples. Critical race theory, like TIPM, actually results in relational understandings across diverse groups. The timeliness of this book is imperative to confronting these challenges and bringing critical consciousness to the public in order to provide a more thoughtful, caring, just, and inclusive society.

We see from the chapters included in this book how comprehensively the authors provide examples and insights for enacting TIPM. The chapters demonstrate the wave-jumping metaphor of TIPM by recognizing the complexities of transforming education, and the need to learn not from our mistakes, but from our attempts at transformation that found challenges or faced disruptions, such as state legislatures' uninformed actions to limit knowledge growth. The wave-jumping metaphor accounts for the essential reflection back to see forward.

Indigenous peoples' oral traditions provide perfect examples of how our experiences of the past inform our futures. Oral traditions and stories are the basis of our knowledge, theories, and transfer of lived experiences to the next generation (Mahuika, 2019). Mahuika writes that Native oral traditions may change in our forms of expression. It is a process of negotiation for people deeply rooted in their culture so that it survives. It reinvents itself over time.

The book chapters follow this storied tradition by sharing lessons, research, and personal lived experiences, all of which provide a necessary pathway for achieving transformation. The research represented here is our new form of storytelling, knowledge sharing, and reclaiming our knowledge. It is exciting to see the breadth of scholarship and stories, such as the stories of salmon and traditional teachings, mascots and representation, land-based learning, Tribal colleges growing their own, intergenerational female leadership, traditional teaching and Indigenous knowledge systems, Native language education, relational leadership models, and several others that I do not have room to name. The depth of research and storywork represented in this book relates to Corntassel's (2008) notion of sustainable self-determination. Corntassel expressed that sustainable self-determination is the transfer of Indigenous knowledge, worldviews, and cultural traditions and practices to the next generation through means determined by Indigenous peoples themselves. It invokes knowledge sharing and storytelling traditions created through contemporary practices, such as research. As Archibald et al. (2019) emphasize, stories are our theories, our research, and our storywork. They assert that the researcher must engage with Indigenous peoples respectfully and responsibly, and develop relationships through stories that are treated with reverence and strengthened through reciprocity. Today, our research represents our stories and storywork. In closing, this book and its authors have made a large contribution toward a visionary goal of late Lakota scholar Vine Deloria Jr. When discussing education, self-determination, and how Native people will rise above the western, assimilationist education, he stated:

> Initiating an accelerated educational system for Indians was intended to bring Indians up to the parity of middle class non-Indians. In fact, this system has pulled Indians into the Western worldview, and some of the brighter ones are now emerging on the other side, having transversed the Western body of knowledge completely. Once this path has been established, it is almost a certainty that the rest of the Indian community

will walk on right through the Western worldview and emerge on the other side also .
. . . When we leave the culture shock behind, we will be masters of our own fate again
and able to determine for ourselves what kind of lives we will lead. (2001, p. 133)

TIPM and the storywork in this book are determining the kinds of lives we aim to
lead and will lead as Indigenous peoples.

REFERENCES

Archibald, J., Lee-Morgan, J., & De Santolo, J. (2019). *Decolonizing research: Indigenous storywork as methodology*. Zed Books.

Corntassel, J. (2008). Toward sustainable self-determination: Rethinking the contemporary Indigenous-rights discourse. *AlterNatives, 33*(2008), 105–132.

Deloria, V., Jr., & Wildcat, D. (2001). *Power and place: Indian education in America*. Fulcrum Resources.

Mahuika, N. (2019). *Rethinking oral history and tradition: An Indigenous perspective*. Oxford University Press.

Pewewardy, C. D., Lees, A., & Clark-Shim, H. (2018). The Transformational Indigenous Praxis Model: Stages for developing critical consciousness in Indigenous education. *Wičazo Ša Review, 33*(1), 38–69. https://doi.org/10.5749/wicazosareview.33.1.0038

Yellow Bird, M. (2005). Tribal critical thinking centers. In W.A. Wilson & M. Yellow Bird (Eds.), *For Indigenous eyes only: A decolonization handbook* (pp. 9–30). School of American Research.

Acknowledgments and Dedication

We would like to first acknowledge our Ancestors, Elders, and families who have allowed for our existence, resilience, and survival to dream of furthering the movement toward unsettling settler-colonial education. We appreciate the lands, waters, and more-than-humans who have carried and continued the teachings we forward through this book.

We would like to acknowledge each of the collaborators, their families, their communities, their students, those who served as reviewers, Dr. Tiffany Lee, Dr. Michael Yellow Bird, Josh Powell, and Ryan Red Corn. Without all of them, this book would not be possible.

We would like to dedicate this book to honor the memory of the Indigenous children and relatives who have recently been found buried near boarding schools in Canada and the United States. We would like to acknowledge the Missing and Murdered Indigenous Women and children. Acts of genocide and assimilation continue to this day. This is why this book is medicine and serves as an effort to continue to decolonize the minds and hearts of Indigenous peoples through Indigenous education.

Editors' note: The editors have attempted to uplift and honor the voices and writing style of each of the contributors. We acknowledge there may be moments where deviation from APA standard writing and spacing takes place. We acknowledge in our efforts to further the Transformational Indigenous Praxis Model that we must decolonize and push to normalize asserting our Indigenous voice and ways of writing. This is our attempt at doing so.

Introduction

*Cornel Pewewardy (Comanche Citizen and descendant of the Kiowa Tribe),
Anna Lees (Waganakasing Odawa, descendant),
Robin Zape-tah-hol-ah Minthorn (Kiowa Citizen and descendant of the
Apache/Umatilla/Nez Perce/Assiniboine Nations)*

In an effort to put forth a conceptual framework to secure positive Indigenous futures through education, we must first acknowledge that Indigenous education has existed since time immemorial, long before European contact and the settler-designed schools that were and are detrimental to the well-being of Indigenous children and communities (Lomawaima & McCarty, 2006; Sabzalian, 2019; Simpson, 2017). We must also recognize that Indigenous educators have consistently resisted and subverted efforts of assimilation and cultural genocide through public education since its onset (McCoy & Villeneuve, 2020). And yet, the historical and ongoing struggles for Indigenous communities in school systems across the United States call for a radical educational reform that includes a decolonized curriculum model for Indigenous children (Brayboy & Lomawaima, 2018; Faircloth & Tippeconic, 2010; Johnston-Goodstar & Roholt, 2017; Lomawaima & McCarty, 2006; Sabzalian, 2019).

Radical reform efforts recognize the systemic racism ingrained in school structures that privilege whitestream communities as dominant and Black, Indigenous, and Communities of Color as disadvantaged (de Oliveira Andreotti et al., 2015; Simpson, 2017). As Indigenous scholars responding to such profound inequity, we engage insurgent research to actualize decolonization through radical reform, defined by Simpson (2017) as "a thorough and comprehensive reform" (p. 48). In these efforts, we put forth the Transformational Indigenous Praxis Model (TIPM) to promote critical consciousness toward efforts of decolonization among educators.

TIPM challenges readers to critically examine how even the most well-intentioned educators are complicit in reproducing ethnic stereotypes, racist actions, deficit ideology, and recolonization. The 2020 presidential election, and the violence that followed, should remind educators of the resurgent fascist politics of contemporary white[1] supremacist and ultra-nationalist movements taking place within the soul of America. For five hundred years, Rhea (2015) contends that "the education of Indigenous peoples who live in nation states formed during this most recent period of global colonization by European powers has been a complex matter" (p. 3). The 2021 emergent uncovering of unmarked graves at boarding schools in the United States and Canada has confirmed the unreported deaths of Indigenous children under the care of the state during forced attendance in settler schools (U.S. Department of Interior, 2021). The inquiry for who has the authority to lead and guide the education of Indigenous peoples at this moment in time is even more fraught. As Rhea (2015) argues:

> The emergence of an international rights mechanism, the United Nations Declaration on the Rights of Indigenous Peoples, has at its heart a challenge to nations built through colonization to move from an institutionally embedded colonial legacy of educating Indigenous populations to "fit in" with imposed, new, nation state arrangements to recognizing the *sui generis* rights of Indigenous peoples. (p. 3)

In this book, we examine how the lack of attention to settler colonialism hinders the analysis of race and white supremacy as insurgent research attempts to support Indigenous rights.

Thus, while relevant to particular political tensions, the need to develop the Transformational Indigenous Praxis Model (TIPM) as a conceptual framework tool to foster continued critical consciousness-building came from decades of collaboration with teachers and school leaders working to serve Indigenous children and communities. The editors and collaborators of this text identify the deficit ideological underpinnings that frame Indigenous students' school experiences and present each chapter through examples of pathway-making across the TIPM continuum trying to unravel the impact of such experiences upon educational sovereignty. We echo the heavy lifting of Vine Deloria Jr. and Daniel Wildcat (2001) by proposing nothing less than indigenizing our educational systems. By indigenization, we affirm what Wildcat describes as the act of making our educational philosophy, pedagogy, and system our own, making the effort to explicitly explore systems of knowledge that have been actively repressed for five centuries. Moreover, we affirm Deloria's strong message that scholars researching Indigenous communities should be required to put something back into the community (Deloria, 1991; see also Brayboy et al., 2012) and we endeavor to fulfill that call.

Expanding on James Banks's (1989) and Michael Yellow Bird's (1998, 2005) models of multicultural education and decolonization, Pewewardy created the TIPM for educators to identify, map, and develop students' critical consciousness using energy, time, and momentum as the supporting framework for critical thinking. The four dimensions of the TIPM designed to engage a process of decolonization are adapted from the four curriculum approaches to curriculum reform conceptualized and developed by Banks, which are Level 1, The Contributions Approach; Level 2, The Additive Approach; Level 3, The Transformational Approach; and Level 4, The Social Action Approach. Yellow Bird's Model of the Effects of Colonialism (1998) depicted examples of colonization in social work and how one may adapt to or resist colonization. The TIPM built on this work to develop a scaffolded process of decolonization specific to the field of education. And building from Yellow Bird's Tribal Critical Thinking Centers, the TIPM has employed *critical conscious study groups* as a medium for facilitating the process of decolonization.

Through a metaphor of wave jumping, educators working to decolonize their practice can gain forward momentum with time and energy even while facing resistance. Thus, as water is always in motion so are efforts toward decolonization; this is not a linear model of upward progression, but rather cyclical and fluid as we navigate ever changing conditions of our social contexts. The TIPM supports educators to reflect and develop their critical thinking and practice, as well as create opportunities to experience their own processes of decolonization. To decolonize and liberate Indigenous education, we must find ways for healing and reengaging Indigenous education by fostering Indigenous consciousness and languages to create bridges between Indigenous and European knowledge bases (Deloria & Wildcat, 2001). The TIPM retraditionalized methodology to promote healing and cultural restoration of Indigenous peoples is based on a decolonial model as articulated by Barbara Leigh Smith and Linda Moon Stumpff (2014):

> The combination of an empowering pedagogy and culturally relevant content on important issues in Indian Country is what makes this approach highly successful with students, teachers, and tribal leaders who see that as an important way to tell their stories. It is an effective method for building student capacity to analyze critical issues facing Native Americans and our society as a whole. (p. 1)

The TIPM serves as a framework to help educators understand various layers of Indigenous consciousness and how critical consciousness can be developed and followed by commitment and action for social transformation. The model provides a scaffolding process to promote critical thinking and working through dimensions of social stratification in terms of power hierarchies brought about through colonized practices based on individuals, cultures, and institutional structures. These commitments will begin inside each one of us as personal change, but transformation toward decolonization will become a reality only when we collectively commit to a movement based on an ethical and political vision and consciously reject the colonial postures of weak submission, victimhood, and raging violence. This transformation, occurring over time, requires long-term commitment to the work with individual and collective efforts to make change in ways of knowing and being and concrete practice. Ultimately, this resurgent approach to decolonizing oneself and systems builds on the time-tested values of our history in efforts to create a postcolonial future.

The TIPM was shared for decades at multiple settings, including national conferences and invited speaking events. With each presentation—followed by discussion, critique, and feedback from colleagues—the authors modified, further developed, and published the TIPM in article form (Pewewardy et al., 2018). The purpose of this volume is to put forth the TIPM as a structure to support educators in decolonizing and indigenizing their practices, and offer examples of how pathway-making across a variety of settings takes form on the TIPM continuum (see Figure I.1.). Next, we offer a brief summary of the TIPM dimensions with examples of resistance educators face as they expand their critical consciousness toward decolonization.

Figure I.1. Transformational Indigenous Praxis Model

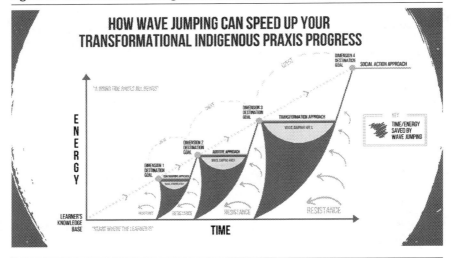

Note. Adapted from "Integrating the Curriculum With Ethnic Content: Approaches and Guidelines," by J. A. Banks, in J. A. Banks & C. A. M. Banks (Eds.), *Multicultural Education: Issues and Perspectives* (pp. 189–207), 1989, Allyn and Bacon; and *A Model of the Effects of Colonialism*, by M. Yellow Bird, 1998, Office for the Study of Indigenous Social and Cultural Justice.

DIMENSIONS OF TRANSFORMATIONAL INDIGENOUS PRAXIS MODEL

Dimension 1: Contributions Approach

The initial dimension of the TIPM portrays experiences of educators who have not yet developed their consciousness to critically examine school structures and curriculum content. Educators in this phase are generally satisfied with school-based education and not yet aware of the settler-colonial impact on education that has worked to eliminate Indigenous peoples from land and water and used schools for the purpose of assimilation. They go with the flow of school movements without any intention to focus time and energy to make forward momentum toward change. In the *contributions approach*, educators may enact the name of this dimension by contributing tidbits of multicultural content to an otherwise white-stream curriculum (otherwise named the "heroes and holidays" approach). Such educators may have good intentions in their work and have not yet gained strong mentorship around critical thinking and praxis.

Resistance. Educators face minimal, if any, resistance in the *contributions approach.* Any efforts put forth in this dimension around multicultural or Indigenous education would be aligned with many school improvement goals and would not disrupt settler-colonial structures of schools or curriculum. Teachers who do face resistance in this dimension may be dismissed by their colleagues for going beyond what is required or wasting time on content that is not part of the curriculum. Objectors to a contributions approach may depict the curriculum as already rigorous with no room for unnecessary goals, even if they are minor contributions of conservative multiculturalism. Educators in this dimension may also receive positive recognition for their good work in addressing school mission and vision goals of diversity without disrupting the school norms—we name this as resistance to a continued progression toward transformation.

Dimension 2: Additive Approach

The second dimension in the TIPM depicts educators with initial curiosity around settler-colonial educational structures with beginning steps toward change through "bursts of critical awareness" (Pewewardy et al., 2018). In the *additive approach* educators recognize that settler-colonial structures of schooling are harmful toward Children of Color and Indigenous children, but the weight of recognizing institutional racism can result in feeling overwhelmed and unclear of where to begin. Educators in this dimension work to integrate multiple perspectives and varying sources of information into curriculum content through practices such as building a multicultural library or recognizing less prominent social movements in their teaching. Educators here clearly intend to surpass deficit ideologies and see families and communities as knowledge holders, but their social justice frameworks are fragile. These educators need strong mentorship and collegial support in order to focus their energy and navigate through the waves of resistance.

Resistance. Educators in this dimension are early on in the development of their critical consciousness, and fragile in their commitments toward social change and resistance. This resistance impacts educators' continued trajectory toward critical consciousness. Colleagues opposing transformational praxis will approach educators in this dimension with dissent around their efforts to indigenize or decolonize curriculum by promoting the standardized curriculum as an easier approach to the work, advancing a narrative that they are adding unnecessary content or showing off to make others look bad. Additionally, district or state mandated standardized curriculum can be portrayed as so rigorous in nature that there is no possible way of adding in additional (critical) content while still meeting the required expectations, and that critical content is inappropriate for school curriculum—often stating that families will not be in support of such efforts. Thus, the work of educators in the *additive approach* dimension can be viewed as barriers to fulfilling their job expectations and the critique they receive in these efforts may be portrayed as a threat to their job security.

Dimension 3: Transformation Approach

In the third dimension, educators demonstrate their practices toward social transformation and have a deep awareness of how settler-colonial policies impact Indigenous children and Children of Color. They recognize the need for decolonizing and critical pedagogies in the curriculum and experiment with implementing such approaches. These educators take on mentor roles to support and collaborate with other colleagues endeavoring to transform the standardized curricula. They have focused their time and attention to move through the waves and surpass resistance as they work toward greater change. In the transformation approach, educators work to uphold axiological, epistemological, and ontological diversity and begin to imagine a postcolonial future. While the process of decolonization may still be murky, these educators make space to conspire with others around how to realize their dreams of a future that remains unknown. The *transformation approach* requires fugitive spaces for colleagues with shared desires to connect and collaborate with each other and community leaders to develop a more radical curriculum (Harney & Moten, 2013; la paperson, 2017).

Resistance. In the *transformation approach*, resistance takes active forms to obstruct educators' endeavors to embody a critical stance. Opponents will position themselves as policy leaders to maintain the status quo and promote a whitestream curriculum under the guise of multicultural education; in this, they may concede to an *additive approach* in some moments to deter substantial change in school structures. When contesting neoliberal policy narratives, educators engaged in the *transformation approach* may be accused of overreacting or making something out of nothing. The opponents then position themselves as trying their best or portraying a state of ignorance where they haven't had opportunities to learn about these issues, so they need to be forgiven and supported in their mistakes. This resistance is difficult to identify and combat without a strong network of support. Continuing on in efforts of transformational praxis becomes exhausting for educators, sometimes referred to as "ethno-stress."

Dimension 4: Cultural and Social Justice Action

At the most advanced dimension, educators demonstrate a deep embodiment of critical consciousness and consistently take active efforts in social justice. Educators enact transformational praxis in both theoretical and concrete ways to make change in the educational experiences of Black and Indigenous communities and other Communities of Color. They engage so consistently that Indigenous and decolonizing pedagogies are embedded in their daily work. They transcend the waves at a steady pace, moving through the resistance fluidly with focused time and energy. Educators in the *cultural and social justice action* dimension find themselves in leadership roles where they mentor others and are recognized as knowledge holders. These educators advance efforts of radical resurgence (Simpson, 2017) within their Tribal Nation communities and across educational settings. They clearly see a postcolonial future, while still working to uncover the path through decolonization. Centering Indigenous knowledges in their teaching, they resist neoliberal and settler-colonial narratives in school policy and curriculum. It can be difficult to remain in this dimension, and even the most critically conscious educators may retreat from leadership roles and move between dimensions to find sustainability in the work.

Resistance. In this advanced dimension of the TIPM, educators face intense resistance. While educators labor determinedly, the resulting change is gradual at best. The resistance in this dimension can sometimes turn violent. And while not frequent enough to gather significant social attention, profound moments in history and contemporary social action movements depict the serious risk that educators advancing *cultural and social justice action* can face (see Indian boarding schools, Wounded Knee, the fish wars, IdleNoMore, NoDAPL, and more). While these examples may be perceived as anomalies, the patterns of resistance that move toward physical harm when Indigenous peoples claim inherent sovereignty are undeniable. Additionally, educators in this dimension face institutional resistance and isolation from colleagues daily, where they are coined difficult to work with or never satisfied with what they have. To enact *cultural and social justice action,* educators must hold deep commitment to their work and be grounded in their belief of a more positive future for the next generation, rather than change to secure a better experience for themselves.

Antidotes to Resistance

To support educators developing their critical consciousness toward transformational Indigenous praxis, we discuss ways to combat resistance throughout the process. As we assess the varying forms of resistance faced by educators, we find it necessary to create spaces of support for educators across dimensions of the TIPM. These spaces allow for mentorship, comradery, and restoration with others who share the same goals and help beginning educators build their awareness around the need for decolonization. Educators cannot sustain aspirations for change alone and must find spaces of interdependence to nurture each others' efforts across institutional settings in what we name *critical conscious study groups.* Having like-minded colleagues within and outside of one's own institution is invaluable to make sense of experiences that are both successful and challenging. Holding regular *critical conscious study groups* with educators across contexts and with varying levels of experience creates space to foster continued critical thinking toward transformation. The examples of pathway-making in this text portray work across the TIPM and depict how the work took form in spite of institutional and societal resistance.

CONTRIBUTIONS FROM COMMUNITIES

This book is organized in four sections to represent a holistic balance in (1) Birth–Grade-12 Education, (2) Teacher Education, (3) Higher Education, and (4) Educational Leadership. While collaborators present their work within these distinct fields of study, we in fact work regularly across context toward shared goals of decolonization.

Our common ground as editors and collaborators is that we have all committed to teaching and learning within Indigenous education that centers community ways of knowing, being, and valuing. To bring clarity and stretch critical thinking, we structure this volume as a series of pathway-making examples across communities to make known the latest developments in Indigenous education and to celebrate the brilliance of Indigenous communities committed to positive futures.

Birth–Grade-12 Education

We open this text emphasizing the profound work occurring with children and communities across generations to enact Indigenous resurgence through education. Chapters in this section depict efforts to sustain Indigenous education in spite of settler-colonial desires of assimilation and erasure. Collaborators offer examples of critical engagements across a range of Indigenous education topics beginning with Indigenous languages, where Geneva Becenti offers research of teacher perspectives regarding teaching Indigenous languages in New Mexico. Examples of community-driven change and nation building toward sustained futures are threaded throughout this section in service to our youngest generations. Anthony Craig and Chelsea Craig illustrate Indigenous education through their pathway-making example of collaboration across communities and Tribal Nation organizations to support public education in Washington state; their work is grounded across generations and guided by Elders. Recognizing that education expands beyond classroom practice, yahnesuaru mohatsi offers an analysis of policy and practice and the importance of collaboration to bring back together education and wellness. Transitioning from community-based efforts, the next section offers examples of pathway-making in the preparation of future teachers.

Teacher Education

Essential to our commitments of radical reform in public education, we feature pathway-making in teacher education across the TIPM continuum. To illustrate how the work of teacher education is closely related to B–12 and community learning settings, Dolores Calderón depicts the need for land and water education in teacher education to integrate a Tribal sovereignty K–12 curriculum. This section also features practical applications from teacher education programs and the experiences of teacher candidates as well as faculty seeking to critically engage transformational praxis. In one example, Anna Lees and Verónica Nelly Vélez describe how an early childhood teacher education program with a minor in education and social justice impacted the work and perspectives of beginning Black and Indigenous teachers and Teachers of Color. And in another context, we encounter the ways in which Jeanette Haynes Writer was faced with patriarchy and privilege by a white male student resisting transformational curriculum in a multicultural education course. Finally, Cornel Pewewardy, Tahlia Natachu, and Anna Lees reflect on experiences in primarily white teacher education programs and hopes for the future. These varied accounts demonstrate the significant potential for change-making through the preparation of future teachers.

Higher Education

As Indigenous children move onward in their educational trajectory, Indigenous higher education scholars have done profound work to decolonize university settings to best serve Indigenous learners seeking advanced degrees. This section opens with Natalie Youngbull centering research focused on faculty leadership at Tribal colleges and universities (TCUs.) TCUs have taken great efforts in securing Indigenous futurities through educational sovereignty, and Youngbull brings to light the ways in which TCU faculty furthers Indigenous education. Examining the experiences of Indigenous students in higher education, Jeff Corntassel and Virginia Drywater-Whitekiller consider how increased efforts of land education in universities are experienced by Indigenous students. And closing the section, Alma M. Ouanesisouk Trinidad and Hyuny Clark-Shim focus on social work education and a multidisciplinary approach. The chapters in this section depict the profound importance of disrupting settler-colonial dominance through efforts to promote Indigenous education in higher education.

Educational Leadership

To enact change, we must foster Indigenous leaders who can apply decolonizing theories and Indigenous methodologies at the institutional level. In the final section of this text, we share important work happening across Tribal Nations and academia to develop Indigenous leadership in education. Dawn Hardison Stevens puts forth an Indigenous leadership philosophy that centers Indigenous values and ways of knowing and being in academic leadership positions. Hollie Mackey, Sashay Schettler, and Melissa Cournia discuss a professional development opportunity with non-Native educators to improve the experiences and connections between the school and Indigenous students. Robin Zape-tah-hol-ah Minthorn shares processes for developing educational leaders within Tribal Nations through the development of Indigenous-based doctoral programs. Offering a personal narrative and indigenized autoethnographic approach, Alex RedCorn describes his process of developing critical consciousness from his time as a classroom teacher to his work in educational leadership. Shawn Secatero depicts a complex representation of a community-driven Indigenous leadership education model, and Carrie Whitlow closes the section exploring the role of intergenerational women's leadership in Tribal Nation organizations through an Indigenous feminist framework. Whitlow features personal stories that must be understood to disrupt colonial models of patriarchy toward Indigenized futures.

CONCLUSION

In this process we have contributed individually within our respective areas in efforts to transform Indigenous pedagogical praxis. What we acknowledge is that we must work collectively as Indigenous scholars and co-conspirators to vision a future that moves in waves for holistic transformation. We hope that these examples of pathway-making honor work happening each day across communities and inspire others to continue on in efforts of Indigenous education that cultivate transformation and thriving futures.

NOTES

1. Moving away from the formatting and style guidelines of APA 7th edition, we enact our rhetoric sovereignty by choosing not to capitalize *white* in this introduction and support contributors throughout this book in resisting other style guidelines that minimize Indigenous futures and continue efforts of colonization.

REFERENCES

Brayboy, B. M., Gough, H. R., Leonard, B., Roehl, R. F., & Solyom, J. A. (2012). Reclaiming scholarship: Critical Indigenous research methodologies. *Qualitative research: An introduction to methods and designs*, 423–450.

Brayboy, B. M. J., & Lomawaima, K. T. (2018). Why don't more Indians do better in school? The battle between U.S. schooling & American Indian/Alaska Native Education. *Daedalus*, *147*(2), 82–94.

de Oliveira Andreotti, V., Stein, S., Ahenakew, C., & Hunt, D. (2015). Mapping interpretations of decolonization in the context of higher education. *Decolonization: Indigeneity, Education & Society, 4*(1).

Deloria, V., Jr. (1991). Research, redskins, and reality. *American Indian Quarterly*, 457–468.

Deloria, V., Jr., & Wildcat, D. (2001). *Power and place: Indian education in America*. Fulcrum Publishing.

Faircloth, S. C., & Tippeconnic, J. W., III. (2010). *The dropout/Graduation crisis among American Indian and Alaska Native students: Failure to respond places the future of Native Peoples at risk*. Civil Rights Project/Proyecto Derechos Civiles.

Harney, S., & Moten, F. (2013). *The undercommons: Fugitive planning and black study*. Minor Compositions.

Johnston-Goodstar, K., & VeLure Roholt, R. (2017). "Our kids aren't dropping out; They're being pushed out": Native American students and racial microaggressions in schools. *Journal of Ethnic & Cultural Diversity in Social Work, 26*(1-2), 30–47.

la paperson. (2017). *A third university is possible*. University of Minnesota Press.

Lomawaima, K. T., & McCarty, T. L. (2006). *"To remain an Indian": Lessons in democracy from a century of Native American education*. Teachers College Press.

McCoy, M. L., & Villeneuve, M. (2020). Reconceiving schooling: Centering Indigenous experimentation in Indian education history. *History of Education Quarterly, 60*(4), 487–519.

Pewewardy, C. D., Lees, A., & Clark-Shim, H. (2018). The Transformational Indigenous Praxis Model: Stages for developing critical consciousness in Indigenous education. *Wíčazo Ša Review, 33*(1), 38–69. https://doi.org/10.5749/wicazosareview.33.1.0038

Rhea, Z. M. (2014). *Leading and managing Indigenous education in the postcolonial world*. Routledge.

Sabzalian, L. (2019). *Indigenous children's survivance in public schools*. Routledge.

Simpson, L. B. (2017). *As we have always done: Indigenous freedom through radical resistance*. University of Minnesota Press.

Smith, B. L., & Stumpff, L. M. (2014). Exploring tribal sovereignty through Native case studies. *Indigenous Policy Journal, 25*(3). http://indigenouspolicy.org/index.php/ipj/article/view/278/271

U.S. Department of Interior. (2021). *Secretary Haaland announces Federal Indian Boarding School Initiative.* https://www.doi.gov/pressreleases/secretary-haaland-announces-federal-indian-boarding-school-initiative

Yellow Bird, M. (1998). *A model of the effects of colonialism.* Office for the Study of Indigenous Social and Cultural Justice.

Yellow Bird, M. (2005). Tribal critical thinking centers. In W. A. Wilson & M. Yellow Bird (Eds.), *For Indigenous eyes only: A decolonization handbook*(pp. 9–29). School for Advanced Research Press.

Part I

BIRTH–GRADE-12 EDUCATION

CHAPTER 1

Native American Language Teachers Going Beyond Their Classrooms

Geneva Becenti (Diné)

At an early age, I was taught *Diné bizaad* not knowing that colonial history tried to assimilate my language and culture. My parents and grandparents instilled in me the values of speaking our language, regardless of how intrusive it was for western society to force English on my relatives. My family only speaks *Diné bizaad* and we are taught our identity first, which came with discipline to always let our relatives know which community we are from. Before my vocal cords formed any words, my parents and paternal grandparents introduced me to *Diyin Diné* (Holy People) and to my relatives. I was born when the Indian Self-Determination and Education Assistance Act of 1975 was created. In *Diné*, this self-determination is translated to *t'áá hwó ají téego,* which is defined as self-reliance, that you do everything on your own, and even when you do not know where and how to do things, you start from somewhere. The act was created for Native people to control their own schools on the reservations. Tribes were given the option to take over any or all BIA program functions (Lomawaima & McCarty, 2002).

Yet, my relatives and community have been governed by the Civilization Fund Act of 1819, where the U.S. government financially supported missionaries to operate boarding schools. The missionaries' goals were to train Natives not to speak their heritage language, and to punish Natives for practicing their Indigenous culture. Through this trauma, my grandparents still spoke our language and practiced our culture. Yet, they did not get to see the work that followed. Policies that protect Native American language, including the state act titled the New Mexico Indian Education Act (NMIEA) of 2003, were created to increase the culturally relevant learning environment and to ensure the maintenance of Native American languages. So, I ask, what transformed between 1819, 1975, and 2003? Although my relatives' language and culture were almost assimilated by the Civilization Fund Act of 1819, the U.S. federal government's Indian Self Determination Act of 1975 finally endorsed Tribal Nations' revitalization of their culture and language by operating their own schools on their own nations. The NMIEA of 2003 continues to build upon the work from the 1970s bilingual education acts. Therefore, I share narratives from Native language teachers that were impacted by state policies such as the NMIEA. Some teachers transformed their classroom teaching through their cultural teachings, which increased the number of Native American language speakers. The case study findings presented in this chapter uncovered some barriers that the teachers continue to work through, and I share my work through the Transformational Indigenous Praxis Model (TIPM) (Pewewardy et al., 2018).

The TIPM offers "a scaffolding process to promote critical thinking and working through dimensions of social stratification in terms of power hierarchies brought about through colonized practices based on individuals, cultures, and institutional structures" (p. 3, Introduction, this volume). Here, I ask: What does cultural relevance mean from state policy? The transformation of education from the historical structure comes with critical questions from the community such as, Who is teaching our youth? From a TIPM viewpoint, our Native American language teachers (NALT) are self-determined speakers, self-identified bilingual teachers, and self-taught Navajo language writers and readers. Not only are they teachers in the classroom, but they also outreach to their community and their students' parents/families. These teachers are going beyond their classroom responsibilities to ensure their students are being supported by their school, district, and community. They wear many hats in teaching our youth by taking on administrative duties, curriculum/assessment specialist roles, community liaisons, professional development facilitators, and advocates. Not only do they have various sizes of hats, but they are also mothers, fathers, grandparents, aunts/uncles, sons/daughters, and colleagues. These outstanding teachers are put in situations where they are asked to create content standards for their heritage language, use common core standards, outreach to educational assistants, and support parent advisory council groups to monitor Title I budgets. So, we pressure our Native language teachers beyond their classroom, then we ask why Native youth are not speaking our language or accuse the teachers of teaching our children wrong. In some cases, community members or other language teachers criticize their teaching style without recognizing they have multiple roles, and their community outreach takes a lot of their family time. My journey has led me to examine state and federal policies that impact Native language learners. Initial research began with Arizona Proposition 203, which led to English immersion for children in schools and required that business meetings be conducted in English only. While this proposition impacts more so on Spanish speakers, Indigenous heritage language teachers have experienced similar challenges through their grandparents or themselves. Regardless of Arizona Proposition 203, the Native teachers advocated for their students and community to continue to teach Native languages and culture. These teachers have dealt with institutional racism and lack of respect by school administrators, but they continue with their endless work in teaching youth their heritage language.

Through testimonies from grandparents who are heritage language speakers, they would say "only if my grandchild spoke in our language." We continue to share why speaking in our language is important. Our NALTs have deep traditional knowledge in relation to historical stories, description of creation stories, political changes, and environmental foundations and are eager to share their knowledge of the act. Native language teachers shared that they paid for their own materials to develop curriculum resources. Once I taught a dual-credit Navajo language, I experienced how creating hands-on activities meant spending your own money to create lesson plans for each language learner. The amount teachers spent on curriculum materials normally is not approved by the administrators. Most teachers who I asked if their school reimbursed them for the curriculum purchases said no. A couple of teachers were fortunate that their school provided materials for their class. Others were not aware that funds were provided to them through Title I. In the efforts of meeting the needs of a grandparent's desire to communicate with their grandchild, there is more work to come.

The purpose of this work is to identify educational policies that impact Indigenous children's ways of living and is focused on Native American language learning in New Mexico. The research presented in this chapter is to help Native language teachers understand multiple ways to interpret state policies. The findings are to help policymakers understand the justification in the implementation of state policies for the betterment of Indigenous language learning. The analysis of western academic research was intimidating and confusing, so I used various conceptual frameworks, such as TIPM and Diné Paradigm, to unpack the western historical structural and institutional methodology. Accordingly, I relearned my own Diné foundation through the work of some Diné scholars such as Benally (1990), Aronilth (1992), and Clark (2009). Also, I felt the spirit of writing by the late Vine Deloria Jr. and Daniel Wildcat's (2001) work from *Power and Place: Indian Education in America*. I took this sentiment to heart from the work of Battiste (2011) and Deloria & Wildcat (2001), as emphasized in Pewewardy et al. (2018): "We need to find ways for healing and rebuilding Indigenous education by restoring Indigenous consciousness and language to create bridges between Indigenous and European knowledge bases" (p. 51). Next, I will describe policies that impact Native American language teaching and how that took form in the context of this study.

BACKGROUND OF THE NEW MEXICO NATIVE AMERICAN LANGUAGE CLASSES AND PROGRAMS IN PUBLIC SCHOOLS

The *1970s Bilingual Education Acts* was implemented into New Mexico's education department for Spanish speakers to learn English. The New Mexico Public Education Department (NMPED) is still using the same policies that were used in the 1970s to learn English over the maintenance of Native American language. To recap the creation of NMIEA, it was to (a) ensure equitable and culturally relevant learning environments, educational opportunities, and culturally relevant instructional materials for American Indian students enrolled in public school, (b) ensure maintenance of the Native American languages, and (c) provide for the study, development, and implementation of educational systems that positively affect the educational success of American Indian students. Between the bilingual education acts and the NMIEA, the Native American language programs were developed to support and revitalize heritage language. There were at least five different types of programs created in the public schools, such as maintenance, enrichment, Indigenous/heritage language, transitional, and dual language immersion.

In this study, I interviewed 11 NALTs. Most of these teachers had bachelor's and master's degrees. I spent time with them over the years and got to know their families and communities. My semi-structured interviews were to learn about the teachers' knowledge on state policies related to the Native American Language programs. They reflected on the state's marginalized language learning. They quickly narrowed down inequalities in the state's unclear standardization, inconsistent district requirements for NALTs' credentials, limited support to provide curriculum materials, and access to professional development. Their narratives have transformed my views on a variety of state policies. The Native language teachers did not allow their narratives to sit on bookshelves collecting dust; instead they wanted their narratives to be shared widely with other language teachers for learning purposes and to bring awareness to policymakers.

Several questions emerged from multiple gatherings such as community meetings, state conferences, and government-to-government summits. Discussions on education included Native American languages. The attendees asked critical questions such as: Is our language being taught in the youth's home or public schools? Who is teaching our Native American youth their heritage language? Do the state policies and the bilingual education program's funds sustain our Native youth's language and culture in public schools?

This chapter intends to bring enlightenment of positivity to appreciate the language teachers who teach our heritage languages. Yes, there are challenges, and it is not easy to talk or write about it. Often, we do not share the success stories. As a result, our communities become divided because of their beliefs in where we teach our heritage language. Should our heritage language only be taught at home, or does it belong at school, or with the community? What about other parts of the world? My understanding through our Diné worldview is that our language is a healing language, that we use it to pray, to heal our community, and to protect nature. As Indigenous people, we have relatives throughout the world. We travel throughout the world to share knowledge, trade, work, and to protect our people and to defend our Mother Earth. Our language needs us to put life into our prayers, which honors our creation stories. And our Ancestors will continue to teach us.

Next, drawing from interviews with 11 teachers, I share teachers' stories aligned with the phases of the NMIEA. To protect the identity of the teachers, I gave them pseudonyms. For years, they dedicated themselves toward teaching their heritage language in schools. For the interviews, I organized the teachers into the three phases of the NMIEA such as pre-implementation, implementation, and post-implementation. Also, I was not able to use all of NALTs' stories.

Pre-Implementation Phase

About five teachers said they started working at their school before the language program started and the NMIEA was established, which is 13–20 years ago. Multiple times, these veteran language teachers were moved from one school to another school due to either low enrollment in Native American language classes or a district's desire to begin language classes in new communities. They experienced a change of leadership (principal and superintendent) and witnessed the district discontinue Native American language classes. One veteran language teacher for 18 years mentioned that she worked in the bilingual program for 4 years. Suddenly, leadership changed, and she was required to develop new materials and no longer had access to existing lesson plans or assessments. Another teacher was moved to another school because of a district reorganization. Even when she applied to stay in the community, the district transferred her into a different school where she was not familiar with the community, which made it harder to teach the community language.

Implementation Phase

The next two teachers shared their 9–19 years' experience, and as they began their career Native American language classes were already implemented. These Navajo language classes are considered electives and as such are not part of the required school courses. Another issue is the language teachers' credentials. One teacher mentioned a school administrator mandated an additional license and certificate to teach Navajo language at a public school. She had three teaching credentials: (1) bilingual teaching license, (2) Teaching English to Speakers of Other languages (TESOL), and (3) 520 Native American language certification. In addition to her license and certification, she had a master's degree and bachelor's degree in education. The school districts were not consistent with their NALTs' credentials. This caused confusion among the teachers; some did not self-identify as a bilingual teacher, nor did they know the Navajo language program that they taught under for years was an extension of the bilingual education program from the 1970s.

Post-Implementation Phase

The last four teachers taught in classrooms that were transformed by multiple NALTs. One mentioned that she taught for 8 years in a semi-immersion structure for 55 minutes each day by only talking in Navajo to her students. The second semester, the Navajo language program provided curriculum mappings to the Bilingual Program coordinator and instructional support teachers. Also, as part of her teaching she shared various state and federal policies on revitalization of Native American languages with her students.

Most of these teachers shared their compassion for teaching their heritage language to their students. They all have challenging and successful stories, such as Paula Nelson, who said, "They don't take the language seriously. . . . Oh, it's just another elective." At the beginning of Paula Nelson's teaching career, she was frustrated by the way the school district and the state treated Navajo language programs. She felt that the school put the Navajo language behind everything else and did not treat it the same as more general subjects, such as math and science. Paula confirmed that the Navajo language is an elective subject at her school and that the [school] authorities do not acknowledge the program as a way of revitalizing the Navajo language. She said, "I can say they [the district and the state] don't take the language seriously. . . . Oh, it's just another elective. What can I say?"

On a positive note, Paula Nelson and Claudia Nakai were thankful that the Navajo Nation created a Memorandum of Agreement (MOA) with their school district to teach Navajo in every subject. Both mentioned that without the MOA their school district would not have Navajo language programs. However, the agreement does not include the objectives of the curriculum for the language programs. The school district has instructional support teachers who create curricula for teachers who need additional assistance in teaching language and culture in their classes.

Along the lines of mentorship, Haskie Smith was not mentored by other Navajo language teachers or given a curriculum to teach from at his school. He took initiative to request assistance from other teachers to share their lesson plans, but these teachers did not assist. He said, "Nobody helped me. Just what I thought would be good. So. My class was like 50/50 culture and language. I did a lot of culture because I knew what to teach." In addition, he mentioned the lesson plans included second language acquisitions but not so much of the theories because he was not familiar with them. On a positive note, the school principal was supportive in his professional development, so he attended the Navajo Studies Conference, the New Mexico Bilingual Education Conference, and the Indian Education Summit provided by the NMIED. Haskie utilized these conference materials into his lesson plans. Although the Navajo Nation language department provides curriculum, he did not agree with some of the lesson plans, so he continued to provide materials for his class. Next, I will explain how the Diné Paradigm serves as a community-based model for Diné communities and how the TIPM may act as a similar resource for other Indigenous researchers and graduate students.

SA'ąH NAAGHÁÍ BIK'EH HÓZHÓÓN DINÉ PARADIGM AND THE TRANSFORMATIONAL INDIGENOUS PRAXIS MODEL

TIPM was not developed until after I graduated with my doctorate; however, this chapter will provide examples to assist graduate students to identify issues through social justice methods of Tribal critical thinking and Indigenous epistemology, and to promote self-evaluation. As a doctoral candidate, I searched for Indigenous scholars to help me construct my conceptual framework. I imagine most Indigenous graduate students are currently reading about or contemplating models to use in framing their research, but, for me, I felt it was most appropriate to use my Diné worldviews. The majority of my relatives who shared their stories were Diné; they expressed their Diné perspectives that are embedded into the Diné Paradigm. Along the way, I continued to discuss my work with my dissertation committee and was mentored by other Indigenous scholars.

Based on my Diné worldviews (Becenti, 2021), I identified key aspects of critical awareness that aligned with the TIPM goals. *Saʼąh Naagháí Bikʼeh Hózhóón,* the Diné Paradigm for Critical Consciousness (DPCC), includes four phases. We begin from phase one, *Nitsáhákees:* to identify the problem by using critical thinking; phase two, *Nahatʼá:* to plan/evaluate issues; phase three, *Iiná:* life/social development; and phase four, *Sii Hasin:* faith/hope outcome. The DPCC is formed with prayers and discussion with relatives. In respect of my relatives (Diné language teachers), I share their lived experiences through cultural knowledge, and I use the DPCC to unpack the issues faced by Native American language teachers in schools.

In Figure 1.1, the NALT is in the center of the *Saʼąh Naagháí Bikʼeh Hózhóón* Diné Paradigm and TIPM. I merged both models to help unpack issues faced by Native American language teachers through cultural worldviews and a critical consciousness lens, and intended for use for external audience research and methods purposes. In Figure 1.1, the circular paradigm helps us to go through each phase forward, not go backward. In Diné cultural protocols, we do not go backwards, and we ask the *Diyin Diné* to help us move forward. We begin by thinking

Figure 1.1. Saʼąh Naagháí Bikʼeh Hózhóón Diné Paradigm and TIPM

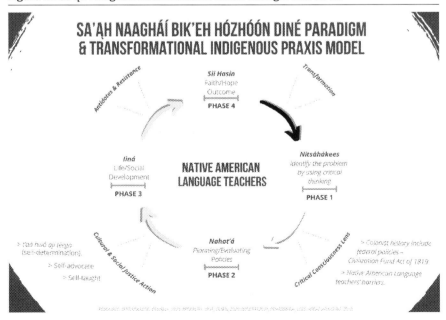

and discussing, to help us understand issues. To prescribe or problem-solve, we need to identify the issues, which do not happen in one sitting or place. Over centuries, we learned to reflect on history, but we cannot dwell on the past; if we do, we get stuck in a cycle of disharmony.

Nitsáhákees [Thinking]: Critical Consciousness Lens

In phase one, we identify the issues through *Nitsáhákees*: critical consciousness lens. As introduced at the beginning of this chapter, my relatives taught me my language without knowing there are assimilation policies from the U.S. federal government such as the Civilization Fund Act of 1819. Unpacking issues is the initiation for the language teachers to recognize the unequal treatment from state-licensed teachers who undervalue their Tribally issued 520 certifications. Teachers who hold a 520 Native American language certification have passed a Navajo language proficiency test from the Navajo Oral Language and Cultural Program of the Navajo Nation. The Nation submitted an official letter to NMPED to confirm the language teacher is proficient to teach in Diné. The 520 certificate holders are not on the same pay scale as the state-licensed teachers, yet their job duties are equal to or more than the state-licensed teachers. The language teachers are not as supported by their principals as the general education teachers, as detailed previously by the lack of resources allocated to their curriculum and multiple layers of credentialing requirements. Sometimes, they were afraid of what would happen if they reported their complaints.

Most teachers were aware of the act but did not know the type of resources included that they could benefit from. NMPED has a helpline for general questions for teachers and the public, but these language teachers are left to advocate for themselves. The act encourages the maintenance of Native American languages, but how do the state and the tribe help their language teachers with complaints from regular teachers and help with inequality within the schools? Also, how do student language learners cope with constant changes with their heritage language classes and teachers? These questions are important points to examine if language teachers are to find success within the public school system.

Nahat'á [Planning/Evaluating Policies]: Cultural and Social Justice Action

In phase two, the language teachers acted on the long effect of oppressions from federal policies on English-Only ramifications within the TIMP dimension cultural and social justice action. Here they felt it was necessary to engage with the NM legislators to state the obvious inequality of treatment through lack of professional development, limited access to existing curriculum materials, inequities of salary, and being removed out of their home community school and transferred into another school. Language teachers acknowledged these issues and progressed to transformation, wherein many of them exercised *t'áá hwó ají téego* (self-determination). For things to be back in order, teachers have stated that they took initiatives to re-create their language curriculum, even though this takes a long time to do. Mostly, these teachers do not get paid for the extra hours spent developing hands-on activities and visual learning components for their students. They have expressed their compassion for their students as they are relatives, and hope that through their efforts toward revitalization there is an increase of Diné speakers.

Iiná [Life/Social Development]: Antidotes and Resistance

In phase three, revitalization also means healing from the traumatic experiences endured from federal and state policies. During my conversations with the Diné language teachers, they were very emotional about how much work they must do to revitalize their heritage language. As a routine aspect of their jobs, each school year the teachers continue to share the horrific stories and U.S. boarding school histories that were shared by their grandparents.

TIPM shows the power of hierarchies that oppress our relatives through policies such as the Civilization Fund Act of 1819, then later the perseverance of grandparents to transform these federal policy barriers into the concept of the Indian Self-Determination Act of 1975, to Arizona's passing of Proposition 203 that led to English immersion in schools. Battiste (2011) along with Deloria and Wildcat (2001) grace us with their work about rebuilding and restoring, while healing how Native Nations use western knowledge with Indigenous knowledge. As the Diné language teachers use their *Sa'ah Naagháí Bik'eh Hózhóón* components to overcome the federal and state policies that tried to assimilate our culture and language, they continue to teach and breath *Iiná* [life] back into our heritage language.

Sii Hasin [Faith/Hope Outcome]: Transformation

In phase four, TIPM reflects the resistance that comes from the narratives of the NALTs. As a long-time advocate for revitalization and sustaining our Diné bizaad, we hope to see the NMIEA of 2003 reflect on the grassroot advocacy work and acknowledge the grandparents as language carriers within the act to respect all language teachers. Transformation of these teachers shows their advocacy through presentations to the New Mexico legislators about the pay difference between state-licensed teachers and Tribally approved 520 certified teachers. Other areas that NALTs mentioned to amend are policies to include equity requirements that emphasize respect for the language teachers regardless of certification type.

To provide a closing to this first chapter, I ask, does TIPM have similar features to the Diné Paradigm (Figure 1.1)? The four phases were embedded with critical dialogues and facilitated NALTs knowledge expansion by recognizing how far the teacherscame with their students and community in using cultural and social justice action and self-advocacy. *T'aá hwó ají téego* is the driving force of moving away from disharmony, as demonstrated through the stories of the NALTs' antidotes and resistance against the colonial histories and policies that impact language. The perseverance and values of well-being come to the forefront. Being mindful of unpacking issues does not happen overnight. Some of our relatives did not survive the U.S. federal policies, yet they had *sii hasin* (faith/hope). The positive outcome is the reflection on the transformation from an issue that came to be through epistemology.

Our worldviews may not be acceptable in western places, but with the TIPM and Diné Paradigm we will move through the western construct and be involved in seeing how the worldviews are similar. Both lenses show us how the western framework has impacted our Diné epistemologies. The U.S. federal government's Indian Self-Determination platform has encroached into the Indigenous education, so the local community has been struggling to sustain their language and culture. The hidden self-determination policies were eventually for Tribal Nations to align their programs and agencies within the U.S. government.

CONCLUSION

Ahéhéé (thank you) for reading this chapter and being one to practice the *Sąʼah Naagháí Bikʼeh Hózhóón* Diné Paradigm and TIPM. Federal policies aimed to enhance the Native children's education toward being a "good citizen" of the United States. However, *Power and Place* (Deloria & Wildcat, 2001) provided some essential tools to analyze the true meaning of self-determination among the Native American population in education. Wildcat listed several action plans to use metaphysics (time, space, and energy) to unpack the issues that surround and are within the Native American communities. Deloria says, "We must remember that every article [contribution] attempting to discuss this problem should be understood as a call for each of us to enter into the exchange of knowledge" (p. 5). Werito (2014) also shares the concept of hózhó to help move toward a positive well-being by *nahatʼá* (planning). By sharing his personal journey, he explains how hózhó works for him. And the *Sąʼah Naagháí Bikʼeh Hózhóón* Diné Paradigm and TIPM show the essential tools to discuss issues and plans and collaborate to combine Diné (Indigenous) methodological practices to retrain Native children from western education and heal our Elders who were forced not to speak Native American languages. We hope to continue to guide our young scholars. *Tʼaá hwó ají téego eí yá.*

ACKNOWLEDGMENTS

I wish to acknowledge Mary Whitehair-Fraizer for reviewing Diné bizaad and culturally relevant content. Ahéhéé shí kis. I also wish to acknowledge Indigenous language teachers across communities who are doing important work to keep our young relatives grounded in culture and community wellness by teaching new language speakers.

REFERENCES

Aronilth, W., Jr. (1992). *Foundation of Navajo culture*. Navajo Community College.

Battiste, M. (2011). *Reclaiming Indigenous voice and vision*. UBC Press.

Becenti, G., (2021). Diné worldviews: Research and methodology. In G. A. Cajete (Ed.), *Sacred journeys: Personal visions of Indigenous transformation* (pp. 83–102). J. Charlton Publishing.

Benally, H. (1990). *Philosophy of education at Navajo Community College: Navajo philosophy of learning*. Board of Regents Report, December 13–14, 1990, Navajo Community College [Diné College], Tsaile, AZ.

Clark, F., (2009). *In becoming Saʹah Naaghai Bikʹeh Hozhoon: The historical challenges and triumphs of Diné College* [Doctoral Dissertation, University of Arizona].

Deloria, V., Jr., & Wildcat, D. R., (2001). *Power and place: Indian education in America*. Fulcrum.

Lomawaima, K. T., & McCarty, T. L. (2002). When tribal sovereignty challenges democracy: American Indian education and the democratic ideal. *American Educational Research Journal, 39*(2), 279–305.

Pewewardy, C. D., Lees, A., & Clark-Shim, H. (2018). The Transformational Indigenous Praxis Model: Stages for developing critical consciousness in Indigenous education. *Wičazo Ša Review, 33*(1), 38–69. https://doi.org/10.5749/wicazosareview.33.1.0038

Werito, V. (2014). Understanding Hózho to achieve critical consciousness: A contemporary Diné interpretation of the philosophical principles of Hózhó. In Lloyd, L. (Ed.), *Diné perspectives: Revitalizing and eclaiming Navajo thought* (pp. 25–38). University of Arizona Press.

Wildcat, D. R. (2001). Indigenizing education: Playing to our strengths. In V. Deloria, Jr. & D. R. Wildcat (Eds.), *Power and place: Indian education in America* (pp. 7–19). Fulcrum.

CHAPTER 2

Indigenous Knowledges to Transform Public Education

Anthony B. Craig (Yakama Nation)
and Chelsea M. Craig (Tulalip Tribes)

PROLOGUE

In this chapter, we share traditional Coast Salish and Yakama teachings. In Lushootseed, x̌əčusadad is "traditional training, education." This encompasses all that makes us who we are. We ask you to recognize that when listening and learning from storytelling, you must access skills different from colonial approaches to "comprehension." When learning from traditional teachings, we must open our minds in order to recognize the messages that can be applied to multiple settings and situations; these are considered personal messages or lessons for each individual. In order to engage in this type of learning, we must decolonize our thinking and recognize the gifts that traditional teachings have to offer. To engage with this chapter, we have listed ways to open your minds to learning Indigenous traditional teachings:

Listen With Your Heart

- Be open to what the "work" or words have to offer.
  - » Apply the teachings, leadership moves, values to your own setting.
- Open your mind to hear the messages.
  - » You must "ground" yourself by coming with a good heart, being present, turning your mind off to all other thoughts.
  - » Ask yourself: What does this mean for me? For our kids, for our schools? What teachings does this help me recall from my Elders?

As a couple, as colleagues, and as coauthors, we situate ourselves as a partnership navigating life and working together. We share teachings we have encountered individually and together. Anthony is a citizen of the Yakama Nation and is also of Coast Salish and Irish descent; Chelsea is a citizen of The Tulalip Tribes and identifies as Coast Salish. We live and work in Coast Salish territory.

While we strive to please our Ancestors, Elders, and community members, we do so by acknowledging that the ideas we share here are not necessarily representative of our broader Tribal communities; instead, we have permission of our own family Elders to represent them and our families. We are learners of our languages and cultures and do not claim expertise. We also believe these teachings can spark thinking and inspire other Indigenous educators, across Tribal nations.

In this chapter we offer a story of Salmon. Salmon is a central being in our Tribal cultures now and has been forever. In the style of traditional stories, we imagine what we can collectively learn from a story of Salmon's return home. This story rises from our engagement with the Transformational Indigenous Praxis Model (TIPM). We see ourselves in Salmon and imagine her consciousness and resilience as our own.

INTRODUCTION

The time has come. Salmon and her relatives are beginning their long, arduous journey home. Using the knowledge from her Elders, the resources she has prepared all year, and the collective energy of her species, she travels toward survival—she seeks life. Like her Ancestors have since the beginning of time, Salmon will defy all odds to fulfill her life's purpose and ensure the survival of her species and provide for her relatives as designed by the Creator. Salmon moves with the teachings of her species— she knows her calling, her teachings, her resourcefulness will lead to her successful journey. She has a way . . . she seeks life.

What must we learn from Salmon? Salmon is unstoppable. Her sense of urgency and sense of purpose move her over, through, and around obstacles. She moves as though life itself depends on her successful navigation. It is her instinct, her movement with her salmon relatives, her teachings making the way.

In the tradition of Sandy Grande's *Red Pedagogy* (2004), in the footsteps of Michelle M. Jacob's "Yakama Decolonizing Praxis" (2013), and most recently with the language and conceptual underpinnings of the TIPM, we offer ideas, practices, and teachings from our own Tribal communities that guide our thinking, action, and vision for Indigenous education.

As part of Red Pedagogy, Sandy Grande (2004) reminds us to be guided by the "engagement between critical theory" and Indigenous education with a basis in hope. This hope "trusts the beliefs and understandings of our ancestors" (p. 28) and the power of traditional knowledges. This hope believes in the strength of and resiliency of Indigenous peoples and communities and acknowledges we have always been peoples of resistance.

Through her "Yakama Decolonizing Praxis," Jacob (2013) offers insights and approaches to healing the "soul wounds" in Indigenous communities caused by settler colonialism. Yakama Decolonizing Praxis is a "critical healing approach" (p. 11) that centers (grassroots) cultural revitalization, knowledge production and reproduction, and community activism. Through the Yakama Decolonizing Praxis,

Tribal communities can hear and respond to the calls of Ancestors while protect-ing sovereignty and Indigenous peoples' rights to culture, language, well-being, and learning.

TIPM is a structure that helps us hold many ideas at once while enacting cultural-based practices, reflecting on our own leadership and impact on today's school systems and for generations to come. Through TIPM we explore individ-ual and collective understanding of the un-learning and re-Indigenizing neces-sary to realize our dreams of rich learning and bright futures for our Indigenous people.

Our story of this work is interwoven with ancestral teachings and ceremonies passed down from past generations, our grandmothers' survivance of the boarding school era, and our mothers' resiliency and strength that has modeled for us viable ways forward for Indigenous people. We have spent the last two-plus decades as formal educators and as learners gathering more traditional teachings to ensure we pass on our lifeways to our grandson, his children's children, and beyond. As a Tulalip-Yakama collective, our drive for change is fueled by a sense of urgency for disrupting and intervening within colonial education systems that continue to attempt to stifle the spirit of our children and thus continue the violent assimila-tion through the settler-colonial complex. Through our leadership and learning, we aim to heal ourselves, our families, and our communities by returning to and strengthening Indigenous learning systems.

An Invitation

In this chapter, we share traditional teachings that have transformed our edu-cational practice toward healing. In sharing these teachings, it is our hope that readers can call to mind the ancestral strength and knowledge present in their own communities. We imagine fellow educators rejecting the violent, assimilative settler logics and practices of western education and thus intentionally centering teachings that remind us of the "education" models present in Indigenous soci-eties since the beginning of time. We further imagine the teachings we humbly offer from our Tribal communities and families existing in a complex ecosystem across Tribal nations, Tribal communities, and amongst our Ancestors as a bold, collective re-Indigenizing movement toward healing and true sovereignty for Indigenous people across our homelands.

Salmon has been traveling for days and days. Along her journey, Salmon grows tired and disoriented—she loses confidence. Calling from the cedar near the river's edge is Blue Jay. Blue Jay is the holder and carrier of knowledge, information, and resources. Blue Jay is calling to Salmon, urging her on, telling her what is ahead and how to navigate. With his knowledge and encouragement, Salmon forges ahead. Blue Jay remains in his post waiting to help Salmon's relatives making their way, too. Like Salmon, Blue Jay is answering his ancestral call to manage information for the benefit of all.

Our teachings are strong. Our Elders remind us that we must be active in accessing, understanding, and applying our Tribal lifeways and knowledges. Our teachings are waiting for us. Recently, an Elder shared with us that our traditional "learning processes" are much more complex than the ways western schooling has conditioned us, where learning is structured around standardized bodies of content delivered through rigid transactions taking place within curricular units, semesters, "school years" or "grade levels." In our traditional ways, according to our Elder, learning unfolds over time; teachings are not exchanged through a "transaction." Instead, there are times when we carry teachings and other times when teachings carry us. "Because of the fires of colonization," it can feel as though the knowledge we need is gone forever. She reminds us that it is within us and has carried us to this point . . . and we must keep going and the teachings will continue carrying us forward. We offer to our readers, decolonization is a process, our teachings are alive and we must all keep moving forward.

Extending from the TIPM, we offer our teachings and examples of the ways these ideas exist in our practice and contexts. To express the strongest version of these teachings possible, we use our Tribal languages Lushootseed (Tulalip Tribes) and Ichishkíin (Yakama Nation) where we are able. Through our languages, our Ancestors and Elders can help us recenter our traditional teachings and lifeways. An Elder has taught us that English is inadequate in expressing our teachings for their full depth and power. We have been reminded that our languages are known to these lands and waters. Our Ancestors communicate with us in our ancestral languages. While neither of us are fluent speakers of our languages, we share dreams for our grandchildren and their relatives to exist in worlds immersed in Lushootseed and Ichishkíin. It is through ongoing and intentional use of our languages that we make such expansive realities possible.

The teachings we offer are part of our ongoing story of educators on the path of transformation, healing, and reclamation. We hope our story helps you in further articulating and making meaning of your own stories. We also hope that by discussing these teachings, we can participate in the work that connects us to our Ancestors and descendants across generations. Through our work to enact ideas put forth by other Indigenous scholars and practitioners, our central purpose is to honor and celebrate the vital teachings from our Elders and Ancestors in Yakama and Tulalip.

TEACHINGS

huyadadcəɬ: Leveraging Ancestral Knowledges and Practices

Our people have always had a way. You already know the way.

—Bernie Kia Kia Gobin (Tulalip)

Over 20 years ago, we were both new teachers in a public school serving the Tulalip Tribal community. We were dreaming of a culturally rich and academically thriving school and unsure how to realize our dreams. It seemed no matter what approach we took, the settler system wore us down. We struggled to navigate as Indigenous educators. Even more frustrating, though, was our inability to create a space worthy of our Indigenous students. During a particularly challenging season of our school year, we sought the counsel of Elders. Chelsea's grandfather sat us down and said, "huyadadcəł. Our way of life. Our people have always had a way. You already know the way."

This teaching, the stern reminder that we were thinking, moving, reacting in ways that contradicted what our Ancestors and Elders expected of us, forever changed our lives. By design, our own schooling, our educator preparation programs, our school's evaluation system had conditioned us to think and teach in ways aligned with and promoted by the settler schooling system. Our frustration was not just with the structures and constraints of the western model of education, it was also internal frustration as we maintained colonized mindsets and practices and struggled to suppress the ancestral calling to abandon harmful practices and center what we knew was necessary to realize our dreams of Indigenous models of teaching and learning.

huyadadcəł is our most fundamental teaching. Within this one idea lies a calling to maintain our ancestral lifeways as the foundation, throughline, and future we aim to help build in our family and communities. huyadadcəł carries with it the ancestral calling to resist assimilation and dream Indigenous dreams. There is a need to think, learn, act, grow, communicate in ways that heal and help return our communities to our traditional ways through education. huyadadcəł holds the power of a community of Ancestors who protected our lifeways and now call us to strengthen and teach our future generations. Our ancestral ways of teaching, learning, and knowing must be the center of all we do. Our ancestral ways of life are already within us and are waiting to be accessed and enacted. Listed here are examples of how we have enacted our ancestral teachings in our practice; we invite readers to build from these examples as appropriate in other contexts.

huyadadcəł in practice

- Daily whole-school morning assembly beginning with a traditional song from the Tulalip people, Lushootseed, collective learning about Tulalip Tribal Values.
- A team of Tulalip Tribal teachers, other Indigenous teachers, and district leaders developed a curriculum that tells the story of the Tulalip people— past, present and future.
- A group of young Tribal Elders ("cultural guides") responsible for sustaining, revitalizing, teaching Tribal lifeways partnered with educators in the local public school to shift instructional practices toward cultural alignment (Craig, 2020).
- Cultural Guides encouraged our staff to participate in community events and celebrations to learn how our students interacted and learned in these community settings (Ginsberg & Craig, 2010).

Guiding questions to push our work

- What Indigenous teachings are central to our traditional and contemporary life?
- What western, colonial ideas must we reject and replace to truly Indigenize our system of teaching and learning/schooling?

daʔdaʔcut: Taking Action Now to Shape Futures

Like Salmon and Blue Jay, each of us must participate and remain active in strengthening our communities. The complex work of decolonizing and Indigenizing will take all of us to learn, grow, and heal. *daʔdaʔcut* is a Lushootseed phrase that means to "be part of the solution." We believe being part of the solution means it is necessary to cultivate and leverage a collective movement with everyone in the community participating in dreaming and building.

As descendants of boarding school survivors and survivors of settler school systems ourselves, it can feel as though we will never know enough or be able to do enough to return our communities to what we might dream. To these feelings of inadequacy, Chelsea's grandfather pointed out that we "already know enough and have enough to start." In starting, we launch a lifelong process of reclaiming lifeways that have always existed and will exist long after we are gone.

Grandpa would have us think of it like one spark, saying, "It only takes one spark to light a fire. Now, get up and do something! Start the fire." If each of us accepts this call, our sparks become flames, our flames join, and we begin to create heat and energy that clears the space we need to build our Indigenous futures.

Building on huyadadceł and daʔdaʔcut teaches us that the work must be done in a collective and must start now. While we may not know the depth and breadth of our original lifeways, we know enough to act now and to act together. We each have a spark that lives within us—that spark is our traditional teachings waiting to be reclaimed and enacted. That spark is our calling to contribute to the future we want for our descendants. We situate our participation in the disruption of and intervention in harmful school structures as participating in ongoing "survivance" where our people thrive in spite of oppressive systems (Sabzalian, 2019). Listed following are examples of how we have enacted our ancestral teachings in our practice; we invite readers to build from these examples as appropriate in other contexts.

daʔdaʔcut in practice

- Educators engage in cycles of critical self-reflection and meaningful relationality with other Indigenous educators and/or community members. Through an "inward gaze" (Paris & Alim, 2017), we must seek to understand the ways we are influenced and shaped by the very school settings we aim to transform. We must work to unlearn and decolonize ourselves, revitalize Indigenous teachings within our own lives to counter colonization that is internalized by youth and educators.

- Live the culture; live in the community for ongoing learning of our languages and cultures. Seek opportunities to read about, study, experience, live traditional and contemporary culture.

Guiding questions to push our work

- What is my spark? What can I contribute to my community's system of teaching and learning?
- What is within my power to stop doing due to misalignment with our community goals and ways?

x̱ṯtwayma and yəhawˑ: Developing and Working Within Collectives

Salmon continues her journey, with the lessons learned from Blue Jay. As she continues her journey she grows tired and is feeling discouraged, worried about reaching her destination. She then remembers that her relatives are traveling with her. Collectively they swim side by side, supporting each other through rough waters. She is traveling WITH her relatives creating movement, resting together when necessary, charting a course. Salmon and her relatives move together and dream together. When we work together, with a sense of urgency and clear purpose, we can accelerate our work for our people. The Salmon people journey together.

huyadadceł and daʔdaʔcut are teachings that remind us to be in community, to value collective action, and to participate in a tribe of people across generations. In contrast, our public schools are structured around individualism. Individual superintendents, principals, teachers, students are measured, evaluated, and expected to think and act as individuals. Settler approaches to learning, growth, success, and schooling value, uphold, and reward such independence. Indigenous students and educators have been harmed by this mismatch in logics and approaches to schooling.

As we continue to access our Tribal languages and cultures more deeply, many notions of collective learning and action are revealed. An Ichishkíin word, x̱ṯtwayma, holds great importance as we work to recenter norms and practices of community, collaboration, and collective action. x̱ṯtwayma translates to "friends and relatives" (Beavert et al., 2009). While this translation from Ichishkíin to English may seem straightforward, when paying attention to our ancestral stories and teachings, it is clear that Indigenous relationality between humans (and our more than human relations) is complex and necessary for our survivance.

As we learn to work together and contribute to improvement and system-building, we have been using a traditional Coast Salish story, *Lifting Up the Sky* (www.hibulbculturalcenter.org/Storytelling/Value-5/). In this story, all living beings must find ways to communicate in order to solve the shared problem of a sky that is too low for people to live a proper life. The word "yəhawˑ" ("proceed") is put forth in order to help organize people and allow them to coordinate their efforts to lift the sky. Through this story we learn of the need to work together, honor the efforts of each community member, and develop intentional strategy to know when to proceed with the collective work. Calls of "yəhaw̓" should remind us that the people successful in lifting the sky can accomplish anything! The work of transforming educational systems to be rich in Indigenous cultures and languages is possible as long as we work together. yəhaw̓! Listed below are examples of how we have enacted our ancestral teachings in our practice; we invite readers to build from these examples as appropriate in other contexts.

x̱ı́twayma and yəhaw̓ in practice

- Using traditional stories helps ground and reimagine our collective work, used in the process of co-constructing our mission and vision with Indigenous educators and community.
- Sharing practices and resources across territories, we utilized this practice and worked with other Indigenous communities, sharing our stories with each other in order to grow our practice and transform schools.
- Tribal educators recognize relationships with students extend across time beyond their classroom and a single school year.
- Recognizing that our students need relationships that feel more like the support from an auntie or uncle, we created support systems for students to have a daily connection with an adult outside of the classroom.

Guiding questions to push our work

- Are there clear, co-constructed understandings of what we are trying to achieve? Do goals help to uphold our teachings, our people, with consideration of seven generations to come?
- Are we building relationships with students allowing for meaningful connections between educators and students—including outside school?

Salmon and her salmon people keep traveling together. They notice there is a change in the river flow; there is becoming less and less water. It doesn't look how they had expected it to look—a dam blocks the way. Salmon looks ahead and she sees Spilyáy (Coyote) there. Spilyáy explains to her that the humans have changed this waterway. They have stopped the flow of the water. They have controlled the life of the river. Our river is not how it used to be. They must get creative and find new solutions. So Spilyáy explains to Salmon and the salmon people how to move to get over the dam. They do, and continue on their journey to their homeland.

spilyáywitasha: Navigating Systems as Tricksters Might

Imagine the idea of spilyáywitasha in the spirit of the late Congressman John Lewis. Inspired by Rep. Lewis, we imagine ourselves seeking "good trouble" and "necessary trouble" to resist oppression and seek change. Spilyáywitasha is an

Ichishkíin word that carries the meaning, "let's get into mischief" or "let's mess around like Spilyáy" (Beavert et al., 2009; Beavert & Underriner, 2017). Spilyáy is a main figure in traditional stories from throughout Yakama territory and into neighboring Tribal homelands. Spilyáy teaches the ways the world works, how to move through the world, and that life is not always to be taken at face value. Our people have long traditions of surviving colonial oppression and violence, navigating with cleverness, humor, and resistance. In order to seek change, we need to move in ways shown to us by Spilyáy and our Elders and Ancestors. We need to move *anakúsh Spilyáy* (like Spilyáy).

Our Elders have taught us the ways the settler systems have shifted over time to maintain power over tribes as we (re)assert sovereignty. Grandpa Bernie Gobin was a long-time warrior for Tribal sovereignty and treaty rights. Grandpa taught us explicitly and through modeling that we must learn how "the system" works, and how to operate within that system by also knowing traditional knowledge and leveraging community energies and expertise. He would often remind us to avoid situating ourselves as victims to a situation or system but to instead "be smarter." *anakúsh Spilyáy*! Listed below are examples of how we have enacted our ancestral teachings in our practice; we invite readers to build from these examples as appropriate in other contexts.

spilyáywitasha in practice

- Tulalip Sovereignty Curriculum is organized purposefully in a way that leaves no excuses for not accessing and utilizing them into the classroom, including videos of Tribal leaders and educators to help teach in classrooms virtually.
- Claim all the possible "spaces" as Indigenous spaces. We believe that Indigenous educators must infiltrate systems in ways that we can critique settler approaches to schooling and replace harmful practices with those aligned with our Tribal lifeways. As Linda Tuhiwai Smith asserts, "There are no neutral spaces for the kind of work required to ensure that traditional Indigenous knowledge flourishes" (Smith, 2012, p. 226). Apply for leadership positions, reshape positions in your institution, create curriculum, hire Indigenous educators, invite Indigenous community members into decision-making spaces.

Guiding questions to push our work

- Are we doing something different? Or are we perpetuating the same way of "doing school" that has always been in place, rooted in settler-colonial logics that not only has not worked for our people but has caused and continues to cause harm?
- Does your mission, vision, and decision-making reflect the values of and include the people you serve?

CONCLUSION

As Salmon was nearing her homelands, she could hear the drumbeat coming from the Big House under the sea. There was a great celebration of all her relatives, reflecting on their hard journey that took determination, guidance from wise Elders, and a collective effort to preserve lifeways for future generations. There were many teachings given at the ceremony, the teachings that have been in place since time immemorial. She could hear another sound coming from above the sea. It was the next generation, the sduhubš (Snohomish/Tulalip) people continuing what was left for them. She could see the respect, sacred practices, and love given to King Salmon. As they too carried on traditional teachings for future generations.

We offer these teachings as starting places. We are humbled by how little we know and excited to imagine the learning ahead. The gifts from our Ancestors and Elders hold infinite hope and possibility. We aspire to extend our practitioner expertise in ways that might emulate renowned Maori scholar, Linda Tuhiwai Smith's *Indigenous Research Agenda* (2012). We strive for educational leadership and instructional practices of Healing, Decolonization, Transformation, Mobilization; like Smith, we work to create the conditions of Survival, Recovery, Development, Self-Determination (2012, pp. 120–121). Like Salmon, we will keep traveling, keep humbly contributing what we can to the survival of our people.

We offer these small parts of the story of Salmon, Blue Jay, Spilyáy, our Elders, our Ancestors, our youth, our future generations, and ourselves in engagement with the TIPM. In the spirit of Marie Battiste, we have written this chapter as a story, as an act of resistance, and to transform ourselves and our work (Battiste, 2013). As we share the teachings from our Elders, we have become new versions of ourselves. We are both affirmed and inspired to learn more. We have written this as an invitation to others to join us in centering, celebrating, and being carried by traditional teachings in order to create new possible futures for our people.

REFERENCES

Battiste, M. (2013). *Decolonizing education: Nourishing the learning spirit.* Purich Publishing Limited.

Beavert, V., Hargus, S., & Rigsby, B. (2017). *Ichishkíin Sinwit Yakama/Yakima Sahaptin dictionary.* University of Washington Press.

Beavert, V. & Underriner, J. L. (2017). *The gift of knowledge/Ttnúwit Átawish Nch'inch'imamí: reflections on Sahaptin ways.* University of Washington Press.

Craig, A. B. (2020). Transforming teaching and learning through Indigenous strengths and ways of knowing. In M. M. Jacob & S. R. Johnson (Eds.), *On Indian ground* (pp. 79–98). Information Age Publishing.

Ginsberg, M., & Craig, A. (2010). Tradition becomes the teacher: Community events enrich educators' professional learning. *Journal of Staff Development, 31*(3), 36–41.

Grande, S. (2004). *Red pedagogy: Native American social and political thought.* Rowman & Littlefield.

Jacob, M. M. (2014). *Yakama rising: Indigenous cultural revitalization, activism, and healing.* University of Arizona Press.

Paris, D., & Alim, H. S. (2017). *Culturally sustaining pedagogies: Teaching and learning for justice in a changing world.* Teachers College Press.

Sabzalian, L. (2019). *Indigenous children's survivance in public schools.* Routledge.

Smith, L. T. (2012). *Cram101 textbook outlines to accompany: Decolonizing methodologies: research and indigenous peoples, by Linda Tuhiwai Smith, 1st edition.* Content Technologies, Inc.

Storytelling Value #5. (n.d.). Hibulb Cultural Center and Natural History Preserve. https://www.hibulbculturalcenter.org/Storytelling/Value-5/

CHAPTER 3

Exploring, Leading, and Managing Indigenous K–12 Education

yahnesuaru mohatsi (Comanche and Kiowa)

Haa maruaweka nu?niha tsa yahnesuaru mohatsi, and I am a citizen of the Comanche Nation. This chapter brings together academic fields of educational leadership, administration, strategic change management, and Indigenous education to provide a systems-level analysis of educational services for Indigenous peoples. It explores the complex yet necessary process of relationship building between communities and political institutions of education to address the key challenges of Indigenous education. Education is the soul of an Indigenous peoples; it is a mirror that empowers them to awaken as forerunning communities of understanding. Investing early in the future of Indigenous education requires community-focused collaboration between individuals and institutions who affect all levels of birth–grade-12 learning. The focus of this chapter is on the action steps or dimensions described within the Transformational Indigenous Praxis Model to ensure high-quality academic programs that are delivered from birth through grade 12 in an Indigenous cultural context.

Promoting relationships between Indigenous communities that receive education and the institutions that design it proves to be politically intricate. Collaboration is difficult because it requires navigating broken and unbroken relationships with an agenda to introduce new learning and deconstruct old learning. Exercising Tribal sovereignty in education requires us to be strategic and diplomatic as we engage in public spaces—whether those conversations be in the classroom one day and in the courtroom the next day (see *Yazzie and Martinez v. State of New Mexico*, 2018. Decision and Order).

This chapter also reflects upon my experiences as a former executive director of Indian Education for the State of Oklahoma about the application of Indian Education having cultural relevance for Indigenous peoples and their respective communities. In order to focus on improving education for Indigenous students in public schools, we must understand the relationship between Indian Education directors and the school communities they serve. This perspective is critical for any individual who intends to impact education for Indigenous communities in a positive manner. This chapter outlines five major areas where these relationships and subsequent navigation skills are challenged, as well as highlights the dimensions for which I have observed these areas within the Transformational Indigenous Praxis Model. By using the first two dimensions from the TIPM, Indian Education directors can illustrate pathways to equitable education and propose visions of highly responsible and compassionate ways to reconstruct Indigenous education.

ENTANGLEMENT BETWEEN POLICY AND PRACTICE

The relationship between policymakers and practitioners, when planning for Indigenous education, always has a natural tension. This entanglement can be described in two ways. One way seeks educational change through a policy perspective; these are the people who believe change is accomplished for Indigenous communities through Tribal, federal, or state policy change. The other is a practical change; these folks focus more on the tangible products and processes that must be factored into the delivery of education. Examples include the design of culturally responsive lesson plans and instructional delivery of knowledge (cultural pedagogy). This relationship is in constant tension because neither communicates to one another with a cyclical flow of knowledge. Tensions grow greater and collaborations fail if partnerships do not cure the impacts caused from information asymmetry.

Policymakers focus on change through academic standards, and in most cases avoid efforts to address curriculum that may impact local control. This is the first area of entanglement, because changing academic standards is only one-third of a comprehensive solution to restorative educational practices that support Indigenous students. The second step beyond academic standards is to invest time and resources into the meaningful design of culturally responsive curriculum informed by directors of Indian Education. These practitioners of Indian Education have subject-matter expertise that justifies the need for investment of resources into curriculum to connect with Indigenous students in a culturally responsive manner. The greatest challenge facing policy change is that people will not forcibly change due to a change in required text. Passing a new law for culturally responsive curriculum is not enough; it never happens with fidelity without the change in practice. On the other hand, the people who prefer practical change are frustrated that policy change doesn't either accurately or feasibly propose how to teach knowledge or new knowledge.

EMPOWERING NATIVE VOICE IN THE POLICY ARENA

The case for community-based participation calls for Indigenous people to be part of the discussion when creating educational policy with Indigenous peoples, if not the leaders of educational policy construction. For example, in 2019 the State of Oklahoma's Department of Education revised social studies standards to expand the expectation that Tribal sovereignty be taught in public schools as early as 3rd grade—whereas it was formerly only taught at the beginning of 11th grade. A critical element of change here was to empower Tribal Departments of Education with the ability to influence the standards revision process. The State Department had three primary committee structures, whereas in the older practice, Tribal Nations would be involved only in the less influential part of the process, meaning symbolic focus groups. From the policy perspective, individuals may be quick to criticize that Tribal Nations do not participate in the revision process and that equates their disinterest in it as a whole. This isn't true. Tribal Nations aren't robustly engaged in the policy-changing process because the terminology and awareness of these functions aren't publicly or easily accessible. Trying to explore the role of state departments of education in Indigenous education could be one method for understanding how educational policy is constructed, modified, and implemented in K–12 schools, particularly in public schools.

LACK OF COLLABORATION AND THE CASE FOR MORE OF IT

Examining student outcomes in public K–12 education can be both an under- and overwhelming experience, especially when a public manager is trying to figure out "what matters" during the consideration of raising student academic achievement. This chapter prepares for an empirical search into the relationship between public managers, who collaborate at different levels of educational authority, in order to see if there is any relationship in educational outcomes that impacts academic achievement. The practical foundation of collaboration as it relates to the discipline of public administration still has a decade's worth of clarifying scholarship to be had; this chapter wants to provide contextual understanding on the importance of collaboration as it relates to K–12 educational outcomes between state educational agency (SEA) Indian Education directors and local educational agency (LEA) Indian education directors. The dynamics by which these public managers interact are not yet understood within the context of actual implementation and coordination of service provision related to engaging with students, families, and other administrative colleagues throughout their respective agencies. In order to better outline these dynamics, it will be beneficial to briefly summarize the K–12 educational policy developments of Indian Education since the inception of the Elementary and Secondary Education Act (ESEA) of 1965. Each subsequent reauthorization and expansion of Indian Education policy has enabled the ability for Tribal Nations to exert their sovereignty within Indian Education policy (McCoy, 2005).

BRIEF K–12 INDIAN EDUCATION HISTORY

In this section I identify some major federal policies that have impacted the state of Indigenous education in general and more specifically for our Tribal communities, students, and families. I begin with the Elementary and Secondary Education act in 1965 and depict a series of policy shifts that led to our current moment.

Elementary and Secondary Education Act (ESEA) 1965 Indian Education

The ESEA was enacted with a national policy intent to "bridge a gap" between children whose socioeconomic backgrounds spanned from impoverished to privileged. President Johnson signed ESEA into law that essentially created a national-educational endeavor to change the relationship between the federal government and state educational agencies throughout the United States. In the original ESEA of 1965, Indian Education did not exist; however, we can assume that federal funds would have impacted American Indian/Alaska Native students through general Title I funding.

PL 89-750 of 1966 and PL 90-247 of 1967 Amendments

Prior to any formal reauthorization of the ESEA, there were two amendments that provided new titles to national educational policy that introduced "Aid to Handicapped Children" and "Bilingual Education Programs," with no specific funds for the purposes of "Indian Education."

The Indian Education Act of 1972

The Indian Education Act (IEA) provided a specific line-item within the U.S. Department of Education (USDE) to create the U.S. Office of Indian Education (OIE), the National Advisory Council on Indian Education (NACIE), and provided empowerment for parent advisory committees for Title IV grant funding for SEA disbursement to LEAs.

Reauthorization: Education Consolidation and Improvement Act (ECIA) 1981

As the first reauthorization of ESEA, the Reagan Administration via Omnibus Reconciliation Act of 1981 expanded the respective roles of education administration between state and local governments with a specific shift of responsibility to state educational agencies.

Reauthorization: Hawkins-Stafford Elementary and Secondary School Improvement Act 1988

In the second reauthorization of ESEA, the Reagan Administration further focused on "specialized concentration grants" to local educational agencies, which created more functional difference between state and local educational agencies as they delivered services. At the time, this was the first inclusion of specific concentrated funding toward providing 1% of basic grant funds to schools for American Indian/ Alaska Native students attending BIA schools on reservations. At that point, no funds were provided to local educational agencies outside of reservation lands.

Reauthorization: Improving America's Schools Act (IASA) 1994

The third reauthorization of the ESEA, during the Clinton administration, introduced a major focus on prescribing authorities for state educational agencies to set state standards, and the local educational agencies would then promote and implement alignment to such standards. The reauthorization devised specific educational components: curriculum and instruction, leadership, improvement, accountability, and so on. At this point, Indian Education funding was changed from Title IV to Title IX with an expectation that American Indian/Alaska Native students would achieve the same standards as the general population.

Reauthorization: No Child Left Behind (NCLB) 2001

The fourth reauthorization of ESEA, during the Bush administration, ushered in a wave of proposed sanctions and corrective actions for state and local educational agencies to adopt "standards-based reform" and design assessments to those standards. Indian Education was retitled in the reauthorization as Title VII "Indian, Native Hawaiian, and Alaska Native Education" for purposes of formula grant funds to local educational agencies.

Reauthorization: Every Student Succeeds Act (ESSA) 2015

The fifth reauthorization of ESEA, during the Obama Administration, emphasized accountability plans that state educational agencies must submit to the U.S. Department of Education. This most recent reauthorization focused on low-performing schools re-designation and distribution of Title I funds, including how subgroups are tracked, school interventions are identified, and English Language Learning. Under ESSA, Title VII "Indian, Native Hawaiian, and Alaska Native Education" was re-designated to Title VI with subparts: (a) Indian Education, (b) Native Hawaiian Education, and (c) Alaska Native Education; under Title VI, funding went directly to LEAs. Each national policy throughout the decades emphasized the necessity for Native/Indigenous control of the educational programs, even to create space for self-determination in public schools. In late 2014, it became overwhelmingly apparent that the federal government must support Tribal sovereignty and self-determination in K–12 public education. This educational emphasis is considered essential to rebuilding Native Nations via Tribal educational agencies, such as Tribal departments of education.

INDIAN EDUCATION COLLABORATION DILEMMA

This chapter is informed from the history of "Indian Education" funding, meaning that throughout each reauthorization since the ESEA of 1965 and Indian Education Act of 1972, the actual funding of Indian Education has set the stage for understanding collaboration between Tribal, State, and Local Educational Agencies. It is important to know that Title VI formula funding no longer "flows" through the state educational agency, which means that state educational agencies possess less interest in monitoring and collaborating with local educational agencies to ensure meaningful implementation of educational services to Indigenous students. Due to the state educational agency having no administrative oversight or compliance capacity relative to Title VI funds, what is the case for collaboration between the state and local educational agencies?

Sometimes school administrators are limited when working and collaborating with Indigenous communities and educators who live within a relational worldview. When relationships are not valued, the opportunities to build connections with Indigenous communities become harder to create and maintain. In some cases, district administrators and Indian Education directors who work with Indigenous education are stuck in the foundational dimension (contributions approach). This dilemma is mostly caused by a difference in worldview, ideology, and teaching philosophy for implementing effective learning practices with Indigenous peoples. This chapter calls for an argument to rethink leadership and management of Indigenous education.

THE CASE FOR CULTURALLY RESPONSIVE AND RELATIONSHIP-BASED PEDAGOGY AND COLLABORATION

Culturally responsive and relationship-based pedagogy and collaboration "set the stage" for more in-depth research into legitimate efforts to examine what relationship-based pedagogy and collaborative behaviors best drive conversations of improving school-based education for all Indigenous students, not just low performers. Teachers and educators with limited knowledge of culturally responsive and relationship-based pedagogy are often unaware of the Indigenous knowledge that children bring into the classroom and of the cultural cues that Indigenous students use to express themselves in the teaching and learning process (Bang et al., 2012; Sabzalian, 2019). The consequences of this misunderstanding usually lead to the inability or ambiguity to address educational disparities adversely affecting Indigenous students (Brayboy & Lomawaima, 2018; Faircloth & Tippeconic, 2010; Johnston-Goodstar & Roholt, 2017).

State and local Indian Education directors serve as the principal glue to bridge the gap between Indigenous and non-Indigenous educators. Their work advances relationships and can cultivate professional learning communities to address gaps in knowledge about Indigenous ways of knowing. In order to stabilize service quality, collaboration will be critical to advancing the cause for continued Indian Education Title funding. No matter how we organize the information, there are still lingering questions around this work. A significant gap in the literature revolves around how state educational agencies influence, partner, and facilitate change through collaborative means and support Tribal and local education agencies. Does collaboration truly cause positive outcomes in

K–12 public education, especially when such collaborations are driven by the state educational agency? How can you maintain effective and meaningful intergovernmental collaborations but still ensure or measure for quality throughout its development? The answers to these questions must go beyond valuing input from Indigenous students and their families; their input must be utilized in the design of new collaborative policies. The future of leading and managing Indigenous education will need teachers and educators to shift the nature of pedagogy in the classroom in a way that enables Indigenous students to participate and learn.

CONCLUSION

As policymakers and practitioners work to address disparities in Indigenous student K–12 experiences and outcomes, it is necessary to work with the educators who are already engaged in culturally responsive teaching and learning as well as relationship-based pedagogy. The importance of doing so is supported by the meta-analysis within the Transformational Indigenous Praxis Model. As mentioned earlier in this chapter, the main challenge for educational administrators of Indigenous education is to focus on advancing from the contributions dimension to the additive dimension. Policy can help all educators move from the contributions dimension to additive dimension in the TIPM and is critical for setting the foundation for greater transformation in the future. The TIPM is about reframing a tool for finding new opportunities and options for rebuilding Indigenous school systems. To reflect this reframing, I suggest how someone can conceptualize educational services for K–12 Indigenous students as the nature and basis of disparities using the framework within TIPM.

I propose viewing Indigenous education issues through three pillars: standards, curriculum, and instruction. Academic standards help level-set understanding across school districts and "open the door" for curriculum to flourish. In the case of Oklahoma, the state department of education revises academic standards every six years. In doing so, the state department of education addresses policy advocates' needs for system-level representation of culturally representative requirements. Curriculum must be culturally responsive and meaningful in the sense that the curricula is representative of any Indigenous student's Tribal affiliation. For example, Comanche and Cherokee peoples' have different lived experiences and history; though both are Indigenous, their stories are unique. It is not meaningful to teach a Comanche student about Cherokee history and expect that Comanche student to connect with the curriculum. Indigenous students must have the opportunity to connect with curriculum that is representative and meaningfully designed to their Tribal affiliation(s). Last but not least, instructional delivery is essential to ensure all the time and effort in standards and curriculum do not go to waste. In order for effective change to be authentic, the instructional delivery and subsequent professional development to Indigenous and non-Indigenous educators must focus on empowering educators to teach in a culturally responsive manner. My observation is that all three pillars have been the exceptional challenge facing K–12 Indigenous education.

James Banks's foreword to Hopkins's (2020) book, *Indian Education for All*, echoed the sentiments for this chapter when he stated that "inclusion conversations must take place between Indigenous community members and mainstream educators in public schools in order to conceptualize and implement Indigenous school reform and a decolonizing education for Indigenous youth" (p. ix).

The hope of this chapter was to encourage and nurture such qualities and possibilities for working together in a concerted effort to ensure the continued resilience of Indigenous education. We must continue to focus on both managers and leadership. Leading and managing are different, but both are important when reframing Indigenous education. The greatest pathway to effectively managing and leading change for K–12 Indigenous education requires extensive, authentic, and meaningful investment of public education resources and dollars into collaborative efforts that strengthen consultation and cooperation at all levels of academic standards, curriculum, and instruction for years to come.

REFERENCES

Bang, M., Warren, B., Rosebery, A. S., & Medin, D. (2012). Desettling expectations in science education. *Human Development*, *55*(5-6), 302–318.

Brayboy, B. M. J., & Lomawaima, K. T. (2018). Why don't more Indians do better in school? The battle between US schooling & American Indian/Alaska Native education. *Daedalus*, *147*(2), 82–94.

Faircloth, S. C., & Tippeconnic, J. W., III. (2010). *The dropout/graduation crisis among American Indian and Alaska Native students: Failure to respond places the future of Native Peoples at risk*. Civil Rights Project/Proyecto Derechos Civiles.

Hopkins, J. P. (2020). *Indian education for all: Decolonizing Indigenous education in public schools*. Teachers College Press.

Johnston-Goodstar, K., & VeLure Roholt, R. (2017). "Our kids aren't dropping out; they're being pushed out": Native American students and racial microaggressions in schools. *Journal of Ethnic & Cultural Diversity in Social Work*, *26*(1-2), 30–47.

McCoy, M. (2005). *The Evolution of tribal sovereignty over education in federal law since 1965*. Indian Education Legal Support Project. http://www.narf.org/wordpress/wp-content/uploads/2015/01/gold.pdf.

Sabzalian, L. (2019). *Indigenous children's survivance in public school*. Routledge.

Part II

TEACHER EDUCATION

Examining Teacher Education and Practice Through the Transformational Indigenous Praxis Model (TIPM)

Dolores Calderón (Mexican/Tigua)

INTRODUCTION

In this chapter, I apply the Transformational Indigenous Praxis Model (TIPM; Pewewardy et al., 2018) to research that examines the impact of Indigenous content and relationships with Indigenous peoples in western teacher practice (both pre-service and in-service). My goal in using TIPM to analyze this literature is twofold: first, to demonstrate the utility of TIPM as an accessible analytical framework that can be used to organize and scale teacher education research and practices according to how supportive they are of decolonizing and indigenizing teacher practices; and, second, to flesh out the four dimensions of TIPM in the context of teacher education work with the largely white teacher workforce in the United States. Specifically, I review literature that documents the impact of infusing Indigenous content and/or relationships with Indigenous communities into mainstream teacher education programs and teacher practice, organizing the literature according to TIPM's four dimensions: (1) contributions approach, (2) additive approach, (3) transformation approach, and (4) culture and social justice action approach. Thus, this chapter demonstrates the utility of TIPM for documenting work that supports Indigenous futures (Grande, 2008; Tuck & Yang, 2012) in the realm of teacher education and practice.

Moreton-Robinson et al.'s (2012) review of literature conducted as part of an official inquiry into the status of Indigenous education in teacher education globally reports that in the United States and Canada, recent teacher education endeavors focus on ideas of decolonizing around (1) Indigenous community involvement, (2) including Indigenous knowledges in school curriculum, (3) increasing Indigenous educational workers, (4) emphasizing Indigenous learning styles, and (5) the differences between school and home cultures. Additionally, Moreton-Robinson et al. (2012) explain that with regards to teacher education,

"North American literature links the decolonization of Indigenous education with the transferring of particular skills to pre-service and in-service teachers" (p. 17). Of note, they find in their review of U.S. and Canadian teacher education research demands that teachers understand ongoing colonialism, but, "[h]ow exactly this sort of knowledge is to be taught to pre-service teachers, however, has not been extensively detailed" (p. 17).

Building from these findings, the literature I examine here documents *how* Indigenous knowledges are being incorporated into teacher education and subsequent professional development, noting successes and challenges. This literature does not represent an exhaustive review of literature documenting impacts of Indigenous content and/or relationships with Indigenous communities on mainstream teacher education programs and practice. Instead, pieces selected here highlight the four dimensions of TIPM and offer examples of how pathway-making across these teacher education examples "takes form on the TIPM continuum" (p. 3, this volume). The analysis I apply in this integrative review is guided by RedCorn's (2020) call for dynamic systems thinking that serves "the critically conscious collective efficacy" (p. 12) in the "professional ecosystem of educators" (p.11) that are working toward ensuring Indigenous futures (Pewewardy & Hammer, 2003). This work is also guided by my participation in a work collective that attends to local Coast Salish community leaders' calls to improve the experiences of Indigenous students in local school districts to strengthen educational opportunities for Indigenous families.

As a researcher of Pueblo and Mexican background from the border, I have a commitment to do work to support local desires in the place I live (Smith, 2013; Wilson, 2008). Brayboy et al.'s (2012) Critical Indigenous Research Methodologies framework in educational research affirms that research should be in service of Indigenous communities and determined by community needs, thus the focus here on white teachers engaging Indigenous informed content. Because Indigenous communities and needs are starting points and constant collaborators (Archibald, 2008; Kovach, 2009; Smith, 2013; Wilson, 2008), the work always speaks back against the "epistemological ethnocentrism" of western knowledge (Thambinathan & Kinsella, 2021) in education, which I trace in literature of teacher education and practice.

INDIGENOUS CONTENT AND RELATIONSHIPS WITH INDIGENOUS PEOPLES

As described in the introduction of this book, the Transformative Indigenous Praxis Model (TIPM) is composed of four stages or dimensions (Pewewardy et al., 2018). Here I examine literature documenting the impact of Indigenous content and relationships with Indigenous peoples in teacher education programs and practice. The first dimension of TIPM, the *contributions approach*, characterizes educators who have not developed critical consciousness of schooling. As previously mentioned, in this dimension teachers are ignorant of the negative impact of settler colonialism on education, its devastating impacts on Indigenous peoples, and "are . . . satisfied with school-based education" (p. 4, this volume). Teachers operating in this dimension might add-in typical multicultural content, or the "heroes and holidays" model (Banks, 1989; Lee et al., 1997; Pewewardy, 1998).

Characteristics of teacher practice that embody the *contributions approach* are the most dominant approach. Teacher attitudes about their profession shape this approach. For instance, the manner in which teachers internalize the profession- alization of the work (Blimkie et al., 2014; Dion, 2009) aligns with existing, nor- mative curriculum that embraces the heroes and holidays approach (Pewewardy, 1998). Relatedly, many teachers express discomfort with Indigenous content (Calderón et al., 2021; Jackson et al., 2016), as the majority of the teaching force in places such as the United States and Canada is white. These teachers internalize dominant narratives of Indigenous absence (Bang et al., 2014) and do not find Indigenous inclusion important (Dion, 2009; Nardozi et al., 2014). Dion (2007) describes this attitude as the "perfect stranger" syndrome, where white teachers profess ignorance of Indigenous peoples and their stories; "Teachers respond with comments that go something like 'Oh I know nothing, I have no friends who are Aboriginal, I didn't grow up near a reserve, I didn't learn anything in school, I know very little or I know nothing at all about Native people'" (p. 330). And yet, even when teachers decide to include Indigenous content, inclusion reproduces ongoing Indigenous dispossession. In other words, the preparation of teachers, whether through teacher education or professional development, determines how this inclusion occurs (Dion 2009; Madden, 2015) and whether the inclusion leads to movement into a more decolonizing dimension in the TIPM.

Madden (2015) and Dion (2009) also describe challenges when pre-service and in-service teachers are led to include Indigenous content that fails to provoke a more critical understanding of settler colonialism as a structure. Madden (2015) describes this as the "limits of empathy" in settler teachers. Madden, drawing from Dion (2009), clarifies:

> Dion (2009) explains that the cultivation of empathy created the conditions for stu- dents to overlook their participation in ongoing colonial relations. They [students] learned "to see themselves as compassionate and honourable" (p.127) in that they were able to "develop appropriate attitudes regarding the suffering [of Aboriginal peoples subject to multiple colonial oppressions], arriving at judgments about fairness, and learning the 'right' rules of moral behaviour" (p. 138). Moreover, Dion observed that students' preoccupation with "feeling sorry for the pitiful [Aboriginal] victim" ob- scured examples of resilience and agency present in counternarratives. It is argued that pedagogical methods intended to foster empathy . . . may also reinscribe colonial ways of knowing about Aboriginal-non-Aboriginal relationships. . . . (p. 9)

Other research identifies the experiences described in the previous quote as mo- ments where teachers maintain their settler innocence (Seawright, 2014; Tuck & Yang, 2012).

However, it is also at this juncture where white teachers have the opportunity to engage Indigenous content differently, allowing them to move into the next stage, the *additive dimension* of TIPM. Otherwise, they remain in a *contributions approach*. Adding Indigenous content is often met with resistance in teacher education and practice. This can include the belief that teaching Indigenous content is a disservice to non-Indigenous students. For example, Blimkie, Vetter, and Brown (2014) interviewed a teacher who shared a common perception, "'I think there are other focus areas that would help me more as a teacher–special education, diversity in general. Not saying Aboriginal topics are not important, but I think there are other focus areas that could help more students as a whole'" (p. 53). This prevailing attitude often prevents teachers from moving to the next dimension.

In the second dimension, or the *additive approach*, educators demonstrate "curiosity around settler colonial educational structures with beginning steps toward change through 'bursts of critical awareness'" (p. 5, this volume). Teachers often feel overwhelmed with the impact of racist curriculum and unsure of how to even begin to approach such controversial topics (Delpit, 2006; Gay, 2018). Teachers working toward incorporating culturally relevant approaches are often working against internalized deficit ideologies about Communities of Color. Pewewardy, Lees, and Minthorn (Introduction, this volume) point out that "[t]hese educators need strong mentorship and collegial support in order to focus their energy and navigate through the waves of resistance" (p. 18). (See also Kohli et. al, 2015; Pewewardy, 2005; Picower, 2012.)

The *additive approach* represents the most common approach of teacher education and teacher professional development that works to include Indigenous peoples and subject matter (Lees et al., in press). Much of the challenge of doing this work in teacher education and practice has to do with the overall poor preparation of white teachers regarding Indigenous content and knowledge generally (Rogers, 2018). At the same time, teacher education spaces that require or encourage Indigenous content in the curriculum are often isolated spaces, not consistently applied regionally (Nardozi et al., 2014). Similarly, required content in K–12 schooling often does not expand beyond the limited ways it is required to be taught in specified curriculums (Smith et al., 2011; Tupper & Cappello, 2008). But it is also in these spaces where Tribes and First Nations assert sovereign influence over education. These instances offer important case studies representative of the transformational approach (Blimkie et al., 2014; Lees et al., 2021; Tupper & Cappello, 2008).

In the third dimension, or the *transformation approach*, educators move beyond multicultural, additive practices that are anti-racist toward praxis that challenge settler colonialism. In this stage, teachers often seek others to help do this work, usually outside of sanctioned education spaces (Kohli & Pizarro, 2016; Navarro, 2018; Picower, 2015) in order to make sense of what decolonization in their educational practice looks like.[1]

Much of this work occurs in context where Indigenous content and relationships with local Indigenous communities are legally mandated (Lees et al., 2021; Smith et al., 2011) and Indigenous communities are serious partners in the work

(Blimkie et al., 2014; Lees et al., in press). Because Indigenous communities and personnel are involved, this work occurs outside what is considered the traditional classroom. Indigenous educators find that taking white teachers to learn with land and water and other Indigenous relatives allows non-native teachers to *see* the realities of settler colonialism, transforming it from an idea to a concrete experience (Bell, 2020; Calderón et al., 2021; Lees et al., in press; Noordhoff & Kleinfeld, 1993). Bell (2020), an Anishinaabe teacher educator, created a land-based learning opportunity for pre-service teachers that immersed them in her home community of Burleigh Falls and Lovesick Lake to engage in decolonial learning. Bell built a curriculum that teaches white teachers to understand Indigenous kinship models that are not human-centric. Bell describes that this work "means teaching to students' mental, physical, emotional, and spiritual capacities" (p. 1). Bell continues, "Spirituality is also about being humble enough to acknowledge that humans are the most insignificant beings on this planet, because we cannot live without the life-givers that are provided for us" (p. 1).

The transformative approach embraces the capacity of Indigenous knowledges to disrupt fundamental notions of the western self—from rejecting individualism (Deloria & Wildcat, 2001) to challenging the human–nature divide (Bang et al., 2012)—such learning in teacher education creates opportunities for teachers/future teachers to build collaborative classrooms and imagine education outside the narrow confines of western schooling (Bang & Marin, 2015; Calderón et al., 2021; Tanaka et al., 2007). In this stage teachers realize that centering Indigenous content and partnership with Indigenous communities is good for all students (Blimkie et al., 2014).

As a result of these approaches, teachers change their pedagogical practice. Pedagogically successful classroom practices for in-service teachers in this dimension might include the use of storytelling, the use of relevant and connected Indigenous cultural content aligned with student and community backgrounds, experiential and observational learning, small-group learning, and a warm relationship established between teachers and students (Kanu, 2016). Moreover, in this stage, teacher-community relationships are transformed. No longer do teachers unidirectionally invite Indigenous communities into the classroom; teachers recognize the need to build relationships with Indigenous communities and knowledge holders in order to facilitate knowledge sharing (Brayboy & Maughan, 2009; Kearney et al., 2014).

Challenges that arise in this stage are that the more white pre- and inservice teachers learn about Indigenous knowledges, the more resistant they become. Some examples of this resistance include an unwillingness to accept Indigenous creation stories (Jackson, 2016; Kanu, 2016), which prevents them from wanting to understand systemic racism, structural poverty, and the ongoing legacy of colonial governance and dispossession for Indigenous peoples (Grande, 2015; Kanu, 2016; Lees et al., 2021; Nardozi et al., 2014). Just as common is educators' reluctance to teach Indigenous content, afraid that they will make mistakes because in their attempt to include Indigenous content they have hurt Indigenous students (Jackson et al., 2016; Kanu, 2016; Nardozi et al., 2014). For instance, one teacher in a Canadian study describes, "'I worry about whether I am going to get it right and not be offensive. Because I don't think any of us would do something deliberately to be offensive, but there's a certain sensitivity and I don't know very much still. What if I get it wrong?'" (Blimkie et al., 2014). These challenges can be overcome, the literature shows, if educators work in partnership with Indigenous communities that is ongoing, resulting in enduring learning opportunities. In the teacher education collective I am a part of, one teacher took a misstep including local Indigenous content, but because of the Tribally led professional development she participated in, she subsequently changed her approach to one that embodies *transformational* praxis: "So the second semester I, like, had to preview . . . like, there are local connections when you talk about local tribes that you don't understand at all, and then trying to inform students in a way that's like something completely outside of your knowledge base where they're the experts" (Calderón et al., 2021, pp. 10–11). The shift to students being experts represents the type of work that leads to *cultural and social justice action*.

Indeed, the most transformative dimension, dimension 4, *cultural and social justice action*, describes those educators that "demonstrate a deep embodiment of critical consciousness and consistently take active efforts in social justice" and also "enact transformational praxis in both theoretical and concrete ways to make change in the educational experiences of Black and Indigenous communities and other Communities of Color" (p. 6, this volume). Educators' daily practices are guided by Indigenous and decolonizing pedagogies, centering Indigenous knowledges and advancing Indigenous self-determination (Garcia et al., 2021). They are often mentors of others endeavoring to TIPM, but as Pewewardy et al. point out, "It can be difficult to remain in this dimension, and even the most critically conscious educators may retreat from leadership roles and move between dimensions to find sustainability in the work" (p. 6, this volume; see also Navarro, 2018; Valdez et al., 2018).

The resistance encountered by teacher educators in this dimension has to do with the ongoing violence of settler colonialism in Indigenous peoples lives. While Indigenous students' academic success increases in classrooms that embody cultural and social justice action (Deyhle, 2013; Kanu, 2016), nevertheless the students are faced with the structural realities of being Indigenous in a settler-colonial context. Kanu (2016) describes:

> This complex array of reasons/issues causing educational under-achievement among so many Aboriginal students requires us to go beyond the integration of Aboriginal cultural knowledge/perspectives, important as it is, and take into account macro-structural explanations of Aboriginal students' chronic educational underachievement. Several factors are lead suspects in this area, including poverty perpetuated by the low participation of Aboriginal peoples in the labour market, frequent mobility due to lack of good-quality affordable housing, and lack of well-resourced secondary schools on many Aboriginal reserves, which forces Aboriginal students to leave their home communities and live in dormitories or with guardians and extended family members in the city in order to further their education. (p. 144)

Kanu's apt description of the ways settler colonialism structures ongoing dispossession leads teachers with this knowledge to confront the barriers in schooling. This can lead to alienation of these teachers (Kulago, 2019). Yet hope is found in the work that names this process as fugitive (Lees & Vélez, 2019; Pewewardy et al., this volume). Indeed, teachers—as they always have—create unsanctioned spaces to collectively do transformative and liberatory work (Navarro, 2020).

Yet school leaders, other teachers, and non-native families often push back on Indigenous-focused content in favor of approaches characterized by the attitude of "there are other children here" (St. Denis, 2011). Certainly, the main thrust of schooling as an agent of the state requires we understand that TIPM can circle back through different dimensions. Cycles of inequity are repeated, yet, as shown above, TIPM traces the trajectory of the work that ultimately embodies *transformation* in the deepest sense.

CONCLUSION

Returning to RedCorn's (2020) dynamic systems thinking, I find TIPM as a framework maps the ability of teacher education and practice to incorporate Indigenous content and communities in concrete ways for white teachers. Using TIPM to examine this literature helps cultivate a "critically conscious collective efficacy" (RedCorn, 2020, p. 12) by making legible good practice. More importantly, this work makes clear the importance of being in good relation to each other and building from a more fundamental desire to provide for the generations to come and to remember, earnestly, those whom we stand on. Reviewing this literature evidences the power of people and place and the importance of sustained relations with Indigenous communities. To support Indigenous resurgence is to support the future of all our relations.

NOTES

1. Note this is distinct from Indigenous teacher education programs (Kulago, 2019).

REFERENCES

Archibald, J. A. (2008). *Indigenous storywork: Educating the heart, mind, body, and spirit.* UBC Press.

Bang, M., Warren, B., Roseberry, A. S., & Medin, D. (2012). Desettling expectations in science education. *Human Development, 55*(5–6), 302–318. doi:10.1159/000345322

Bang, M., Curley, L., Kessel, A., Marin, A., Suzukovich, E. S., III, & Strack, G. (2014). Muskrat theories, tobacco in the streets, and living Chicago as Indigenous land. *Environmental Education Research, 20*(1), 37–55.

Bang, M., & Marin, A. (2015). Nature–culture constructs in science learning: Human/non-human agency and intentionality. *Journal of Research in Science Teaching, 52*(4), 530–544.

Banks, J. A. (1989). Integrating the curriculum with ethnic content: Approaches and guidelines. In J. A. Banks & C. A. M. Banks (Eds.), *Multicultural education: Issues and perspectives* (pp. 189–207). Allyn and Bacon.

Bell, N. (2020). Land As teacher: Using learning from the land and Indigenous people to shape tomorrow's teachers. *Education Canada, 60*(1). https://www.edcan.ca/articles /land-as-teacher/

Blimkie, M., Vetter, D., & Haig-Brown, C. (2014). Shifting perspectives and practices: Teacher candidates' experiences of a First Nation, Métis and Inuit infusion in mainstream teacher education. *Brock Education, 23*(2), 47–66. https://journals.library.brocku.ca/brocked /index.php/home/article/view/384

Brayboy, B., Gough, H. R., Leonard, B., Roehl, R. F., & Solyom, J. A. (2012). Reclaiming scholarship: Critical Indigenous research methodologies. in S. Lapan, M. T. Quartaroli, & F. J. Riemer (Eds.), *Qualitative research: An introduction to methods and designs* (pp. 423–450). John Wiley & Sons.

Brayboy, B. M. J., & Maughan, E. (2009). Indigenous knowledges and the story of the bean. *Harvard Educational Review, 79*(1), 1–21. https://doi.org/10.17763/haer.79.1 .l0u6435086352229

Calderón, D., Lees, A., Swan Waite, R., & Wilson, C. (2021). "Crossing the bridge": Land education teacher professional development. *Professional Development in Education, 47*(2-3), 348–362. https://doi.org/10.1080/19415257.2021.1891957

Deloria, V., & Wildcat, D. (2001). *Power and place: Indian education in America*. Fulcrum Publishing.

Delpit, L. (2006). *Other people›s children: Cultural conflict in the classroom*. The New Press.

Deyhle, D. (2013). Listening to lives: Lessons learned from American Indian youth. In J. Reyhner, J. Martin, L. Lockard, & W. S. Gilbert (Eds.), *Honoring our children: Culturally appropriate approaches for teaching Indigenous students* (pp. 1–10). Northern Arizona University.

Dion, S. D. (2007). Disrupting molded images: Identities, responsibilities and relationships— teachers and Indigenous subject material. *Teaching Education, 18*(4), 329–342.

Dion, S. D. (2009). *Braiding histories: Learning from Aboriginal peoples' experiences and perspectives*. UBC Press.

Garcia, J., Shirley, V., & Grande, S. (2021). Grounding Indigenous teacher education through Red Praxis. In *Oxford Research Encyclopedia of Education*. https://doi.org/10.1093 /acrefore/9780190264093.013.1112

Gay, G. (2018). *Culturally responsive teaching: Theory, research, and practice*. Teachers College Press.

Grande, S. (2008). Red pedagogy: The un-methodology. In N. K. Denzin, Y. S. Lincoln, & L. T. Smith (Eds.), *Handbook of critical and Indigenous methodologies* (pp. 233–254). Sage.

Grande, S. (2015). *Red pedagogy: Native American social and political thought*. Rowman & Littlefield.

Jackson, C., de Beer, J., & White, L. (2016). Teacher's affective development during an Indigenous knowledge professional teacher intervention. In *Proceedings: Towards effective teaching and meaningful learning in mathematics, science and technology. ISTE International Conference on Mathematics, Science and Technology Education, 23–28 October 2016. Mopani Camp in Kruger National Park, Limpopo, South Africa* (pp. 494–504). Unisa Press.

Kanu, Y. (2016). Integrating Aboriginal perspectives for educational wellbeing: Minimizing teacher candidate resistance. In F. Deer & T. Falkenburg (Eds.), *Indigenous perspectives on education for well-being in Canada* (pp. 139–156). ESWB Press, University of Manitoba.

Kearney, E., McIntosh, L., Perry, B., Dockett, S., & Clayton, K. (2014). Building positive relationships with indigenous children, families and communities: Learning at the cultural interface. *Critical Studies in Education, 55*(3), 338–352.

Kohli, R., Picower, B., Martinez, A. N., & Ortiz, N. (2015). Critical professional development: Centering the social justice needs of teachers. *The International Journal of Critical Pedagogy, 6*(2), 7–24.

Kohli, R., & Pizarro, M. (2016). Fighting to educate our own: Teachers of color, relational accountability, and the struggle for racial justice. *Equity & Excellence in Education, 49*(1), 72–84.

Kovach, M. (2009). *Indigenous methodologies: Characteristics, conversations, and contexts.* University of Toronto Press.

Kulago, H. A. (2019). In the business of futurity: Indigenous teacher education & settler colonialism. *Equity & Excellence in Education, 52*(2-3), 239–254.

Lee, E., Menkart, D., & Okazawa-Rey, M. (Eds.) (1997). *Beyond heroes and holidays: A practical guide to K–12 anti-racist, multicultural education and staff development.* Network of Educators on the Americas.

Lees, A., & Vélez, V. N. (2019, July). Fugitive teacher education: Nurturing pedagogical possibilities in early childhood education. In *The Educational Forum, 83*(3), 309–324. Routledge.

Lees, A., Laman, T. T., & Calderón, D. (2021). "Why didn't I know this?": Land education as an antidote to settler colonialism in early childhood teacher education, *Theory Into Practice, 60*(3), 279–290, https://doi.org/10.1080/00405841.2021.1911482

Lees, A., Wilson, C., Swan-Waite, R., & Calderón, D. (in press). Indigenous land education: A model for teacher professional development. In C. Gist & T. Bristol (Eds.), *Handbook of research on Indigenous teachers and teachers of color.* American Educational Research Association.

Madden, B. (2015). Pedagogical pathways for Indigenous education with/in teacher education. *Teaching and Teacher Education, 51*, 1–15.

Moreton-Robinson, A., Singh, D., Kolopenuk, J., Robinson, A., & Walter, M. (2012). *Learning the lessons? Pre-service teacher preparation for teaching Aboriginal and Torres Strait Islander students.* Australian Institute for Teaching and School Leadership.

Nardozi, A., Restoule, J. P., Broad, K., Steele, N., & James, U. (2014). Deepening knowledge to inspire action: Including Aboriginal perspectives in teaching practice. *in education, 19*(3), 108–122.

Navarro, O. (2018). We can't do this alone: Validating and inspiring social justice teaching through a community of transformative praxis. *Curriculum Inquiry, 48*(3), 335–358.

Navarro, O. (2020). Fugitive learning through a teacher inquiry group: Urban educators humanizing their classrooms & themselves. *The High School Journal, 103*(3), 157–175.

Noordhoff, K., & Kleinfeld, J. (1993) Preparing teachers for multicultural classrooms. *Teaching and Teacher Education* 9(1), 27–39.

Pewewardy, C. (1998). Fluff and feathers: Treatment of American Indians in the literature and the classroom. *Equity & Excellence, 31*(1), 69–76.

Pewewardy, C., & Hammer, P. C. (2003). *Culturally responsive teaching for American Indian students.* ERIC Clearinghouse on Rural Education and Small Schools.

Pewewardy, C. (2005). Shared journaling: A methodology for engaging white preservice students into multicultural education discourse. *Teacher Education Quarterly, 32*(1), 41–60.

Pewewardy, C. D., Lees, A., & Clark-Shim, H. (2018). The Transformational Indigenous Praxis Model: Stages for developing critical consciousness in Indigenous education. *Wičazo Ša Review, 33*(1), 38–69. https://doi.org/10.5749/wicazosareview.33.1.0038

Picower, B. (2012). *Practice what you teach: Social justice education in the classroom and the streets.* Routledge.

Picower, B. (2015). Nothing about us without us: Teacher-driven critical professional development. *Radical Pedagogy, 12*(1), 1–26.

RedCorn, A. (2020). Liberating sovereign potential: A working education capacity building model for Native Nations. *Journal of School Leadership, 30*(6), 493–518.

Rogers, J. (2018). Teaching the teachers: Re-educating Australian teachers in Indigenous education. In P. Whitinui, C. Rodriguez de France, & O. McIvor (Eds.), *Promising practices in Indigenous teacher education* (pp. 27–39). Springer.

Seawright, G. (2014). Settler traditions of place: Making explicit the epistemological legacy of White supremacy and settler colonialism for place-based education. *Educational Studies, 50*(6), 554–572.

Smith, B. L., Brown, S., & Costantino, M. (2011). *Since time immemorial: Developing tribal sovereignty curriculum for Washington's schools.* Enduring Legacies Native Cases Initiative. http://nativecases.evergreen.edu/sites/nativecases.evergreen.edu/files/case-studies/sincetime immemorialcase.pdf

Smith, L. T. (2013). *Decolonizing methodologies: Research and Indigenous peoples.* Zed Books Ltd.

St. Denis, V. (2011). Silencing Aboriginal curricular content and perspectives through multiculturalism: "There are other children here." *Review of Education, Pedagogy, & Cultural Studies, 33*(4), 306–317.

Tanaka, M., Williams, L., Benoit, Y. J., Duggan, R. K., Moir, L., & Scarrow, J. C. (2007). Transforming pedagogies: Pre-service reflections on learning and teaching in an Indigenous world. *Teacher Development, 11*(1), 99–109.

Thambinathan, V., & Kinsella, E. A. (2021). Decolonizing methodologies in qualitative research: Creating spaces for transformative praxis. *International Journal of Qualitative Methods.* https://doi.org/10.1177/16094069211014766

Tuck, E., & Yang, K. W. (2012). Decolonization is not a metaphor. *Decolonization: Indigeneity, Education &Society, 1*(1), 1–40.

Tupper, J. A., & Cappello, M. (2008). Teaching treaties as (un) usual narratives: Disrupting the curricular commonsense. *Curriculum Inquiry, 38*(5), 559–578.

Valdez, C., Curammeng, E., Pour-Khorshid, F., Kohli, R., Nikundiwe, T., Picower, B., & Stovall, D. (2018, July). We are victorious: Educator activism as a shared struggle for human being. *The Educational Forum, 82*(3), 244–258.

Wilson, S. (2008). *Research is ceremony: Indigenous research methods.* Fernwood Publishing.

CHAPTER 5

Early Childhood Teacher Education for Transformation

Anna Lees (Waganakasing Odawa, descendant)
and Verónica Nelly Vélez (Mexican/Panamanian)

For us, the work of preparing future teachers is grounded in hopes for reclamation of holistic education within public school systems. We imagine education that centers community values, knowledges, and ways of being where children's whole selves are embraced by educators who value all that their families and communities offer. Schooling in the United States has largely been structured to intentionally distance children from families and communities and is void of curriculum connections to land, water, and place (Brayboy & Lomawaima, 2016; Lomawaima & McCarty, 2006; Sabzalian, 2019).[1] For many Black, Indigenous, and other People of Color (BIPOC), relationships with the natural world ground traditional ways of teaching and learning (Cajete, 1994; Deloria & Wildcat, 2001; Marie & Watson, 2020). We argue that land education is foundational in teacher education to foster teachers' critical consciousness across the Transformational Indigenous Praxis Model (TIPM) continuum. In this chapter, we offer a brief overview of established work around land education and the need for Indigenous methodologies as a framework for teacher education. From this conceptual anchor, we offer examples of our efforts to embed these approaches in an early childhood teacher education program and how those efforts have impacted BIPOC teacher candidate development.

LAND EDUCATION

Land education in early childhood and teacher education offer the potential to reimagine school-based education by reinstating traditional ways of teaching and learning. Nishinaabeg scholar Leanne Simpson (2014) paints a clear picture of this in her telling of the Michi Saagiig Nishnaabeg story, "Kwezens makes a lovely discovery." In this story, kwezens discovers the gift of maple syrup by observing squirrel in early spring. She shares her discovery with her mother, grandmother, and aunties. While she faces some struggle in showing her matriarchs how squirrel retrieved the sap that so brilliantly turns to sugar, she had a loving foundation of kinship to support her process of coming to understand with and from land. In early childhood education, we may name this as inquiry, outdoor learning, or community-based education; for us, we see this as the essence of what education should entail for all children.

We are not alone in describing land education. Many scholars have put forth extensive work to articulate land education in theory and to demonstrate what it looks like in practice. Lakota scholar Vine Deloria Jr. and Yuchi member of the Muscogee Nation Daniel Wildcat offer *Power and Place: Indian Education in America* (2001), depicting the need for Indigenous students to have an education that recognizes Native spirituality and deep connections with earth. Glen Coulthard, Dene, articulated Indigenous relations with land through sovereignty and self-determination that reject politics of recognition in his text *Red Skin White Masks: Rejecting the Colonial Politics of Recognition* (2014). Mexican/Tigua scholar Dolores Calderón underscores how Indigenous land education diverges from place-based education in social studies (Calderón, 2014). Anishinaabe scholar Megan Bang, and many of her colleagues, portray examples of children coming to know through land education (see among others Bang et al., 2014; Barajas-López & Bang, 2018; Marin & Bang, 2018). Unangax̂ scholar Eve Tuck and non-Indigenous scholars Kate McCoy and Marcia McKenzie (2016) put forth multiple representations of land education across contexts. And Indigenous African scholar Fikile Nxumalo has written prolifically on how land education with young children disrupts settler colonialism (see among others Nxumalo, 2019).

We build on this work to consider how land education can guide teacher education programs to engage candidates in building their critical consciousness to disrupt standardization toward transformational praxis. We describe how an early childhood teacher education program partnered with an education and social justice program to engage principles of land education and decolonizing theories in the preparation of future teachers. We offer examples of this collaborative endeavor as well as its impact on the experiences of BIPOC teacher candidates and alumni, and we end by stressing the necessity of land education and decolonization to drive the preparation and praxis of future teachers.

GROUNDING OUR SHARED JOURNEY: THEORIES, METHODS, AND PRACTICES

Determining an appropriate methodology to drive inquiry about teacher education has been an important point of reflection for us, as we come to this work from different places, spaces, and ways of knowing the world. Lumbee scholar Bryan Brayboy and colleagues' (2012) Critical Indigenous Research Methodologies (CIRM) has offered a framework to make sense of how and why we have approached our work in this way. CIRM is grounded on tenets of relationality, responsibility, respect, and reciprocity, and "is driven by service and is tied to well-being, rather than an approach that views knowledge accumulation as the end goal" (p. 435). We have collaborated on numerous projects, each of which wrestled with tensions and possibilities of bringing together critical theories and understandings that have guided our research and shaped our journeys through the academy. Our collaborations deepened our commitment to CIRM, especially its insistence to examine our relationships to the university, to each other, to research, and particularly to the communities and places where we work–situated on the ancestral homelands of Coast Salish Peoples and contemporary territories of the Lummi Nation and Nooksack Tribe.

Our shared projects made clear that CIRM is vital for understanding the complexities BIPOC teachers face in schools, while simultaneously providing a conceptual, analytical, and practical path for imagining an education they and their communities deserve. By working to secure Indigenous futurities inclusive of sustainable, reciprocal socio-ecological relations, CIRM makes possible the pursuit of a holistic education that all BIPOC teachers need to thrive, especially given the continued whitestreaming of public schooling (Sabzalian, 2019) and teacher education (Jackson & Kohli, 2016) that continues to reorder settler-colonial logics at present.

Our Coming Together

The journey of how we've come together is an important starting place to understand the context in which this work has evolved. After more than a decade of community organizing in California, Vero, a non-Black and non-Indigenous Chicana, entered the Secondary Education and Education and Social Justice (ESJ) programs at Western Washington University. A year later, Anna, a Waganakagsing Odawa descendent with Scottish, German, Italian, English, and African American ancestry, began as faculty in the Early Childhood Education (ECE) Program. We connected quickly that year through shared advising of students enrolled in ESJ and leading numerous activist student groups on campus. This coming together in support of students built our kinship that eventually led to an overlap of our academic programs.

Program Description and Design

The ECE program offers prenatal-to-grade-3 teacher certification. Courses follow the trajectory of child development beginning with infants and toddlers, moving into preschool years, and concluding with an elementary internship; the program embeds field experiences at each phase of child development. The ESJ minor integrates theory and practice to equip aspiring teachers and other educational professionals with the skills and knowledge for understanding the complex relations of culture, power, systems of oppression, and movements for social justice, particularly in and connected to schools. Over 5 years of collaboration and shared commitments toward decolonization, the ESJ minor has been embedded in the ECE program where all ECE candidates can earn the minor with the addition of one foundational course.

Given the unique opportunity to combine programs, *structurally* and *curricularly*, we felt it important to capture the benefits and challenges of combining

ECE and ESJ through empirical inquiry. We were especially interested in how BIPOC ECE/ESJ teacher candidates and early career teachers made meaning of their experiences at the intersection of both programs to shape their relationship to teaching and the structures of schooling. The goal was to demonstrate to what extent the ECE/ESJ programs enhanced BIPOC candidates' readiness to surpass standardization and implement critical and decolonizing pedagogies as classroom teachers and ECE professionals. We've examined experiences of BIPOC ECE/ESJ teacher candidates over the last 3 years (see Lees & Vélez, 2019; Lees et al., 2021). We've included interview data from five student participants who self-identified as Women of Color, four as Latinx, and one as Asian-American. This informed our understanding of teacher candidate development across the TIPM.

TOWARD A DECOLONIAL CONSCIOUSNESS IN EARLY CHILDHOOD EDUCATION

Our work of teacher education remains imperfect as we balance current contexts of standardized schooling and desires for futures where BIPOC students, families, and communities thrive in educational settings. Here, we depict tenets of our program with *voices from the field*, which offer examples from interviews with BIPOC candidates to depict their development across the TIPM.

Structures for Relationality

The ECE/ESJ programs are grounded in values of relationality. This is made evident through advising, particularly in the ECE program, wherein students are grouped together as a cohort and share activities and courses throughout the program. The cohort and advising approaches are directly related as the design of admitting one cohort each year allows for relationships to develop and remain sustained through the duration of student enrollment. Research affirms the importance of cohorts for BIPOC students, noting their value in supporting student adjustment and promoting a sense of belonging, especially on predominantly white campuses (Kulago, 2019; Lucas & Robinson, 2002). Cohort models can also encourage built-in program and faculty support, creating more effective connections to assist students over time (Lucas & Robinson, 2002). Both of these benefits were evidenced in the ECE/ESJ programs. Relationality was prioritized and structured in faculty-to-student communication and in student-to-student community-building. This took form through formal structures that connected faculty with candidates prior to entrance, where they could take beginning courses in the program to build relationships and understanding before formally applying. It also took place through informal social gatherings with students, staff, and faculty where candidates could connect across cohorts, share experiences, and offer advice while coming to know their faculty outside of the classroom setting.

Voices from the field. The selected quotes depict BIPOC candidates' consciousness around the importance of relationality as a necessary foundation toward success in primarily white teacher education programs. They discuss the impact of the cohort model and strong connections with faculty and staff as essential to their retention in the program and the field. While we do not align these sampled quotes with the TIPM, we put forth that cohort models in teacher education with critically conscious faculty and staff can serve as Critical Conscious Study Groups, as called for by Pewewardy and colleagues (2018). Advancing practice across the TIPM continuum cannot occur outside of community. The following quote makes clear that BIPOC candidates found the cohort model akin to a nurturing community space: "When you get to a university I think that it's very overwhelming. And like for me, it was because I've always counted on having that close relationship with my teacher. . . . And even if you're not like that, I just think it's overwhelming to go into something so big and like you're not really noticed anymore. So having the cohort is really helpful because we're all doing the same thing." Building on this, another candidate explicitly named the connection between cohort and community: "It was definitely more personal with like [faculty]. Really talking about what you wanted to do. This is what it means to be part of a community, you know, within your department." Speaking to the impact of relational advising, this candidate makes clear the importance of faculty and staff collaboration:

> I'm kind of shy. So, I just email [ECE Staff] and then she's super, like, "oh yeah! I'm happy to see you!" I don't have to wait weeks to see her. We just sit down and she tells me, you know, how are you doing and everything. She pops up my schedule and checks up with me about all of my classes. If there's anything that she can do, like email the teachers, if I'm not comfortable enough to email them.

Critical and Decolonizing Theories

As teacher educators, we believe future teachers must have a strong theoretical foundation to their practice in the classroom. We have embedded theories of decolonization and critical pedagogies in course readings with opportunities for candidates to enact these ideas into their practice. In foundational ESJ courses and introductory ECE courses, candidates read works by Linda Smith, Eve Tuck, Kate McCoy and Marcia McKenzie, bell hooks, and Paulo Freire (among others). They make sense of this scholarship as it relates to their work in service to young children and families with peer and faculty facilitation, and then design and implement learning experiences in field settings toward decolonial curriculum. For example, they read about land education (Tuck & McKenzie, 2014) and then design and implement an environmental provocation in a preschool partner site. These have included water walls where children collect rainwater for water play outdoors, or installing light tables to examine natural materials in an effort to bring the outdoors in.

They also read theories and examples of land education (Bang et al., 2014; Calderón, 2014; Nxumalo, 2019) during their elementary internship where they develop and teach an interdisciplinary unit connected to the state-mandated Tribal sovereignty curriculum. In these units, teacher candidates engaged children in a mapping lands and waters activity and connected with stories from neighboring Tribal Nations.

Voices from the field. Describing their development across the continuum as a continual process of development, we share quotes from teacher candidates at the additive domain around understandings and application of Indigenous theories:

I think before taking ECE classes in general, I didn't think about that too much and Indigenous perspective as well, like, that was also something new to me that I was learning about and I still, like, need to learn more about. It's like a learning process . . . I think it also just, like, reminds us that change is necessary as we learn more and not to be just stuck in the same method of, like, learning and teaching all the time. We should adapt and make sure that it's fitting the needs of our students.

I think that exposure to the curriculum for my students was a great first step for them. Most of them have never heard of the local tribes and communities. Introducing them to the term "Native Americans" instead of "Indians" was also a good vocabulary shift; we need to continue teaching students ways, big or small, to be culturally responsive and respectful. Words and labels matter.

Here, we depict teacher candidates' experiences in a family and community class that emphasized the need for decolonial practice through a transformation approach as defined on the TIPM: "And for community, I would say they really emphasize that. I think it was the family partnerships class that [faculty] taught. And that one was more kind of just understanding where your students come from. And understanding a lot of the different structures, like discrimination, you know, like topics around the school system."

Beginning to engage with her practice at the transformational domain of the TIPM, this candidate discussed understandings of holistic education for young children: "I feel what I've been getting about being a teacher . . . is more than just teaching instruction, it's actually helping the students learn about the world. And how they should view it. I hear that so much in all of my classes. It's not just seeing them academically but helping them as a whole child."

Community Partnerships

Our work as teacher educators residing away from our traditional homelands is only made possible through collaboration with local community leaders. These collaborations take many forms across the varied communities where teacher candidates come from and where field placements occur; and through these experiences we model for candidates approaches for building and sustaining reciprocal community-based partnerships. Here, we highlight partnerships with the nearest Tribal Nation and migrant farm working communities. Building relationships with Coast Salish and Latinx educators from these communities has been an essential aspect of faculty professional development. Developing relationships with people from this place allowed us to better understand and make sense of lands and waters to prepare future teachers.

These collaborations have developed to offer candidates a literacy field experience in a Tribal Nation early learning program where they plan and implement activities with young children connected to seasons and cultural practices such as hunting and feasting, weaving, and gifting. They also led to a partnership with a local community college for a transfer pathway for Latinx teachers from migrant farm working communities to gain their teaching certification and return home to teach.

Voices from the field. At the contributions approach, students express their initial awareness of perspective taking as an important beginning: "I keep going back to perspective taking because it's just something new. And I'm like, 'Oh, I wonder why people see certain things this way.' And I'm wondering why I never saw it this way before. . . . I think that is a new perspective where you kind of have to check your own biases and values and just reflect on, like, why do I think this way and how do different groups." At the additive approach, teacher candidates express how program content fostered their understandings of how community should be included as part of the curriculum and family engagement: "I think it's made me want to be a teacher that's very intentional in what they're teaching. And really creating, like . . . setting, like . . . expectations for my students. Being like, again, intentional with the curriculum. And just be very aware of who my students are, you know. What's the community that I'm reaching. That's important." Finally, aligned with the transformation approach and a desire to transform school structures, this candidate considered how she can serve families in her future teaching based on her knowledge of community ways of being.

> I've worked picking blueberries before. . . . So, I would have that . . . like, I know your parents . . . for conferences and stuff . . . we can do it later at night once they get out of work and have time to relax a little bit and stuff. I feel I could connect with them a little bit more 'cause I know the situation and all of that, rather than someone who is Mexican but doesn't really know the place, doesn't know the valley.

Next, we depict examples of teacher candidates developing and applying their understandings of inquiry-based curriculum with young children to foster complex thinking and sustainable futures.

Inquiry

Teacher education research establishes the necessity to prepare teachers as activists and advocates of social justice (Apple, 2011; Au et al., 2005; Picower, 2011; Souto Manning, 2019). These efforts underscore a critical need for teacher education programs to resist a national trend to prepare teachers as technicians within narrowed curriculum standards that align with high-stakes tests (Iorio & Parnell, 2015; Nxumalo et al., 2011; Tesar, 2015). Instead, they urge us to engage teacher education as movement-building toward a more humane future that fosters children's wondering and critical thinking connected to locally specific ways of knowing, being, and valuing. Sharing commitments to critical and decolonial pedagogies, the ECE/ESJ programs emphasize inquiry-based curriculum, where candidates are prepared to serve children's holistic development while resisting standardized schooling. Candidates develop their understandings through a variety of readings (Anderson et al., 2017; Nxumalo, 2019; Vasquez, 2014) and opportunities for application in field experiences.

During preschool internship, candidates work with a small group of children to facilitate a 10-week inquiry project around relationships with the natural world. Supported by classroom teachers, candidates connect with families and community members to observe children's interests and wonderings to facilitate their critical thinking and development across domain areas. These projects have led children to visit and listen to trees who live outside of the designated play area, record their observations, and retell the stories throughout the project. In another example, children negotiated tending to a community garden and an identified problem of bugs and insects eating the growing vegetables—ultimately, they fostered space for both plant and animal relatives to thrive.

Voices from the field. The impact of inquiry in ECE teacher preparation has resulted in teacher practice at the transformational and social justice action domains of TIPM in powerful ways with young children, as demonstrated by these teacher candidates:

> I have a deeper appreciation for the land and water aspect after teaching it. I think it helps us see other living things as our equals and it has the power to humble our society through a different perspective. It also makes me think about the process of give and take; a capitalist society only focuses on the take and often forgets about the reciprocity required to sustain a healthy environment. (transformational)

> I think it's important to acknowledge the land and water around us and this curriculum can start a discussion that leads into bigger and important issues (controversy about reservations, conflicts in government, social relationships with different groups of people, etc.) Even though my students are 7 or 8 years old, they have the capability to start talking about complex problems and being part of a community that supports activism. (social justice action)

It is important to note that candidates also struggle to apply programmatic commitments in their practice even at a beginning contributions approach due to standardization, as evidenced by this reflection: "There is literally no space. You have to do math, you have to do reading, you have to do writing . . . I didn't get to do the stuff that I wanted to do . . . Not as much of the social justice education." To support teacher candidates in sustaining their commitments to social transformation, teacher educators must also demonstrate their commitment to such efforts and take action toward continuing their own development.

Continued Faculty Development: Collaborating Toward Decolonial Futures

Our efforts to prepare critically conscious educators requires us to commit to our own continued development of criticality. Doing this work in kinship has furthered our development in the work and expanded our perspectives. Because we come from different places, with different experiences as educators, and through different doctoral programs and methodological and theoretical framings, we have done extensive work to learn from each other how our respective fields of study matter for teacher education. This occurs daily through conversations and course planning, and more formal collaborations by merging the ECE and ESJ programs. Most recently, with Dolores Calderón, we collectively taught the ESJ capstone course titled "Theorizations of Space and Place in Education," which deepened our analysis of how place-based and other forms of environmental education can position themselves as culturally or politically neutral while perpetuating forms of European universalism, settler colonialism, white supremacy, and extractive capitalism.

These shared endeavors have made clear that teacher educators must take seriously their commitments and actions toward postcolonialism in their preparation of future teachers. TIPM is as much a model of critical consciousness building for *us* as it is for teacher candidates. We were intentional in our commitments and ongoing self-reflexivity to shift our accountability away from the university and toward the communities we, and our students, would partner with in the preparation of young children. For example, we deliberately co-taught in order to have the time and space to come together, better understand the theories we wanted to integrate in our programs, and pilot pedagogical practices for teacher candidates. In addition to teaching, we write together, linking theories, empirical student data, and ongoing reflections to consider pedagogical innovations and revise conceptual frameworks that deepen our work toward decolonization. Our journey is far from over. We persist in our development, guided by TIPM and the humble recognition that we still have much to learn from each other and from our communities.

NOTES

1. Given the brevity of this chapter, we cite scholars throughout this chapter whose work underscores our arguments but, by no means, represents the full body of literature.

REFERENCES

Anderson, D., Comay, J., & Chiarotto, L. (2017). *Natural curiosity: The importance of Indigenous perspectives in children's environmental inquiry*. Ontario Institute for Studies in Education.

Apple, M. W. (2011). Global crises, social justice, and teacher education. *Journal of Teacher Education, 62*(2), 222–234.

Au, W., Bigelow, B., Burant, T., & Salas, K. D. (2005). Action education: Teacher organizers take quality into their own hands. *Rethinking Schools, 20*(2), 11–14.

Bang, M., Curley, L., Kessel, A., Marin, A., Suzukovich III, E. S., & Strack, G. (2014). Muskrat theories, tobacco in the streets, and living Chicago as Indigenous land. *Environmental Education Research, 20*(1), 37–55.

Barajas-López, F., & Bang, M. (2018). Indigenous making and sharing: Claywork in an Indigenous STEAM program. *Equity & Excellence in Education, 51*(1), 7–20.

Brayboy, B. M. J., & Lomawaima, K. T. (2018). Why don't more Indians do better in school? The battle between US schooling & American Indian/Alaska Native education. *Daedalus, 147*(2), 82–94.

Brayboy, B. M., Gough, H. R., Leonard, B., Roehl, R. F., & Solyom, J. A. (2012). Reclaiming scholarship: Critical Indigenous research methodologies. *Qualitative Research: An Introduction to Methods and Designs*, 423–450.

Cajete, G. (1994). *Look to the mountain: An ecology of Indigenous education*. Kivaki Press.

Calderón, D. (2014). Speaking back to manifest destinies: A land education-based approach to critical curriculum inquiry. *Environmental Education Research, 20*(1), 24–36.

Coulthard, G. S. (2014). *Red skin, white masks: Rejecting the colonial politics of recognition*. University of Minnesota Press.

Deloria, V., Jr., & Wildcat, D. (2001). *Power and place: Indian education in America*. Fulcrum Publishing.

Iorio, J. M., & Parnell, W. (2015). *Rethinking readiness in early childhood education: Implications for policy and practice*. Springer.

Jackson, T., & Kohli, R. (2016). Guest editors' introduction: The state of teachers of color. *Equity & Excellence in Education, 49*(1), 1–8.

Kulago, H. A. (2019). In the business of futurity: Indigenous teacher education & settler colonialism. *Equity & Excellence in Education, 52*(2-3), 239–254.

Lees, A., & Vélez, V. N. (2019, July). Fugitive teacher education: Nurturing pedagogical possibilities in early childhood education. *The Educational Forum, 83*(3), 309–324.

Lees, A., Vélez, V., & Laman, T. T. (2021). Recognition and resistance of settler colonialism in early childhood education: perspectives and implications for Black, Indigenous, and Teachers of Color. *International Journal of Qualitative Studies in Education*. https://doi.org/10.1080/09518398.2021.1891319

Lomawaima, K. T., & McCarty, T. L. (2006). *"To remain an Indian": Lessons in democracy from a century of Native American education*. Teachers College Press.

Lucas, T., & Robinson, J. (2002). Promoting the retention of prospective teachers through a cohort for college freshmen. *The High School Journal, 86*(1), 3–14.

Marie, T., & Watson, K. (2020). Remembering an apocalyptic education: Revealing life beneath the waves of Black being. *Root Work Journal*, 14–48.

Marin, A., & Bang, M. (2018). "Look it, this is how you know:" Family forest walks as a context for knowledge-building about the natural world. *Cognition and Instruction, 36*(2), 89–118.

McCoy, K., Tuck, E., & McKenzie, M. (Eds.). (2016). *Land education: Rethinking pedagogies of place from Indigenous, postcolonial, and decolonizing perspectives*. Routledge.

Nxumalo, F. (2019). *Decolonizing place in early childhood education*. Routledge.

Nxumalo, F., Pacini-Ketchabaw, V., & Rowan, M. (2011). Lunch time at the child care centre: Neoliberal assemblages in early childhood education. *Journal of Pedagogy, 2*(2), 195.

Pewewardy, C. D., Lees, A., & Clark-Shim, H. (2018). The Transformational Indigenous Praxis Model: Stages for developing critical consciousness in Indigenous education. *Wíčazo Ša Review, 33*(1), 38–69. https://doi.org/10.5749/wicazosareview.33.1.0038

Picower, B. (2011). Resisting compliance: Learning to teach for social justice in a neoliberal context. *Teachers College Record, 113*(5), 1105–1134.

Sabzalian, L. (2019). *Indigenous children's survivance in public schools*. Routledge.

Simpson, L. B. (2014). Land as pedagogy: Nishnaabeg intelligence and rebellious transformation. *Decolonization: Indigeneity, Education & Society, 3*(3).

Souto-Manning, M. (2019). Transforming university-based teacher education: Preparing asset-, equity-, and justice-oriented teachers within the contemporary political context. *Teachers College Record, 121*(6), 1–26.

Tesar, E. (2015). Te Whāriki in Aotearoa New Zealand: Witnessing and resisting neo-liberal and neo-colonial discourses in early childhood education. In *Unsettling the Colonial Places and Spaces of Early Childhood Education* (pp. 108–123). Routledge.

Tuck, E., & McKenzie, M. (2014). *Place in research: Theory, methodology, and methods*. Routledge.

Vasquez, V. M. (2014). *Negotiating critical literacies with young children*. Routledge.

CHAPTER 6

White, Christian, Male Privilege and Colonialism

Contending With Chief Wahoo in the Multicultural Education Classroom

Jeanette Haynes Writer (Tsalagi, Cherokee Nation citizen)

The battle to end the use of the harmful and denigrating American Indian sports mascots has carried on for more than 50 years. While scholars and organizations have focused on the impact of such icons on students, the literature has not addressed the effect on Native American faculty, as well as institutional policies and procedures, when the mascot enters the university classroom.

In this chapter I delve into the issue of an education-major student flaunting the derogatory American Indian sports mascot, Chief Wahoo, consciously and deliberately in an undergraduate university course I taught. Using the Transformational Indigenous Praxis Model (TIPM), specifically drawing from Dimension 3, "Transformation Approach," and Dimension 4, "Cultural and Social Justice Action," I discuss the steps I took and the processes and policies in place that facilitated movement toward accountability of the student to his white settler privilege, and accountability of the teacher education program (TEP), College of Education, and the university to combat racialized imagery, student hostility, and settler colonialism toward me as a Native professor and Native Peoples at large. Finally, to highlight TIPM's "wave jumping" concept, I address the murky and constantly shifting waters that I negotiated in tackling the mascot incident.

In the following section, I convey the story of the mascot incident with the student in my university course. As well, I present the initial steps I took to bring attention to the student's questionable behavior in relation to his future work as an educator and his problematic actions toward me as a Native professor.

CHIEF WAHOO ENTERS THE CLASSROOM: THE MASCOT INCIDENT

During what seemed to be a typical teaching day, I made my rounds to the small discussion groups in the Multicultural Education class. The groups were discussing Harro's (2013) "Cycle of Socialization" and the impact of messages on our social identity formation. I sat down with another group of students, and out of the corner of my eye, I saw him. A feathered headband and toothy smile exploded from the bright red face peering from the top of Isaiah's ball cap—Chief Wahoo. Wahoo watched me as the students conversed about the reading and asked each other critical questions—except Isaiah, who hadn't read deeply. Isaiah tried to be humorous about messages in a remark to a colleague. I said calmly to him, "As a Cherokee woman, what message do you think your hat is giving me?" Isaiah took off his hat, looked at it, and said, "I don't know. I just bought it because I like the color." Student colleagues at our table were silent and watched me carefully, as did the students in the adjoining group. I asked a question to refocus us on the reading. My pedagogical move was not to address the issue at the moment with Isaiah. Nonetheless, Isaiah's colleagues were presented with a learning opportunity from the question I posed to Isaiah, a question he thought he had cleverly dodged.

Two weeks later, as I approached my faculty office suite, Isaiah stopped me to explain that he did not have his assignment draft for class that would begin soon. I again noticed Chief Wahoo watching me from Isaiah's cap. I motioned to him to step inside the office suite where no one else was present. I said to him, "You have that cap on again. It is very racist and offensive. I don't want you wearing that to class." He took it off and apologized. I told him that it was quite hurtful to me.

We moved back to the issue of Isaiah not having the assignment draft. After discussing his lack of preparedness for class, I turned to the issue of mascots: why they are problematic; that much is written about the mascot issue; why it is hurtful to me and that I did not want him to wear the hat or other American Indian mascot items around me. I presented him with a parallel situation of another racialized group and asked him if he would wear such a hat. He said, "No." I responded, "This is the same thing." I let him know that if he did not understand or would like to know more, I would be happy to provide resources and would welcome a dialogue with him—this was part of our multicultural education work. I advised Isaiah that 95% of Native students are in public schools (National School Boards Association, 2020) so he will have contact with Native students and families through his coaching of sports whether he realizes it or not. The wearing of such demeaning imagery would be hurtful and harmful to his students. I conducted the conversation in a calm voice and demeanor.

Immediately following this second incident, I sent an email detailing the two incidents to the college administrator who handled student issues: "I spoke for a second time to an EDUC 315 student about his wearing of a racist sports mascot—Chief Wahoo of the Cleveland Indians—in my presence . . . What might be my options if this continues to happen? I am quite concerned since this student wants to work (coach) in schools." After sending the email, I began investigating university policies.

A short time after I spoke to Isaiah for the second time, I was in the classroom preparing to start our class. In walked Isaiah with his Wahoo hat. Isaiah wore the hat throughout class, even when I sat at his small group table for several minutes. He proceeded to bring attention to his hat throughout the class session. After class, I sent another email to the college-level administrator: "I am wondering if I should make an appointment with the General Counsel [university attorney] to investigate his and my rights."

The above narrative presented the mascot incident and my actions through administrative channels to hold the student accountable. In the following, I lay out the mascot issue, identifying it within the conceptual framework of settler colonialism and anti-Indianism.

LITERATURE REVIEW & CONCEPTUAL FRAMING

Mascots

Over the years various scholars and organizations, such as the National Congress of American Indians (2013), National Indian Education Association (2009), Society of Indian Psychologists (1999), and the American Psychological Association (2005), have developed position statements on the detrimental impact of mascots on students, specifically, and Native Peoples, in general.

Native scholars and their allies have identified the harm American Indian sports mascots have on Native and non-Native pre-K–12 students and university-level students (Freng & Willis-Esqueda, 2011; Fryberg et al., 2008). Problems surrounding mascots include reinforcing stereotypes of Native Peoples as "savage" (Fenelon, 2017) and denigrating Native Peoples while claiming to honor them (Davis, 2010), leading to cultural violence (Pewewardy, 2000). King (2010) specifically identified the root of the mascot controversy—anti-Indianism. Anti-Indianism provides mascot supporters the ability to "disregard the lives and voices of Indians, consciously and callously work against their interests, and by design undermine the possibility of equality, dignity, and humanity for Native Americans" (p. 146).

In a comprehensive review of research concerning the direct and indirect psychosocial effects of Native American mascots on Natives and non-Natives, Davis-Delano, Gone, and Fryberg's (2020) review emphasized:

> Although most people in the U.S. do not perceive Native American mascots as problematic, all of the academic studies undertaken to study the psychosocial effects of these mascots demonstrate either direct negative effects on Native Americans or that these mascots activate, reflect, and/or reinforce stereotyping and prejudice among non-Native persons. (p. 630)

Settler Colonialism and Anti-Indianism

Colonialism is historically rooted and carries into Native Peoples' present reality on a daily basis through its explicit and implicit embedded nature (Brayboy, 2005) within various U.S. institutions and systems, including the media, religion, economics, and education (Harro, 2013). Assessing settler colonialism as the process of laying claim to land, Wolfe (1999) also describes it as structural, while Tuck and McKenzie (2015) describe it as ongoing.

Cook-Lynn (2001) defines anti-Indianism as the exclusionary ideologies and practices leading to Native non-existence and refutation of nationhood. The subtle slights and explicit offenses toward Native Peoples blame them for historical trag-edies and contemporary problems. And, "[f]inally, Anti-Indianism is that which exploits and distorts Indian cultures and beliefs. All of these traits have conspired to isolate, to expunge or expel, to menace, to defame" declares Cook-Lynn (2001, p. x). While U.S. higher education institutions operate on Native lands, Native absence is starkly apparent in low numbers or lack of Native faculty and staff; dis-regard of Native participation in institutional decision-making and policy devel-opment; and scarcity of non-stereotypical and accurate Native curricular content.

Deconstructing the roots undergirding the mascot incident is necessary to identify, expose, and challenge settler colonialism and anti-Indianism, within not only the EDUC 315 classroom, but also within the larger context of a TEP embed-ded in a settler-centered higher education institution. If not disrupted, the exclu-sion and disregard of Native faculty and the imposition of a deficit lens on Native students, their communities, and their Peoples will continue.

As a female Native faculty member, my identity impacts my work, such as in the interface with Isaiah's white Christian male privilege, and my identity also serves to undergird my purpose to transform the academy. Within my profession-al role in the settler-centered institution, I experience forward movement, but also arduous resistance, as discussed below.

MY IDENTITY, MY WORK, MY PURPOSE

I am Tsalagi (a citizen of Cherokee Nation), my home is located in northeastern Oklahoma within the Cherokee Nation. In my professional work I hold the rank of full professor in the Department of Curriculum and Instruction (C&I) at New Mexico State University (NMSU). I am a guest upon the lands where I work and, as such, I have a responsibility to Peoples here. As the first Native professor hired in the College of Education, at the present I am the only tenured Native professor at my institution. I work with three other culturally invested and identifiable Native faculty and staff to address Native issues on campus and to serve New Mexico's 23 Tribal Nations. I define my presence and leadership at NMSU as an attempt to Indigenize the academy because I truly believe "something productive will hap-pen as a consequence" (Mihesuah & Wilson, 2004, p. 5), aligning with TIPM's "Transformation Approach" (Pewewardy et al., 2018) as I attempt to "transform and indigenize [the] curriculum and pedagogy and also consider ways to enact systemic change" (p. 56). It is Native cultural continuance and intellectualism that I protect and move forward, not the desires of settler colonialism, not the wants and purposes of institutional anti-Indianism.

The Multicultural Education Course and Isaiah's Privilege

My academic department is responsible for preparing teacher candidates for licen-sure. Education majors must pass the Multicultural Education (MCE) course to be eligible for admittance into the TEP to become teacher candidates. I have taught the undergraduate MCE course since arriving at NMSU. In the course students examine how race, class, gender, sexual orientation, language, ability, and spirituality intersect and impact the experiences and opportunities of students. But first, they must examine their socialization process and examine how they access power or are denied it in their own dominant or subordinate social identities (Harro, 2013). As I have designed it, the course expands each student's knowledge base through engagement with academic literature and provides opportunities for students to apply the literature or see it "in action" so they may recognize systems of power and/or challenge points of privilege held. Affiliated with the MCE course is the first assessment and documentation of the TEP Dispositions for each student; dispositions are the "habits of professional action and moral commitments that underlie an educator's performance" (Council for the Accreditation of Educator Preparation, 2020).

Isaiah was rather oblivious to power as privileged by his dominant social identities. In his introduction to colleagues at the beginning of the course and from class conversations, Isaiah identified himself as a baseball player, so he was quite familiar with Chief Wahoo, and was, obviously, a Cleveland Indians fan. He also identified himself on different occasions, verbally and in written form, as being Christian, along the evangelical tradition. Being Christian was a very strong aspect of Isaiah's identity and socialization. He shared that he was not sure if he wanted to teach or preach.

In the Social Identity assignment based on Harro's (2013) "Cycle of Socialization," Isaiah named his race as "American" and named his Christian identity as subordinate (being invisible or having little social power). He also did not work his race or religious identities through Harro's cycle, so avoided critically examining the dominant nature of these privileged, intersected identities. Osage/Cherokee theological scholar George Tinker (1993) asserted that missionary-based Christianity is not relegated to the past but the "cultural imposition" continues into the present (p. 113) due to the "pervasiveness of a culturally ingrained sense of white superiority" (p. 114). Without his willingness, and, perhaps, his lack of scholarly capacity to examine his race and missionary-based Christian identity, as well as his male privilege, he avoided any need or responsibility for personal growth and transformation. The protection and operation of these identities can conceivably explain why Isaiah did not find it necessary to engage with me on the mascot issue.

Wave Jumping: Actions and Resistance

As mentioned in the Introduction of this book, Pewewardy et al. put forth in TIPM the concept of "wave jumping" where "educators working to decolonize their practice can gain forward momentum with time and energy even while facing resistance" (p. 3). There was indeed evidence of forward wave motion in my action to address the incident at an administrative and program level, impressing onto others that the incident was not simply a course-bound issue reflective of a student's poor behavior. When tackling the issue with department-level administrators, I front-loaded scholarly literature based on my uncertainty that the administrators understood the harmful nature of the mascot issue or would take it seriously. I was happily surprised to be fully supported. A meeting was quickly arranged with Isaiah by one of the administrators and a program assistant director to hold him accountable for his actions. When Isaiah asserted his right to self-expression in wearing the Wahoo icon, the administrator informed him of my right to seek assistance with the Office of Institutional Equity.

Forward motion was gained as well in the ally-ship of departmental faculty colleagues who also teach the MCE and other critical pedagogy and social justice courses. In tandem, we were able to leverage TEP policy and the TEP Dispositions Assessment to address students' behavior, like Isaiah's. When he chose not to engage with me in the learning opportunity, I was able to document Isaiah's disrespect and unwillingness to learn and engage as per criteria in the TEP Dispositions Assessment. Of note, years before, I chaired the committee to oversee the development of the original dispositions assessment. For this newest iteration of the dispositions assessment, I piloted the assessment at the request of the TEP Director. Both assessments were developed to assist education majors and teacher candidates in their development to be effective for all students or hold them accountable should they not develop the necessary professional attitudes, skills, and abilities.

While flow in a forward motion occurred, I also am quite cognizant of the backward wave motion found within the protection and maintenance of settler colonialism and anti-Indianism, and the continued resistance to Native realities and futurities. Backward wave motion occurred when the non-Native college-level Administrator of Color initially read and reified a status quo policy "from a developmental and administrative perspective," that embraced the "freedom of expression/speech" of Isaiah. It was later that she located Isaiah's actions as potentially violating the university's code of student conduct and creating a hostile environment in the classroom. Whether it be administrators, faculty, or students like Isaiah, I am disappointingly reminded, "If members of the public cannot understand the problem with Native American mascots, they certainly will not understand sovereignty or other issues that affect the quality of Native American lives" (Davis, 2010, p. 28).

Backward wave motion was apparent when, even though department-level and program-level administrators called a face-to-face meeting with Isaiah to address the incident, he was not required to engage with me to learn about Native Peoples and the harmful nature of American Indian sports mascots. My personal invitation to Isaiah to discuss American Indian mascots was rebuffed. Did he ever have to engage on the subject of Native Peoples, or did he leverage his white settler, Christian male privilege with other instructors whose social identities normalized and meshed with Isaiah's? Was he admitted to the TEP? If so, was his anti-Indianism challenged or left to advance in the classroom of settler-centered faculty and in an anti-Indianist institution that refuses to engage with Native faculty and staff?

Although the mascot incident and response took place within a Curriculum and Instruction Department's TEP, implications to address the harmful nature of American Indian sports mascots reaches across departments and units within colleges and other schools of education. The mascot issue has extended implications for educational administration, counseling, or educational psychology, and kinesiology and athletic training.

This particular mascot incident speaks to the constantly shifting waters within my educational institution to either confront or maintain settler colonialism and anti-Indianism. Shifts and variations within institutional waters include the time and place (i.e., city, state, or region) where such incidents occur; the institutional context and climate (which includes the praxis of diversity, institutional policies, procedures, etc.); and the institutional participants (students, faculty, administrators, and professional staff).

I understand I must continuously reflect and commit to additional work as related to TIPM's "transformation approach" and "cultural and social justice action" dimensions to further my own critical consciousness and extend my Indigenizing actions to transform the learning context for education majors in not only the Multicultural Education course, but the TEP and institution at large. As a Native professor, I seek alignment with TIPM's Dimension 4: Cultural and Social Justice Action, to "exhibit advanced knowledges and proficiency in [my] practice and also patience and humility in [my] teaching" (Pewewardy et al., 2018, p. 57)

CONCLUSION

In this book, Pewewardy, Lees, and Minthorn contend that "the lack of attention to settler colonialism hinders the analysis of race and white supremacy" (p. 2, this volume). Without a critical analysis of the workings of settler colonialism in education majors and teacher candidates, as well as within faculty in higher education institutions, Native erasure continues. Tuck and Gaztambide-Fernández (2013) argue that, "Indigenous futurity does not require the erasure of now-settlers in the ways that settler futurity requires of Indigenous peoples" (p. 80). In Isaiah's dismissal of the engagement and learning opportunity I offered—his learning obligation to be effective for all students—he asserted the assumed superiority of and leveraged the power located within his white settler, Christian male privilege to erase me as a Cherokee woman who follows traditional spiritual teachings, and to erase my authority and scholarly expertise as a female Native professor. If Isaiah would not engage with me, as one who carried power as a professor, would he or how would he engage with Native students, families, and communities?

It remains for me a concern that those like Isaiah continue to make their way through TEPs and obtain licensure because few TEP faculty are prepared to recognize within non-Native students the ideologies of settler colonialism and anti-Indianism. This is because those ideologies and practices reside as well within university and TEP faculty who have not been challenged or challenged themselves.

Through this mascot incident transformative action took place as I confronted the issue through administrative channels using the policies in place at the university, administrative power and authority to address the issue, and developmental tools like the TEP Dispositions Assessment to leverage programmatic documentation and accountability of an education major who intends on applying for the TEP. I asserted myself as a Cherokee woman and scholar to Indigenize the academy and to confront anti-Indianism using the literature on mascots. Some advancement of a Native presence was gained, but as with the wave-jumping concept, resistance was also apparent in the settler colonialist approach to policy (i.e., the interpretation of a student's freedom of expression rather than the psychological harm such mascots foster), and perhaps lack of follow-through in the TEP to attend to Isaiah's professional and critical multicultural development. I am, however, emboldened and transformed by addressing such harmful transgressions in that I confronted a student who could be harmful to Native children and communities. Nonetheless, I am also painfully aware of what it means to be a Native American faculty member in an institution built on and maintaining settler colonialism, an institution that refuses to engage with Native faculty and staff, and a College of Education that refuses to allow me to use my experiential and scholarly knowledge to develop and teach a course to prepare eventual teacher candidates to work with Native students and teach accurately and appropriately about Native Peoples. With such a course I could have a meaningful effect through the preparation of teachers to challenge anti-Indianism and settler colonialism, and the harmful effect of American Indian sports mascots.

The scholarly literature on American Indian sports mascots has demanded a halt on the use of such icons due to the harmful effect for specifically Native American students and Peoples. More examination is needed of the effects of the demeaning mascots to a broader population. Due to the hostile nature of the appearance of the mascot in the multicultural education classroom, I call for research to interrogate the impact of American Indian sports mascots on pre-K–12 teachers and college and university faculty to better understand the covert and overt oppression against educators and the possibility of institutional responses to such oppression.

REFERENCES

American Psychological Association. (2005). *Resolution recommending the immediate retirement of American Indian mascots, symbols, images, and personalities by schools, colleges, universities, athletic teams, and organizations.* https://www.apa.org/about/policy/mascots.pdf

Brayboy, B. M. J. (2005). Toward a ribal critical race theory in education. *The Urban Review, 37*(5), 425–446.

Cook-Lynn E. (2001). *Anti-Indianism in modern America: A voice from Tatekeya's earth.* University of Illinois Press.

Council for the Accreditation of Educator Preparation. (2020). *Glossary.* http://caepnet.org/glossary?letter=D

Davis, L. R. (2010). The problems with Native American mascots. In C. R. King (Ed.), *The Native American mascot controversy: A handbook* (pp. 23–31). Scarecrow Press, Inc.

Davis-Delano, L. R., Gone, J. P., & Fryberg, S. A. (2020) The psychosocial effects of Native American mascots: A comprehensive review of empirical research findings. *Race Ethnicity and Education, 23*(5), 613–633.

Fenelon, J. V. (2017). *Redskins?: Sports mascots, Indian nations and white racism.* Routledge.

Freng, S., & Willis-Esqueda, C. (2011). A question of honor: Chief Wahoo and American Indian stereotype activation among a university based sample. *The Journal of Social Psychology, 151*(5), 577–591.

Fryberg, S. A., Markus, H. R., Oyserman, D., & Stone, J. M. (2008). Of warrior chiefs and Indian princesses: The psychological consequences of American Indian mascots. *Basic and Applied Social Psychology, 30,* 208–218.

Harro, B. (2013). The cycle of socialization. In M. Adams, W. J. Blumenfeld, R. Castañeda, H. W. Hackman, M. L. Peters, & X. Zúñiga (Eds.), *Readings for diversity and social justice: An anthology on racism, antiSemitism, sexism, heterosexism, ableism, and classism* (pp. 45–52). Routledge.

King, C. R. (2010). Defensive dialogues: Native American mascots, anti-Indianism, and educational institutions. In C. R. King (Ed.), *The Native American mascot controversy: A handbook* (pp. 145–162). Scarecrow Press, Inc.

Mihesuah, D. A., & Wilson, A. C. (Eds.). (2004). *Indigenizing the academy: Transforming scholarship and empowering communities.* University of Nebraska Press.

National Congress of American Indians. (2013). *Ending the legacy of racism in sports and the era of harmful 'Indian 'sports mascots. National Congress of American Indians.* https://www.ncai .org/attachments/PolicyPaper_mijApMoUWDbjqFtjAYzQWlqLdrwZvsYfakBwTHpMAT cOroYolpN_NCAI_Harmful_Mascots_Report_Ending_the_Legacy_of_Racism_10_2013 .pdf

National Indian Education Association. (2009, October 10). *2009-05: Elimination of race-based Indian logos, mascots, and names.* Retrieved from https://www.niea.org/niea-2009 /elimination-of-race-based-indian-logos-mascots-andnames?rq=mascots

National School Boards Association. (2020). *The condition of Native America students.* Retrieved from https://www.nsba.org/ASBJ/2020/December/condition-native-american-students

Pewewardy, C. D. (2000). Why educators should not ignore Indian mascots. *Multicultural Perspectives, 2*(1), 3–7.

Pewewardy, C. D., Lees, A., & Minthorn, R. (2022). *Unsettling settler colonial education: The Transformational Indigenous Praxis Model.* Teachers College Press.

Pewewardy, C. D., Lees, A., & Clark-Shim, H. (2018). The Transformational Indigenous Praxis Model: Stages for developing critical consciousness in Indigenous education. *Wičazo Ša Review, 33*(1), 38–69. https://doi.org/10.5749/wicazosareview.33.1.0038

Society of Indian Psychologists. (1999). *Statement on retiring Native American mascots.* Retrieved from https://60a73858-fd8d-431a-89df-8d957fe23d9b.filesusr.com/ugd/6c5978_00a885e f5ae142bc9b1fea146318255a.pdf

Tinker, G. E. (1993). *Missionary conquest: The gospel and Native American cultural genocide.* Fortress Press.

Tuck, E., & Gaztambide-Fernandez, R. A. (2013). Curriculum, replacement, and settler futurity. *Journal of Curriculum Theorizing, 29*(1), 72–89.

Tuck, E., & McKenzie, M. (2015). *Place in research: Theory, methodology, and methods.* Routledge.

Wolfe, P. (1999). *Settler colonialism and the transformation of Anthropology: The politics and poetics of an ethnographic event.* Cassell.

CHAPTER 7

Indigenous Teacher Education

Reflections of Pathway-Making Through Primarily White Institutions Toward Indigenous Futures

Tahlia Natachu (Zuni), Cornel Pewewardy (Comanche Citizen and descendant of the Kiowa Tribe), Anna Lees (Waganakasing Odawa, descendant)

We are three Indigenous educators who have come together for more than a decade as teachers and students. Tahlia Natachu is youth development coordinator for a Tribal community education program, Dr. Cornel Pewewardy is professor emeritus who continues to teach and lead community education efforts, and Dr. Anna Lees is associate professor of early childhood education who works closely with local Indigenous Nations. Our relationships began with Dr. Cornel Pewewardy serving as advisor to Dr. Anna Lees during her doctoral studies. Upon her faculty appointment, Anna served as advisor to Tahlia Natachu through the Native American Student Union. Upon completion of a bachelor's degree in English, Tahlia entered an American Indian urban teacher preparation program where Cornel had been a lead designer. Throughout these years and to date, we have stayed connected and committed to goals of Indigenous education. We've come together through this chapter to depict our desires for Indigenous teacher education, personal experiences as teacher candidates and teacher educators, and our efforts to enact traditional teachings.

TRADITIONAL TEACHINGS FROM INDIGENOUS EYES

Traditional teachings have always employed the extraordinary capabilities latent in each human being—a "being of being rather than thinking, acting, and world-making as if we were transcendent or 'possessive' modern subjects" (Chandler & Reid, 2018, p. 1). Extraordinary results of teaching and learning are being realized by returning to traditional knowledge bases and protocols for Indigenous students. Traditional teachings for Indigenous students are a discourse for exploring, mapping, training, and using the innate abilities within the human body and mind systems. The purpose of this chapter is to unlock traditional knowledge bases to the extraordinary potentials inherent in each one of us as Indigenous teachers.

Until 1900, Indigenous teachers in the United States were those most likely to teach Indigenous students. Indigenous communities upheld complex educational systems. Knowledge instruction came through participation of community shared values, age- and gender-specific customs and protocols, kinship guidance and protection, and understanding territorial space within the context of encampments and seasonal movements (Cajete, 2014). For Indigenous peoples, learning on the move has always been about "ongoing re-collective and re-membering of dynamic social and spatial relationships" (Bang, 2020, p. 1). Traditionally, most Indigenous peoples taught their young how to be good, respectable persons and good relatives to the four-legged, winged-ones, and water-beings. Interconnectedness empowers learners to value their community, work, play, and to communicate and solve problems together as members of a group (Alfred, 2009). While traditional teachings from Indigenous eyes is unmatched in its presentation of principles, the keys to practice depend on the psychological development from which theory is framed. And this work must account for generational traumas inflicted by boarding schools and continued settler-colonial school structures as systems of assimilation aimed at dismantling our cultures and Nationhood. The task at hand is to understand how do we, as Indigenous teachers, enact philosophy and theory to guide our students to give back to community and understand teaching and learning as an act of reciprocity.

INDIGENOUS THEORIZING

Traditional teachings from Indigenous eyes is a timeless construct—by no means is this chapter a complete cookbook for teaching Indigenous students. We are also aware of whitestream standards for publication, teachings, and research; we echo Killsback (2020) where he "intentionally omitted numerous ideas and teachings that are strictly reserved for Cheyenne eyes and ears. . . . We as Indian people have a right to privacy and to protect our cultures" (p. xxix). In addition to teachings we found unfit for publication, we recognize literature and community-based efforts of Indigenous teacher education not included in this chapter.

We believe that to serve Indigenous students, traditional teachings must be applied to our contemporary reality (Alfred, 1999). However, American Indian/ Alaska Native (AI/AN) K–12 teachers comprise 0.5% of the total teacher population (National Center for Education Statistics [NCES], 2011), and less than 1% of higher education faculty are AI/AN (NCES, 2020). Given the whitestream nature of teacher education programs, most Indigenous teachers never enter the classroom or else leave the profession early in their career. Teachers of Color are more likely to enter teaching through alternative pathways and leave the profession due to poor working conditions (Carver-Thomas & Darling-Hammond, 2019). Yet, we maintain optimism toward better futures.

This chapter shares our experiences and perspectives around efforts to prepare and retain Indigenous teachers. Each of us have employed traditional teaching practices not only to survive in whitestream schools, but to uphold Indigenous values, knowledges, and ways of being. We affirm the scholarship of Higgins et al. (2015) when they argue that Eurocentrism simultaneously centers and obscures whiteness resulting in teachers' misconceptions about culture. Like Jordan and Schwartz (2018), we challenge tacit ideas about empathy that pervade both whitestream culture and teaching, for which they suggest a more nuanced consideration of empathy in teaching and learning. And we recognize how false empathy takes form in classrooms through everyday interactions (Warren & Hotchkins, 2015).

As we put forth a call for traditional teachings in Indigenous teacher education, we are clear that our teachings are being "retrieved," not "re-invented" (O'Meara & West, 1996). To decolonize our teaching, educators must consider what traditional teachings can be most effective within contemporary classrooms. Kulago (2019) asserts that critical Indigenous consciousness is necessary to successfully navigate mechanisms of settler colonialism by speaking up and making Indigenous perspectives known. Accordingly, we have witnessed that most teachers are positioned at the beginning dimension of TIPM, which may be the most important for "unlearning" the colonial process of Eurocentric philosophies. For many teachers, the TIPM's "pedagogical scaffolding" (Dion, 2009, p. 176) disrupts settler colonialism in the classroom. According to Tuck and Ree (2013), "decolonization necessarily involves an interruption of the settler colonial nation-state, and of settler relations to land" (p. 647). Tuck, McKenzie, and McCoy (2014) suggest that "land education calls into question educational practices and theories that justify settler occupation of stolen land, or encourage the replacement of Indigenous peoples and relations to land with settlers and relations to property" (p. 8). Indigenous pedagogy must be guided by Indigenous values, knowledges, and ways of being to build upon previous generations in relationship to place.

SITUATING OUR PROCESS

We came together writing this chapter as Indigenous teachers to portray our teaching experiences and how we see ourselves Indigenizing the profession. We have been exploring our own identities and agencies as teachers to determine what drives our pedagogy and perceptions of teaching and learning processes. Inspired by Marin et al.'s (2020) use of Wilson's (2008) talk story approach, we reflected on our experiences and collective commitments through talking in relationship with each other. We framed questions to guide our discussion, recorded our talk story, and edited the transcription. Our intention in sharing our dialogue in this way is to make visible a process for navigating the TIPM and to demonstrate the importance of doing this work in relationship across generations.

OUR REFLECTIONS ON INDIGENOUS TEACHER EDUCATION

How Have We Each Come to This Work?

Cornel. I came into the teaching profession by default, meaning I was so far down in the pool of applicants for the Native teacher program at Northeastern State University. By default, some candidates far into the top-10 applicants were not able to fulfill their commitment to the program. Graduating in 1976 with a bachelor's degree in elementary education and health, I could not find a teaching job in Oklahoma. My dark phenotype, long hair, and earrings may have something to do with not getting any teaching interviews in Oklahoma. Thus, I applied out of state in New Mexico and found a counseling position with Crownpoint Boarding School on the Navajo reservation in New Mexico. My first college course was teaching at the University of Minnesota in Native American Studies, while I was the principal of the American Indian Magnet School in St. Paul, MN. My entry to a tenure-track faculty appointment was at Cameron University and later at the University of Kansas where I received tenure as Associate Professor in the KU School of Education. At Portland State University, I was able to switch disciplines and secured a tenure-track position as director of the Indigenous Nations Studies at Portland State University, bringing to campus the American Indian Teacher Program.

Anna. After an initial major in engineering, I completed my teacher education at our local community college in rural northern Michigan where a 4-year teacher education program offered satellite courses. I then spent 3 years teaching preschool and kindergarten near my home community and 2 years teaching overseas in the United Arab Emirates. During this time, colleagues spoke poorly about Indigenous children and families living in poverty. I saw most teachers failing to teach, or learning how to teach, children from backgrounds different than their own. Without theoretical foundations to understand why, I quickly realized that teachers are not adequately prepared to serve diverse communities. This led to my doctoral studies where I was able to build a theoretical understanding of Indigenous education and engage research around how Indigenous community members believe teachers should be prepared. That research continues to drive my work regarding Indigenous community partnerships for teacher education.

Tahlia. Early on in my own education, I loved helping my peers grasp the lessons and concepts we were covering in class. My teachers from elementary school to high school, who were primarily non-Native, would allow me to teach my peers when their efforts were unsuccessful. When my classmates would exclaim, "Oh! Now I get it," I would be filled with pride and satisfaction knowing that they can continue on with their education and that I helped. This inspired me to become a teacher, specifically in my own community. I went into my undergraduate studies knowing exactly what to major and minor in and when Cornel and Anna guided me into the American Indian Teacher Program at Portland State, I knew I was doing exactly what I was meant to do. Immediately after graduation, I moved back home and took a language arts teacher position at our local middle school. I absolutely loved being able to teach the youth in my community and connect with them in ways I did not experience during my student teaching in Portland. That's when I knew there was something magical and inherent when Indigenous teachers teach their Indigenous students. I taught for 2 years before moving into my current position as the Youth Development Coordinator in a community education program. I felt so much guilt for leaving the classroom but felt so suffocated by the scripted curriculum, standardized tests, and generic standards. I am now able to connect with youth and their families and provide education around holistic health in a culturally relevant way. Though I feel more fulfilled, I still wonder how we can do the same in our school district.

What Were Our Intentions in Pursuing a Career in Teaching?

Cornel. Teaching became enjoyable to me when I was in the School of Education at KU. Really diving into the pedagogy of teaching and learning was rewarding having conducted multiple literature reviews and studying effective teaching practices of Indigenous students. This was the juncture of my career where I started to write more articles on culturally responsive teaching for Indigenous learners. As I became the director of the Indigenous Nations Studies Program at PSU, I enjoyed creating new courses within my content area and assigning aspiring graduate students teaching appointments. One of the most rewarding ideas was to create a Teaching Circle, a small yet dedicated circle of graduate students and faculty dedicated to improving their teaching pedagogy at PSU. This Teaching Circle morphed into the Critical Consciousness Study Group, which helped test and reshape TIPM.

Anna. My intentions pursuing teaching evolved over time. As an undergraduate, I loved working with children and I found joy working with families and communities. Through my master's degree, I wanted to deepen my understandings of children's language development, and entering my doctoral program I had developed deep commitments to transforming teacher education. This trajectory mirrors the TIPM where my critical consciousness developed with experiences and gained momentum fostered by strong mentors and colleagues. Beginning as faculty, I had strong theoretical foundations and strengthened my practice in varied educational settings, which sustained my work in the academy. My work spanned from not yet aligning with the TIPM as I lacked critical consciousness to question settler-colonial schooling, to efforts that span TIPM dimensions to "social justice action." Commitments of decolonization and Indigenous postcolonialism drive my work in teacher education, and these commitments are sustained through collaboration with community leaders and Indigenous colleagues.

Tahlia. My intentions around teaching felt more like an obligation. I knew I had the potential to be a good teacher for my younger relatives. I also saw and felt the impact when you had an Indigenous teacher. The few Zuni teachers I had were the ones I learned the most from and had meaningful relationships with. They didn't just teach me their content, they taught me about life and showed me that there was someone in my community outside of my immediate family that cared about me. I wanted to continue developing that environment in education and I knew that was how I could best serve my community; that's why it felt like an obligation.

What Were Our Experiences in Teacher Education?

Cornel. Creating the TIPM guided my own teaching pedagogy as well as helped me understand the positionality of most of the teacher education candidates in their teaching practice. I have witnessed that most public school teachers, many of which were Indigenous students, situated themselves in the first "Contributions" dimension of TIPM. This entry dimension of "unlearning" Eurocentric consciousness also challenges the existing relations of settler-colonial domination. For those learners fortunate enough to transcend upward to the next dimension of critical thinking and praxis, many learners jumped to the "Additive" dimension wherein learners began to change their structural framework in teaching, trying to decolonize themselves but without regular practice; they still embraced Eurocentric thinking with fixed structures of human living systems. The third "Transformation" dimension demonstrated significant paradigm shifts of conscientization (as theorized by Paulo Freire) by regularly decolonizing and advancing their teaching practice, while trying to mentor others desiring to decolonize their minds. The fourth "Cultural and Social Justice" dimension embraced transformational praxis by analyzing settler-colonial constructs, creating genius virtues by becoming the teacher of teachers and protectors of sacred knowledge while engaging insurgent research with a deep commitment to self-determination action (decolonization and critical consciousness).

Ultimately, a colonized mind is far more destructive than that of the body. Today, Indigenous teachers are caught between creating space for Indigenous self-determination and the whitestream methodology of oppression as a weapon of domination. It is essential to perceive discouragement and crumbling by some members of the cohort, but that is where other group members lift them up and help them get back on the right path, or the Red Road. This method requires thorough reflection, training, and practice.

Anna. My experiences as an undergraduate teacher candidate were somewhat unremarkable. The aspects worth noting were the quality advising offered by the community college and making a teaching degree accessible within our community. The program did not include critical perspectives of education or any effort to understand Indigenous or multicultural education; this program did not align TIPM dimensions. As a teacher educator, I have had excellent mentorship. Colleagues have embraced Indigenous education within our ECE program in compliance with state legislation. One example is a Tribal early-learning field experience where teacher candidates work with Indigenous preschool teachers to develop Tribally specific lessons guided by seasonal and cultural practices; these lessons fall within the "contributions" and "transformation" dimensions of the TIPM offering Indigenous children positive and locally relevant school-based experiences. I have also worked with Tribal early-learning programs to design curriculum in relations with lands, waters, and seasonal community practices. This work aligns with the "social justice action" dimension of the TIPM; we are working to decolonize school-based learning and create thriving experiences today.

Tahlia. My experience in teacher education is bittersweet. I went into the program feeling so special and motivated because I never knew there were programs specifically designed for Indigenous teachers. I knew this program's values aligned with mine because their goal for each candidate was to receive a Master's in Education and a teaching license so that they could get Indigenous teachers into communities. I walked into my first class of the program and realized I was one of three Candidates of Color and one of two Indigenous candidates. I put that first impression aside and looked forward to the material; I could not wait to read and learn about all the Indigenous pedagogy and theories and how to apply it in the classroom. However, as the weeks went on, I realized that I would be receiving mainstream teacher education. I met with advisors within AITP and found out that our Indigenous teacher candidates were spread thin across the entire education department and that there was no specific class for us. I was heartbroken and throughout the program I experienced and confronted racial injustices being perpetuated within the curriculum. I still aimed to do all my work through an Indigenous lens, even when the friction became almost unbearable. This experience strengthened my belief that Indigenous teachers need to be in cohorts with additional support and education. Though I was hurt, I was even more motivated to successfully complete the program and go back to my community.

How Do We Enact Indigenous Education?

Cornel. Designing and teaching university courses on disrupting and dismantling settler-colonial practice is my immediate goal. An entry point could be to integrate an Indigenous taxonomy and knowledge base into teacher education programs. Because I witness most teachers and teacher candidates at the foundational dimension of TIPM, we have to reframe the methodology and pedagogy for preparing teachers to effectively teach Indigenous students. My long-range goal is to consciously guide TIPM and creatively plan and produce "back to the future" Indigenous ways of knowing into the teacher education knowledge base, and by doing so, pass on to the next generation its accumulated wisdom, language, and cultural skills necessary to develop and maintain, which reshape and give cultural meaning to Indigenous children's reality.

Anna. In addition to the experiences already described, I'll share other efforts I have taken to enact Indigenous education with children and teacher candidates. A powerful representation of Indigenous education occurs in a summer

Indigenous STEAM program with Anishinaabe educator Dr. Megan Bang. This program enacts land education through intergenerational engagements; spending full days outside learning with and from children, Elders, and more-than-human relations. Designed to cultivate Indigenous resurgence and communal thriving, the program works to foster children's development, knowledge systems, and ethical leadership by learning to uphold their responsibilities to sustain social and ecological balance, which offers a representation of practice aligned with what Dr. Pewewardy has named "Social Justice Action." This program guides my efforts to infuse land education in teacher education. As I have gained success integrating Indigenous education within our ECE program, I have worked to recruit more Indigenous candidates. Encouraging Indigenous students to enter teacher education at a primarily white institution has been done with caution on my part. It was not until I felt our curriculum was relevant for Indigenous children, teachers, and communities that I recommended Indigenous students apply. While our ECE program remains imperfect, we are currently preparing three Indigenous teacher candidates and offering commitment within the program to support their future teaching.

Tahlia. When I was in the classroom, I prioritized relationship building. I wanted my students to know that building relationships with themselves, with me, with their peers, with their families, and with their community was just as important as their academics. I tried to share that perspective with the rest of the teachers and staff in the building. Some were very responsive and also embraced the value, while others did not. I felt like I did not have the words or education to explain what I felt deep inside. I knew that our students already possessed the skills and knowledge to be successful and happy and our job as teachers was to guide them to those realizations. It wasn't until I left the schools and came into my current position where my feelings were validated. Our program's approach is strengths-based and rooted in culture. We believe that our community has the knowledge and answers to develop strong, healthy youth who are connected to their culture. When you approach things in this manner, you gain community partners and trust. Then everyone is on the same page to help our youth and bring their contributions to the overall picture. This is the framework that needs to be promoted in teacher education programs because it is inherent in Indigenous communities.

SYNTHESIZING OUR REFLECTIONS FOR
INDIGENOUS TEACHER EDUCATION

Our shared narratives and engagement in Indigenous education are maintained through shared commitments toward thriving Indigenous futures. The TIPM offers a framework to support educators developing their critical consciousness and decolonized praxis. Through this, teacher education can work to (1) integrate Indigenous knowledges, (2) dismantle settler-colonial paradigms, and (3) engage a continual examination of commitments to transformation and decolonization. We close this chapter with a synthesis of our hopes for Indigenous teacher education.

Integrating an Indigenous knowledge base into teacher education is a slow and continuous process. As Wildcat (2006) echoes Vine Deloria Jr's scholarship on Indigenous knowledge systems, "he did not view Indian knowledge systems in the past tense as artifacts or relics . . . but rather as knowledges that should be taken seriously for contemporary and practical purposes" (p. 425). Thus, dismantling settler-colonial paradigms in whitestream teacher education programs is physically and spiritually taxing and causes ethno-stress for anyone trying to Indigenize structures on their own, and we hope that Indigenous teacher education can create structures for educators to engage this work collectively across generations. We have witnessed beginning achievements toward these ends in teacher education programs by using and implementing TIPM. We have implemented TIPM in pre-service teacher education programs and professional development trainings for 3 decades that warrant continuous development toward decolonizing teacher education programs. Our chapter drew upon decolonizing methodologies, Indigenous theorizing, and whiteness scholarship to support the scaffolding of TIPM in working toward the transformational goals of wave jumping. TIPM requires continuous examination and testing of its implications. This process requires deep reflection and self-critique that bring new, positive experiences as well as resistance when trying to Indigenize teacher education. As we envision positive Indigenous futures for all, we see the TIPM as an important framework to foster educator consciousness to enact traditional forms of Indigenous education with the generations to come.

CONCLUSION

We conclude by acknowledging the complexities for Indigenizing teaching and learning and our decolonizing work in confronting our own colonial mentality, moral indifference, and historical ignorance that offers a critical Indigenous counter-narrative. Working within settler-colonial systems of education, we critique these systems to better understand our ancestral Indigenous teachings that support Indigenous education and identity development. It is our ancestral responsibility as Indigenous teachers to enact teaching and learning where Indigenous self-determination and sovereignty are not transmitted accidently, but by design. Therefore, we share this chapter with a spirit of humility and reciprocity.

REFERENCES

Alfred, T. (2009). *Wasasa: Indigenous pathways of action and freedom.* Ontario: University of Toronto Press.

Alfred, T. (1999). *Peace, power, righteousness: An Indigenous manifesto.* Oxford University Press.

Chandler, D., & Reid, J. (2018). Being in being: Contesting the ontopolitics of Indigeneity. *The European Legacy, 25*(3), 251–268. https://www.tandfonline.com/action/showCitFormats?doi=10.1080%2F10848770.2017.1420284

Bang, M. (2020). Learning on the move toward just, sustainable, and culturally thriving futures, cognition and instruction. *Cognition and Instruction, 38*(3), 434–444. https://doi.org/10.1080/07370008.2020.1777999

Cajete, G. (1994). *Look to the mountain: An ecology of Indigenous education.* Kivaki Press.

Carver-Thomas, D., & Darling-Hammond, L. (2019). The trouble with teacher turnover: How teacher attrition affects students and schools. *Education Policy Analysis Archives, 27*(36), 1–32.

Dion, S. (2009). *Braiding histories: Learning from Aboriginal peoples' experiences and perspectives.* University of British Columbia Press.

Higgins, M., Madden, B., & Korteweg, L. (2015). Witnessing (halted) deconstruction: White teachers' perfect stranger' position within urban Indigenous education. *Race Ethnicity and Education, 18*(2), 251–276.

Jordan, J. V., & Schwartz, H. L. (2018). Radical empathy in teaching. *New Directions for Teaching and Learning. 153*, 25–35.

Killsback, L. K. (2020). *A Sacred people: Indigenous governance, traditional leadership, and the warriors of the Cheyenne Nation.* Lubbock, TX: Texas Tech University Press.

Kulago, H. A. (2019). In the business of futurity: Indigenous teacher education and settler colonialism. *Equity & Excellence in Education*, 1–16.

Marin, A., Stewart-Ambo, T., McDaid-Morgan, N., White Eyes, R., Bang, M. (2020). Enacting relationships of kinship and care in educational and research settings. In A. I. Ali & T. L. McCarty (Eds.), *Critical youth research in education: Methodologies of praxis and care* (pp. 243–264). Routledge.

National Center for Education Statistics. (2020). *The Condition of Education 2020* (NCES 2020-144). https://nces.ed.gov/pubsearch/pubsinfo.asp?pubid=2020144

National Center for Education Statistics. (n.d.). *Number of public school teachers, number and percentage of public school teachers who entered teaching in 2011 or 2012, and percentage distribution of new public school teachers, by race/ethnicity: 2011–12.* https://nces.ed.gov/surveys/sass/tables/SASS1112_2014_03_t1n.asp

O'Meara, S., & West, D. A. (1996). *From our eyes: Learning from Indigenous peoples.* Garamond Press.

Tuck, E., McKenzie, M., & McCoy, K. (2014). Land education: Indigenous, post-colonial, and decolonizing perspectives on place and environmental education research. *Environmental Education Research, 20* (1), 1–23.

Tuck, E., & Ree, C. (2013). A glossary of haunting. In S. H. Jones, T. E. Adams, & C. Ellis, *Handbook of Autoethnography* (pp. 639–658). Left Coast Press.

Warren, C. A., & Hotchkins, B. K. (2015). Teacher education and the enduring significance of "false empathy." *The Urban Review, 47*(2), 266–292.

Wildcat, D. R. (2006). *Indigenizing American Indian policy: Finding the place of American Indian education.* University of Missouri-Kansas City.

Wilson, S. (2008). *Research is ceremony: Indigenous research methods.* Fernwood.

Part III

HIGHER EDUCATION

CHAPTER 8

Tribal College and University (TCU) Faculty as Native Nation Builders

Natalie Rose Youngbull (Cheyenne & Arapaho/Assiniboine & Sioux)

INTRODUCTION

E-pevaʼe éšeevaʼe! Natalie Rose Youngbull na-heševehe. I am an enrolled citizen of the Tsistsistas (Cheyenne) and Hinonoʼei (Arapaho) (C&A) Tribe of Oklahoma and descended from the Ft. Peck Assiniboine and Sioux Tribes of Montana. I was raised in El Reno, Oklahoma, within my C&A Tribal community. As an assistant professor in the College of Education at the University of Oklahoma, I reside and engage in academic spaces within the traditional homelands of the Hasinais (Caddo Nation) and Kirikirʔiːs (Wichita & Affiliated Tribes). My chapter focuses on the programs I managed when I served as the Faculty Development Program Officer (FDPO) at the American Indian College Fund (College Fund), located in Denver, Colorado, the traditional homelands of my C&A people.

Since the establishment of the first Tribal college just over 50 years ago, Tribal colleges and universities (TCUs) have experienced expansive growth within a relatively short timeline. While TCUs continuously plan for institutional expansion and growth, one of their primary aims is seeking to serve the needs of their respective Tribal communities. As Tribal communities continue to reclaim and revive traditional knowledge systems, TCUs play a pivotal role in the reclamation and revitalization process through centering Indigenous teachings, wisdom, practices, and language within existing degree programs and in developing new degree programs. Tribal college leaders understand that faculty development is fundamental to expanding academic program offerings and developing culturally relevant curriculum. This is particularly true with Indigenous faculty who come from the community, as it is likely that these faculty uphold the traditional culture, values, and ways of being that the TCU is grounded in (Tippeconnic & McKinney, 2003). Therefore, faculty development has long been an area of emphasis for TCU leadership. Tribal college presidents and chief academic officers/academic deans seek out and encourage faculty members to pursue graduate and terminal degree programs in their respective fields of study. Some TCUs have established institutional faculty development funds to assist faculty with expenses such as tuition and fees, and weekly travel to/from their hometowns and campuses.

Though TCUs maintain a majority Native student enrollment, Native faculty make up less than half (43%) of the total faculty body across all Tribal colleges (AIHEC AIMS, 2020). There is a gap between Indigenous TCU faculty and non-Indigenous TCU faculty with graduate degrees, as 21% of Indigenous faculty hold master's degrees compared to 32% of non-Indigenous faculty (AIHEC AIMS, 2020). The numbers drastically drop for faculty with doctoral degrees, with only 4% of Indigenous faculty with doctorates compared to 14% of non-Indigenous faculty (AIHEC AIMS, 2020). This fact surprises many people who are not familiar with TCUs, but it comes as no surprise to those from within that are culturally and academically connected to Tribal communities. Educational attainment continues to be a struggle within Native communities, hence the need for Tribal colleges. The struggle for more Native/Indigenous faculty at TCUs is related to the issue of academic credentials. Due to their unique status and size, TCUs spend substantial amounts of time and effort focused on achieving and maintaining accreditation. Though many Native/Indigenous instructors/faculty have traditional knowledges, they are required to achieve certain western academic credentials to actually hold a faculty position. The purpose of this chapter is to highlight how efforts toward TCU faculty development over the past 15-plus years has strengthened Native Nation building. I draw upon the definition and description of Native Nation building provided by Brayboy et al. (2012) as being inclusive of "legal and political, cultural, economic, health and nutrition, spiritual, and educational elements with the well-being, sovereignty, self-determination, and autonomy of the community as the driving force for nation building" (p. 13).

POSITIONALITY/CONNECTION TO THE WORK

As the FDPO at the College Fund, I administered all faculty fellowship programs and faculty development opportunities available for Tribal college faculty. My work included TCU site visits to promote the fellowships and existing faculty development opportunities, along with checking in with previous and current faculty fellows. These site visits were essential to my understanding of faculty development needs within Tribal colleges, as I became familiar with current TCU campus structures and environments. In my visits and check-ins with TCU faculty, I listened to and engaged with them about their needs for more resources and opportunities to explore and grow in scholarly spaces within their respective TCU settings. Though my role was heavily administrative, I also mentored TCU faculty through their dissertation writing process. I observed how many of the Indigenous faculty fellows' dissertation topics were aligned with the latter dimensions of the Transformational Indigenous Praxis Model (TIPM)— Dimension 3, Transformation approach, and Dimension 4, Cultural and Social Justice Action—by centering Indigenous and Tribal-specific epistemologies to support and develop more land-based curriculum and culturally grounded degree programs.

Beyond the faculty fellowship programming, I had the opportunity to develop and enhance faculty development opportunities for TCU faculty. Through feedback from previous and current faculty fellows, I developed two faculty development opportunities: (1) research conference funding to encourage conference attendance of TCU faculty in their respective fields, and (2) an annual intensive writing retreat to assist the development of publishable manuscripts. These opportunities seamlessly contribute to strengthening the annual TCU Faculty Research Convening and the Tribal College and University Research Journal (TCURJ), the first peer-reviewed interdisciplinary journal to focus on research by TCU faculty and for Tribal colleges and communities. These faculty development opportunities provided tangible avenues for Indigenous TCU faculty to more fully operate within the TIPM Dimension 4: Cultural and Social Justice Action by advancing their critical consciousness to continue the decolonization of existing structures, curriculum, and pedagogy within Tribal colleges (Pewewardy et al., 2018).

TRANSFORMATIONAL INDIGENOUS PRAXIS MODEL IN A TRIBAL COLLEGE/UNIVERSITY CONTEXT

The Transformational Indigenous Praxis Model underscores the need for critical thinking in decolonizing and Indigenizing western-based curriculum. Pewewardy et al. (2018) state that the model is meant to be used as a tool to engage students and educators in deep reflection toward the development of critical consciousness to examine structures of their own and others to gain a greater understanding of how to further develop social justice education. The TIPM has the potential to foster critical conversations about the state of Indigenous education within Indigenous communities. In particular, the TIPM sheds light on the transformation occurring at many Tribal colleges toward incorporating more Indigenous knowledges into existing curriculum and new curriculum and programs. Tribal college faculty, both Indigenous and non-Indigenous, are being tasked with centering Indigenous knowledges in their own pedagogical approaches and across degree programs. Per the Tribal college context, TCU faculty critical consciousness falls within the TIPM dimensions 2–4. TCU faculty that fall within the Additive dimension are typically non-Indigenous, teach standard courses, and embrace the Tribal college mission and vision, but still apply Eurocentric pedagogical approaches. In particular, Indigenous faculty fellows fall within Dimension 3: Transformation Approach and Dimension 4: Cultural and Social Justice Action, as they incorporate Indigenous knowledges and research methodologies into their thesis/dissertation research projects. A few Indigenous faculty fellows have wave-jumped from Dimension 3 to 4 by utilizing their own ancestral knowledges and working directly with Tribal Elders and knowledge keepers through their thesis/dissertation research projects to develop Indigenous/Tribal-specific research models and conceptual frameworks. These new models and frameworks are central to developing Indigenous and Tribally centered degree programs for Tribal colleges.

TCU FACULTY FELLOWSHIP PROGRAM

Since 2004, over 100 Tribal college faculty members have completed a master's or terminal degree in the humanities, humanistic social sciences, education, and STEM fields with fellowship funding through the American Indian College Fund (https://collegefund.org/) in partnership with generous donors. Faculty fellowships and development opportunities were available to both Indigenous and non-Indigenous faculty, with an emphasis on funding Indigenous faculty. The fellowship program provided faculty with (1) funding to cover expenses related to their degree programs, (2) mentoring through monthly check-ins with the faculty development program officer at the College Fund, (3) writing support, networking, and mentorship through retreats hosted by the College Fund, and (4) teaching/administrative duty reductions within their respective institutions negotiated through a contract with the faculty fellow and the College Fund. The intent was to impact institutional growth.

The fellowship program provided the opportunity to gather faculty fellows at two scheduled retreats throughout the fellowship year. The first retreat served as an introduction to the fellowship program and was held at the beginning of the academic year. Faculty fellows had the opportunity to present their thesis and dissertation research topics and receive feedback from their fellow peers and two faculty scholar mentors. Faculty fellows' thesis/dissertation advisers were also invited to attend these presentations to participate in the feedback discussion, as it provided an opportunity for the dissertation chair (who may have been non-Indigenous) to interact with Indigenous scholars and learn about the significance of the faculty fellows' research topics. The second retreat was an official writing retreat where faculty fellows worked with Indigenous scholar mentors to develop and strengthen specific sections of their dissertation. Faculty fellows received feedback from their fellow cohort peers, scholar mentors, and the program administrator throughout the multiple-day writing retreat.

Not only did the faculty fellowship program provide generous funding toward total expenses, there was also a contract signed by the faculty fellow and TCU leadership to agree to provide institutional support such as course reduction and more time to work on coursework and dissertation. Teaching was the primary focus for most TCU faculty, and they often carry a heavy teaching load each term, with an average teaching load for the academic year being 30 credits/units. However, many faculty teach higher academic loads due to teacher shortages and student needs to complete necessary coursework for progress toward degree completion. Additionally, TCU faculty are expected to offer more student office hours, an average of 10 hours/week, and be on campus during business hours throughout the week. Due to the size of many TCUs, faculty wear many hats including student advising, committee service, outreach, and assessment planning (Tippeconnic & McKinney, 2003). Though research is not an expectation for all TCU faculty, many faculty members are identified and encouraged by their leadership to pursue graduate and terminal degrees to be able to support growth and development efforts of Tribal colleges. The fellowship program contract was an important piece of the program as it served as an understanding between the faculty member, TCU leadership, and College Fund (funder) that the Tribal college provided specific institutional resources and support. Institutional resources and support were manifested in the form of course reduction(s) throughout the fellowship academic year, physical space for uninterrupted writing time (beyond the faculty member's office space, as it is where students, staff, and faculty can find the faculty fellow), and extended time during the work week to focus on writing, such as every Friday as a writing day. As the fellowship administrator, I met one-on-one with faculty fellows every month to check-in on their dissertation writing progress and offer support in the form of reviewing and providing feedback on written sections of the dissertation, troubleshooting issues/concerns regarding progress and/or necessary support, and providing encouragement and acknowledgment of their progress.

Native Nation Building

I refer to TCU faculty as Native Nation builders because their efforts through teaching, research, and service within a Tribal college context are directly contributing to Native Nation building. Similar to the TIPM, Native Nation building needs to work toward social justice and be beneficial to the community, land, and people (Brayboy et al., 2012). (Re)claiming Indigenous knowledge systems (IKS) is central to this effort and vision for Nation building (Brayboy et al, 2012). TCU faculty enact Native Nation building through the reclamation of IKS within program and curriculum development, pedagogical approaches, community-based research agendas, and Indigenizing student success and leadership. The following two examples illuminate the success of Indigenous faculty development efforts toward Native Nation building in the areas of Indigenous-based conceptual models/ frameworks and Native student success.

Indigenous-Based Conceptual Models/Frameworks

As Tribal colleges continue to uphold their missions of teaching Tribal histories, cultures, and languages, TCU faculty are tasked with decolonizing curriculum and incorporating Indigenous knowledges throughout degree programs. In recognizing the opportunity to decolonize curriculum, several Indigenous faculty fellows focused their thesis/dissertation topics on developing Indigenous-based conceptual models and frameworks. Indigenous faculty relied upon their own ancestral knowledges and worked with local Elders and knowledge-keepers to design these models and frameworks. In this example, Indigenous faculty fellows operated in Dimension 3: Transformational Approach by centering Indigenous ways of knowing and references to language, culture, and land in the development of these Indigenous-based conceptual models and frameworks. Specifically, Indigenous faculty fellows designed these models and frameworks with Indigenous students in mind with the overarching goal of decolonizing curricular and pedagogical approaches within Tribal colleges.

Native Student Success

Indigenous faculty are the heartbeat of Tribal colleges. Beyond the typical expectations of high-quality teaching, service, and potential research activity, Indigenous faculty are expected to lead efforts in sustaining and incorporating traditional knowledges and languages throughout their work because of their personal backgrounds and commitment to Native Nation building (Tippeconnic & McKinney, 2003). Given this standing, Indigenous faculty are essential to the well-being and success of all TCU students, and particularly for Native students. In many discussions with faculty fellows, they acknowledged that their commitment to the faculty role centered on student success. Indigenous faculty fellows, in particular, described how they were creating pathways to graduate school for Indigenous students by openly sharing experiences about their graduate and doctoral programs. Indigenous faculty fellows also shared how students would see them working on their dissertations on campus and engage with them about their research topics and how to pursue graduate school. In these exchanges, Indigenous faculty operated between Dimension 3: Transformation Approach and Dimension 4: Cultural and Social Justice Action as they actively served as role models and mentors for Native students interested in continuing on to graduate school in their educational pathways. By interacting with Indigenous TCU faculty fellows, Native students see reflections of themselves in the faculty ranks and pathways toward achieving that goal.

RESISTANCE TO TCU FACULTY DEVELOPMENT

The Transformational Indigenous Praxis Model acknowledges the resistance that educators face while on the pathway toward cultural and social justice action. This resistance is a product of active decolonizing efforts within higher education institutions (Pewewardy et al., 2018). The very existence of TCUs is a decolonizing higher education project as these institutions have faced considerable resistance to their missions and visions from settler institutions and organizations. TCU faculty face this resistance as they develop Tribally- and culturally-based curriculum, pedagogical approaches, and research projects that further Native Nation building efforts. This section details two examples of resistance experienced by TCU faculty; each resistance example is followed by a related example of how a faculty fellow has overcome resistance through their educational pursuits and professional development.

Resistance Example #1

The accreditation process is necessary for TCU establishment and future expansion as it provides opportunity for more funding sources. However, the work required for achieving and maintaining accreditation is tasking and forces faculty to wear many hats. All TCUs are accredited by two regional accrediting organizations, the Higher Learning Commission (HLC) and the Northwest Commission on Colleges and Universities (NWCCU). Recently, a group of faculty and staff from Sinte Gleska University (SGU) presented at the annual TCU Faculty Research Convening hosted by the College Fund. Essentially, they were exploring what makes a Tribal college *a Tribal college* if their accreditation process is the same as mainstream higher education institutions. It is an important topic of discussion as there is no policy for TCU representation on the accreditation team, but a typical TCU accreditation team might include one individual who may have a loose connection to a Tribal college.

Sinte Gleska University faculty/staff representatives were exploring the option to pursue institutional accreditation from the World Indigenous Nations Higher Education Consortium (WINHEC), an organization dedicated to providing support for Indigenous achievement through higher education. Several Indigenous-based degree programs across Tribal colleges have program level accreditation from WINHEC, but no TCU has pursued full institutional accreditation. This decision is most likely influenced by the potential impact upon current and future federal and outside funding sources. The exploration of a more appropriate accrediting agency for TCUs is an example of how SGU faculty are in the process of wave-jumping from Dimension 3: Transformation Approach to Dimension 4: Cultural and Social Justice Action as they seek to decolonize the accrediting process of Tribal colleges through an Indigenous educational accrediting agency.

TCU Faculty Fellow Example #1: Reclamation of IKS Through Doctoral Journey

An Indigenous faculty fellow developed their dissertation topic through work with their Tribal cultural committee, which consisted of Elders and knowledge keepers. The project entailed an intergenerational transfer of language, traditional knowledge, and practices. The dissertation chair was a non-Indigenous faculty member who was not knowledgeable about Indigenous research methodologies and approaches but was supportive of the faculty fellow's research topic and methodological approach. The faculty fellow was intentional from the beginning of their study in situating their results within the broader work of the cultural committee. They explained that the cultural committee was like a co-author of their dissertation. The faculty fellow worked directly with the cultural committee to receive approval on findings and descriptions to include within the dissertation, and only included what was agreed upon by the cultural committee. In essence, the faculty fellow wrote two dissertations—one to complete the requirements for the doctoral degree, and one to preserve Tribal language and traditional knowledge. This example details how an Indigenous faculty fellow's research project was grounded in cultural and social justice action as they designed their study FOR and conducted it WITH the Tribal community, not for or designed by the degree-granting institution.

Resistance Example #2

A reoccurring challenge faced by many faculty fellows who pursued terminal degrees was the resistance they experienced within their own institutions through their fellowship year and after receiving their doctorate degrees. Faculty fellows endured complaints from colleagues who did not understand the demands of writing a dissertation and the need for course reductions within the fellowship year, and faced challenges with leadership in efforts to develop a research agenda beyond their dissertation and fellowship year. Though TCU leadership supported faculty fellows through the fellowship academic year, faculty fellows were expected to return back to their full teaching and service loads with no option to negotiate for research activities to be incorporated into their faculty contract after receiving their terminal degrees. There was a lack of understanding of how the doctorate journey developed TCU faculty scholarship capacity and interest in building research agendas as part of their work along with teaching and service. Unfortunately, this internal resistance is a result of settler accreditation standards and outdated TCU faculty contracts. This type of resistance prevents TCU faculty from wave-jumping from Dimension 3 to Dimension 4 by obstructing their ability to continue developing the critical consciousness toward research agendas that truly center the well-being of Tribal communities and nations.

TCU Faculty Fellow Example #2: Growing Our Own Leaders

An Indigenous faculty fellow was encouraged to pursue their terminal degree from their TCU president and a colleague, who also served as a mentor to the faculty fellow. The mentor was also an Indigenous scholar and guided the faculty fellow through their doctoral program, as the faculty fellow utilized a model developed by the scholar mentor for their research project. The TCU president and colleague were grooming the faculty fellow as a future candidate for the Tribal college presidency. As the faculty fellow ascended from full-time instructor into roles such as the Dean of Student Affairs and Dean of Academic Affairs, they were instrumental in establishing financial aid policies and processes, student learning assessment plans, and developing student affairs practices for accreditation. Being a graduate of another Tribal college, the faculty fellow was committed to their Tribal college's growth and expansion within their Tribal community. Recently, the faculty fellow was chosen as the new president of the institution, becoming the first Indigenous faculty fellow to ascend to the presidency of a Tribal college. This example exemplifies the success of Tribal colleges' efforts to "grow their own" from within their institutions. In this new role, the former faculty fellow, now Tribal college president, is in the process of wave-jumping from Dimension 3 to Dimension 4 by having the knowledge, experience, mentorship, and commitment to their Tribal nation/community to transform their TCU environment toward advancing Native Nation building efforts.

CONCLUSION: VISIONING ACADEMIC FUTURES
FOR INDIGENOUS TCU FACULTY

As Tribal colleges continue to Indigenize educational pathways and environments for their communities, Indigenous faculty are essential to this effort as they are equipped with ancestral knowledges, language, and maintain cultural and/or social responsibilities within their respective communities. Academically, Indigenous faculty embody a critical consciousness of existing educational landscapes and have training to build connections between Indigenous and western knowledge bases to advance institutional goals. Indigenous TCU faculty are committed to strengthening Native Nation building through designing more Indigenous-based undergraduate and graduate program offerings, developing research agendas in collaboration with the Tribal nations and communities, and creating educational and scholarly pathways for TCU students. Indigenous faculty at Tribal colleges are ready to expand decolonization efforts toward Dimension 4 and mentor fellow colleagues and students along the path toward cultural and social justice action within Tribal colleges.

Incorporate Research and Scholarly Activity into TCU Faculty Contract

As more Tribal college faculty develop as scholars, there is a need to modify the TCU faculty contract to incorporate research and scholarly activity into the roles and responsibilities along with teaching and service. Indigenous TCU faculty have responded to the request from TCU leadership to pursue graduate and terminal degrees to expand program offerings. Yet, there is no option in the faculty contract to continue scholarly activity once the fellow has received their terminal degree. Faculty fellows have indicated there is no change to their roles and responsibilities within their contracts after the fellowship year. The message faculty fellows have received is to return back to their regular teaching and service activities, even after the transformative experience of the thesis/dissertation journey. Faculty contracts differ across Tribal colleges regarding advising and service at the program, department, and university levels, but there are shared expectations about the total number of credits a full-time faculty member must teach for the academic year. One reason previous faculty fellows moved on from their respective Tribal colleges was due to a lack of support from leadership to continue developing their research agendas. A major goal of the faculty fellowships is to assist TCUs with developing their faculty into future leaders from within the Tribal college. Tribal college leadership needs to acknowledge and honor faculty requests to engage in research and scholarly activities as part of their faculty contracts.

Continual Development of Indigenous TCU Faculty in Scholarly Spaces

It is of the utmost importance to support the continual development of Indigenous TCU faculty in scholarly spaces "to apply their advanced level of critical consciousness to actively transform and decolonize educational structures, curriculum, and pedagogy" (Pewewardy et al., 2018, p. 57). Indigenous faculty are central to Tribal colleges fulfilling their missions and visions, as they hold the knowledge, connections, and training to transform their respective Tribal colleges into educational spaces that more fully serve Tribal communities. As Tribal community members, Indigenous faculty serve as direct connections from the community to the institution. As Indigenous faculty have more opportunity to develop within scholarly spaces, they will be able to strengthen Tribal colleges' efforts toward Native Nation building.

REFERENCES

American Indian Higher Education Consortium (2020). *American Indian measures of success: AIHEC AIMS annual report* [Unpublished dataset]. AIHEC.

Brayboy, B. M. J., Fann, A. J., Castagno, A. E., & Solyom, J. A. (2012). Postsecondary education for American Indian and Alaska Natives: Higher education for nation building and self-determination. *ASHE Higher Education Report, 37*(5).

Pewewardy, C. D., Lees, A., & Clark-Shim, H. (2018). The Transformational Indigenous Praxis Model: Stages for developing critical consciousness in Indigenous education. *Wíčazo Ša Review, 32*, 38–69. https://doi.org/10.5749/wicazosareview.33.1.0038

Tippeconnic, J. W., & McKinney, S. (2003). Native faculty: Scholarship and development. In M. K. P. Benham & W. J. Stein (Eds.). *The renaissance of American Indian higher education: Capturing the dream* (pp. 241–255). Lawrence Erlbaum Associates.

CHAPTER 9

Learning On and From the Land

Indigenous Perspectives on University Land-Based Learning Pedagogies

Virginia Drywater-Whitekiller (United Keetoowah Band of Cherokee Indians) and Jeff Corntassel (Cherokee Nation)

In this chapter, we apply two Indigenous concepts. The first, cultural resilience theory, means to use strengths-based, cultural factors to situate and ground us as relatives to the land (Drywater-Whitekiller, 2017). The second concept, community resurgence, is related to the first in that it speaks to the reattachment of our bodies, minds, and spirits to the land (Simpson, 2017). Indigenous land-based relationships are central to community knowledge systems, stories, governance, economies, languages, ceremonies, food sovereignty, and sacred living histories. When discussing "land as pedagogy," Simpson (2017, p. 154), Anishinabe scholar and activist, states, "Like governance and leadership and every other aspect of re-ciprocated life, education comes from the roots up. It comes from being enveloped by land." These intimate, place-based relationships form the basis for our respon-sibilities and governance as sovereign Indigenous nations.[1] However, since first contact, colonial entities and individuals have attempted to dominate Indigenous landscapes in order to maintain a permanent presence, often at the expense of Indigenous nations and peoples. Yet, despite shape-shifting colonial efforts to erase Indigenous peoples from settler-dominated landscapes, Kanaka Maoli scholar J. Kēhaulani Kauanui (2016) describes the inherent dynamics of "enduring Indigeneity" in which Indigenous nations and peoples "exist, resist, and persist."

We are interested in exploring the dynamics of "enduring Indigeneity" fur-ther by examining how cultural resilience theory and community resurgence ap-proaches help Indigenous student success in post-secondary institutions in both the United States and Canada. Additionally, what is the potential for decolonizing approaches, such as the Transformational Indigenous Praxis Model (Pewewardy et al., 2018), to further promote Indigenous student success through critical think-ing and transformative actions? In this chapter we examine the complexities of land-based pedagogies and contexts as well as their implementation within the university system, while also considering some of the challenges faced during the global COVID-19 pandemic. Based on Drywater-Whitekiller's interview and focus group results of Indigenous post-secondary students in both the United States and Canada (Drywater-Whitekiller, 2017, 2019, 2020), as well as our experiences teaching land-based classes, we offer some deeper perspectives and nuance to the notion of reconnecting to the land as well as community. We begin by reviewing literature on land-based learning, cultural resilience theory, and community resurgence in order to assess how these theoretical approaches help yield additional insights into student success within a university context.

LAND-BASED LEARNING AND PEDAGOGIES: A LITERATURE REVIEW

To fully exemplify the interrelation of how land lends to pedagogy and pedagogy, in turn, relates back to the land, we apply this circular concept to two themes that are found in the literature. Indigenous forms of land-based learning and pedagogies often evoke "the spiritual, emotional, and intellectual aspects of Land" (Styres et al., 2013, pp. 37–38). In a comprehensive review of 50 articles that directly address Indigenous land-based learning on Turtle Island, Bowra et al. (2020, pp. 4-6) identify five overarching themes that arise from the literature: land as first teacher, centering relationships, holistic perspectives, land as a place of reflection, and Indigenous resistance to colonial structures. Two themes that most closely align with our work on student success are land as relationship (Bang et al., 2014; Borrows, 2017; Burnette et al., 2018; Goodyear-Kaōpua, 2013; Mowatt et al., 2020; Simpson, 2017; Styres et al., 2013; Tuck et al., 2014; Yerxa, 2014) and Indigenous resistance to colonial structures (Bartmes & Shukla, 2020; Corntassel & Hardbarger, 2019; Fellner, 2018; Wildcat et al., 2014).

After reviewing several key works discussing how land-based learning and pedagogies have been implemented across Turtle Island, recurring themes of resilience and resurgence warrant further exploration regarding their applicability to student success. In the following section we examine how cultural resilience theory has been applied to Indigenous peoples. We apply a particular lens in how being grounded in the land serves as support and buffering for American Indian/Alaska Natives combatting the ongoing effects of colonialism.

Cultural Resilience Theory

Cultural resilience theory is a conceptual application that is strengths-based and has no specific context in space and time. In other words, Indigenous peoples have always employed cultural resilience in everyday living, with one watchful eye on the future and another that has stayed on our past. Among other synonyms, cultural resilience is also referred to in the literature as protective factors (Locklear et al., 2018) and cultural buffers (Walters & Simoni, 2002) which encompass multidimensional, spiritual, and social systems that are grounded in the land, communities, and Indigenous identity (Cajete, 2015). This ever-evolving perception utilizes traditional beliefs, values, norms, and pathways to assist us in overcoming obstacles that continue to diversify and intensify in the 21st century.

In contemporary times, cultural resilience is used as an innate defense mechanism that combats ongoing postcolonial challenges that take the form of a mythical trickster who threatens to change and transform the course and narrative of our story. Consequently, an ongoing battle for Indigenous peoples involves the connection to the land, reminding us that manifest destiny is not limited to our past (Rogin, 2017), but remains an ongoing threat to the survival of our distinct cultures. For example, Arctic Indigenous communities, that face foreboding circumstances associated with climate change, are threatened with diminishing food sovereignty associated with oceanic wildlife. To compensate, coping mechanisms via collective reciprocity involved shared ancient and new stories that situated and confirmed traditional ties to place and identity (Sakakibara, 2017). Similarly, to address environmental stability associated with the effects of climate change, international Indigenous youth employed cultural resilience in an educational context designed to protect and preserve relationships with lands, water, and wildlife (Mark, 2016). However, just as the river can and does change its course due to the forces of nature and the dominant will of humans, cultural resilience posits itself in the fluidity of Indigenous resilience, emerging again and again, forever changing but still the same.

Resilience and resurgence share some similarities but also have notable distinctions. To exemplify, we introduce and examine approaches of how Indigenous resurgence, leading to community resurgence, has been utilized by different scholars and activists. Of important note is the application of reattachment to the land as a means to ground, center, and replace previous colonized mindsets.

Community Resurgence

Indigenous resurgence reframes decolonization away from a direct focus on dismantling colonial institutions and toward a more community-centered emphasis on turning away from the state in order to engage more fully on the complex interrelationships between land-based relationships, and cultural practices that reinvigorate everyday acts of renewal and regeneration (Corntassel, 2021, p. 73). According to Leanne Simpson (2017, p. 44), "resurgence must be concerned with the reattachment of our minds, bodies, and spirits to the network of relationships and ethical practices and generates grounded normativity. It means the reattachment of our bodies to our lands, regardless of whether those lands are rural, reserves, or urban."

Overall, resurgence has several dimensions to it which emphasize land and water-based governance (through grounded normativity), decentering the state and settler colonialism, and engaging in everyday acts of renewal, remembering, and regeneration (Corntassel, 2021, p. 74). With its focus on grounded normativity and everydayness (Corntassel, 2012; Corntassel et al., 2018; Coulthard, 2014; Daigle, 2019; Simpson, 2017), resurgence has the potential to describe and explain the transformative potential of land-based learning on Indigenous students.

We have found the application of the community resurgence to the land aptly fits within the Transformational Indigenous Praxis Model (TIPM) as a means to

Indigenize and liberate educators and students. In particular, the TIPM's foundation of cultural and social justice sets the underlying tone for cultural resilience theory as well as community resurgence, as described in the next section.

The Transformational Indigenous Praxis Model

The Transformational Indigenous Praxis Model (TIPM) developed by Cornel Pewewardy, Anna Lees, and Hyuny Clark-Shim (2018) offers some important insights into dimensions of critical consciousness that educators can aspire to embody "cultural and social justice action" (Dimension 4). Dimension 3 of the TIPM, which is the Transformation Approach, has both a collective and individual effort to recognize "Indigenous epistemologies as primary perspectives for a land-based curriculum" (Pewewardy et al., 2018, p. 56). This consciousness-raising approach to curriculum can help challenge the racism, racial microaggressions, and biased curriculum that often "push" Indigenous children out of school (Johnston-Goodstar & Roholt, 2017). Overall, the TIPM offers some insights into the ways that "everyday acts of resurgence" can occur as well as the ways that land-based learning can lead to liberatory praxis.

Overall, the TIPM along with cultural resilience, resurgence, and land-based pedagogies offer some insights into the potential success of Indigenous students within a university setting.

To summarize, cultural resilience theory, viewed as the use of Indigenous cultural factors that are rooted in historical practices, continues to be used in contemporary times. In turn, cultural resilience complements and supports community resurgence, which focuses on reacquaintance and relationship with the land. We viewed both of these concepts through the Transformational Indigenous Praxis Model's Dimension 3 approach which speaks to the need to situate these Indigenous epistemologies for use in land-based teaching curriculums. To expound, we begin by providing a brief overview of Indigenous methodologies, that are inclusive of decolonization approaches and practices, and encompass theoretical other ways of knowing.

INDIGENOUS METHODOLOGIES

Maori scholar Linda T. Smith (2012) asserts that "decolonization . . . is about centering our concerns and world views and then coming to know and understand theory and research from our own perspectives and for our own purposes" (p. 41). While there is no one template for decolonizing methodologies, Thambinathan and Kinsella (2021) offer four key areas for qualitative researchers to decolonize their research practices: exercising critical reflexivity, reciprocity and respect for self-determination, embracing "Other(ed)" ways of knowing, and embodying a transformative praxis, which closely parallels Pewewardy et al.'s TIPM. Overall, these decolonizing and Indigenous approaches provide a larger roadmap that we use to align with our research methods.

Applying the strengths-based theory of cultural resilience, Drywater-Whitekiller (2010) conducted individual interviews with Tribally diverse university students in three states, two of which had high numbers of Tribal representation, and the third was a university setting with an exclusive federally recognized Tribal student body. Criterion-based sampling was employed as the recruited participants needed to be American Indian and in their final year of undergraduate academic studies. Through narrative analysis, the informants were encouraged to engage in storytelling concerning their direct, lived experiences.

A second study was performed with similar methodology, which was supported by a Canada Fulbright grant at a public university located on Coast Salish territories. The participants reflected diverse representation from First Nations, Metis, and Inuit populations (Drywater-Whitekiller, 2020). As a guest on Coast Salish territories, the researcher sought guidance from university resident Elders, whose pronounced presence was solidified in the university's infrastructure as part of the Truth and Reconciliation Commission of Canada's (2015) *Calls to Action*.

As described and expounded upon in the next section, both studies described below utilized Indigenous methodologies that resulted in seven diverse and three similarly related themes regarding cultural resilience as a means to retain in higher education. The three preeminent factors encompassed related context and meaning in spite of the geographic, Tribal status, and cultural diversities of the informants.

FINDINGS AND DISCUSSION

Results of Focus Groups and Interviews by Major Themes

The use of cultural resilience in higher education retention was studied by Drywater-Whitekiller via individual interviews conducted with Tribally diverse American Indian (2010) and First Nations, Metis, and Inuit student informants (2019, 2020). The American Indian study involved the following question: What cultural factors have assisted you in obtaining higher education? The findings produced seven themes that spoke to the lived experience and importance of employing cultural factors to aid in college completion. It is important to note that none of these factors were mutually exclusive, but each was interwoven, interrelated, and at times, interchangeable. The results indicated the following cultural critical factors as related to retention in higher education:

- Tribal identity
- Elders
- Family support
- Ceremonial rituals and sacred ceremonies participation
- Oral traditions
- Support networks
- Spirituality beliefs and practices

The importance of connection to the land was interconnected with home, and the concept of "home" was interconnected with identity as Indigenous persons. Moreover, similar to the findings by Corntassel and Hardbarger (2019) and Mark (2016), the land was viewed as an educator to provoke Indigenous pathways and thinking (e.g., geographic locales, landmarks, and physical sacred sites). However, when the participants and/or their Ancestors were subjected to forced removals and displacements, interdependent person/land teaching relationships took precedence. Succinctly described by Cajete (2015), a forced relocation of American Indian tribes away from their homelands caused a "soul death" that could only be remedied through time and meaningful ties to the land that had been lost (p. 48). For the informants in this study whose tribes were subjected to political removals, cultural resilience was demonstrated by personal cultural relations (i.e., with family, indigenous persons, oral storytelling) which always circled back to the land.

Finally, the second study that involved First Nations, Metis, and Inuit students included the inquiry: What personal and/or cultural motivating factors have helped you to enter and stay in university? The results revealed the following six themes (phrases encased by quotation marks represent the informant's direct voice):

- Motivation: "I possess the strength of my Ancestors and all that I do is for my Ancestors";
- Importance of mentor/mentee: "Allowing me to go full circle";
- Social justice and advocacy: "Getting involved with other causes";
- Socio-economics: "[Higher education] is "able to give us better";
- Trauma/post-trauma: The "emotional toll" of culture shock, isolation, and survival; and
- Indigenous identity: "Know your people and know the general history of Indigenous people."

When comparing the themes from both the U.S. and Canadian studies, we uncovered three that were similarly related, as found in Table 9.1.

Indigenous identity was a key feature that emerged from both findings. American Indian participants viewed identity as connected to family and Tribal communities; others viewed this concept as traditions and culture, while some referred to phenotypes of introspection and external criticalness of "What an Indian is supposed to look like." However, most often, Indigenous identity was an amalgamation of all factors revealing holistic perceptions. Furthermore, the students desired to give back in some capacity to their families and communities, and assumed a personal responsibility to preserve and continue Tribal cultures and traditions.

The informants in the Canadian study were non-traditional students who were knowledgeable concerning their family and band history. And they also had a solid plan for their use of a college degree. However, concern was generated that younger students may not be so assured. This was especially worrisome if they were brought up in urban settings and may not know their culture/language, or

Table 9.1. U.S. and Canada Thematic Cultural Resilience and Resurgence Similarities

U.S. Tribal Informants	Canada First Nations, Metis, and Inuit Informants
Tribal identity (particularly as viewed by self, majority society, and other American Indians).	Indigenous identity: "Know your people and know the general history of Indigenous people."
Elders (respect for the role and wealth of the keepers as conduits of the culture).	Motivation: "I possess the strength of my Ancestors and all that I do is for my Ancestors."
Support networks (critical to provide physical resources and sage advice from others who had lived experience in higher education).	Importance of mentor/mentee: "Allowing me to go full circle."

have an awareness that there is a difference between legislative identities (e.g., treaties that determine status as Indians and Indigenous identities/culture). Adding to these complexities, one student mentioned "the need to understand and think like a colonizer" while another emphasized higher education requires that "we learn how to think and write in a different way." However, this did not appear to imply that one should no longer be Indigenous, but was instead presented as beneficial advice for navigating what were seen as strange and foreign cultural institutions.

In essence, when one identifies as being "othered" it would make sense that to be successful in mainstream institutions, it is important to learn and employ tactics used by the organizational culture. However, this does not mean that developing stealth skills in this area causes one to be exempt from continuing to be seen by others as different or inferior. In this vein, further exploration warranted how the informants in the U.S. study coped with microaggressions that were aimed at them based upon their identity and mainstream assumptions regarding American Indian/Alaska Natives. More pointedly, the next section addresses the findings regarding protective factors of place and connection to the land for Indigenous persons in what became known as the United States of America.

Microaggressions Buffered by Land-Based Pedagogy and Family/Community Ties

Utilizing the same data in the American study, Drywater-Whitekiller (2017) discussed how American Indian students employed cultural resilience as associated with the interconnection of land and Indigenous identity to cope with microaggressions. Defined as elusive forms of racial bias and discrimination experienced by members of marginalized groups, microaggressions were reported by Sue et al. (2007) as being a part of everyday life for racial minority populations. The nuances associated with Indigenous students pursuing higher education and experiencing microaggressions are now making their appearance in the literature (e.g.,

American Psychological Association, 2014; O'Keefe & Greenfield, 2019; Shotton, 2017). However, less is found concerning how cultural resilience, particularly as related to the land, can help to steady and ground student learners, leading to their success. Based upon these painful experiences, healing was also found in the affirmations that were answered by the question: What does home mean to you? The rich, descriptive findings indicated the following thematic cultural resilience defense mechanisms employed by Indigenous students:

- The land as inter-connected to spirituality, identity formation, and indigenous pedagogy;
- Family and community kinship ties that strengthened identity and the sense of belonging; and
- Generational historical oral and written stories connecting the land to cultural memory (Drywater-Whitekiller, 2017, p. 160).

In sum, "home" took on the meaning of culture and identity; culture was connected directly or indirectly to the land, and the land was always in some way connected to the community. These types of resilient anchoring were available to those who had ready access to them; otherwise they were recalled in memory. However, this does not negate feelings of invisibility, loneliness, and isolation for students attending mainstream institutions. This was particularly profound for those who were geographically distanced from their communities, land, culture, and at times, away from their family connections. As described in the following section, this caused some to find creative substitutions in their temporary displacements to aid in the connectedness to the land; these creative substitutions also facilitated a sense of belonging, which is important to future Indigenous student success within university contexts.

Isolation Buffered by Land-Based Consciousness

The interviews reflected issues such as age, gender, learning disabilities, and lacking access to persons associated with their band/Tribal culture and homeland caused some to feel as if they were different and "othered." Isolation, especially as related to feelings of difference and invisibility, is an ongoing factor associated with low attrition rates of Indigenous college students (Amy et al., 2015; Hawk, 2020; Lopez, 2018). Belonging was situated within a sense of place, particularly in "foreign" environments found in many mainstream higher education institutions. Accordingly, for Indigenous peoples, land is not considered a commodity but consists of a relationship with place (Champagne, 2007) and for students to feel that they belong at university this relationship must be continuously fostered. This fits within a circular pattern of connection and inclusion of all, and this collectiveness is a common thread found throughout the study. Drawing on land-based pedagogies to challenge microaggressions as well as feelings of isolation lends support to both cultural resilience approaches and to resurgence theory with an emphasis on everyday forms of connection with land, culture, and community.

A threat to inclusiveness was posed by feelings of isolation, which were particularly pronounced as related to age, gender, displacement, and disability. For the informants, personal grounding and balance came from Indigenous ways of knowing through improvisation and spiritual direction to support others and self. To illustrate, one non-traditional student expounded upon how she felt invisible and alienated on the college campus. As with her mother, she was raised in various boarding schools, and concreteness in describing home was challenging as educational institutions primarily served as the place where she was housed growing up. The incentive to attend college was revealed to her in a vivid, spiritual account in a personal dream. She relayed that a man came and stood beside her, telling her he had two gifts for her—that is, if she wanted them. When she affirmed positively, he asked her to hold out her hand, and emphasized, "These are *yours*, now take a look at them." When she slowly opened her hand, she found a bachelor's and master's degree and knew that this was an omen that she should pursue higher education.

Raised on the prairies and missing his home, one informant stated he felt very lonely due to being older, male, and having no peers that he found as related to his age, experience, and band affiliation. For him, cultural resilience, based upon the teachings and examples personified by his grandmother, was to give back by serving as a peer mentor for those that he referred to as "the young ones coming up."

Finally, cultural resilience was a major factor in drawing strength from Ancestors for a non-traditional female student whose home connection was in the mainland. Finding herself residing in a coastal area for the purpose of attending university, she faced an ongoing struggle with isolation and difference. She shared how she found it puzzling that other students seemed to easily grasp the course content that took her much longer to understand. It was through the assessment center that she discovered an undiagnosed learning disorder and received guidance on how she learned best. This led to enforcing her purpose to receive a college education while realizing not only was the degree possible, it was also now, more than ever, within her reach.

In sum, the pursuit of higher education meant more to the informants than individual and personal goals. And it required more than individual and personal strengths to stay balanced to continue in their academic studies. Instead, the informants employed the interconnection of collectiveness, especially as pertaining to reaching back to culture, community, and land, while reaching forward to give hope to others who will inevitably follow. Just as they, too, were conscientious to follow in the footsteps of their Ancestors.

CONCLUSION

As we write this chapter, we are in the midst of a global COVID-19 pandemic which has been especially devastating to multiple Indigenous nations across Turtle Island. Despite the challenges of COVID-19, cultural resilience and resurgence approaches offer strengths-based insights regarding the ways that Indigenous students in both the United States and Canada confront adversity, such as microaggressions. Based on our findings, land-based learning often mitigated the harmful impacts of microaggressions experienced by Indigenous students. Additionally, even when connections to "home" are not direct, it is clear that the land, spirituality, identity, and Indigenous pedagogies are intertwined and help explain the depth of student resilience amidst hardship. In this light, oral and written stories connecting the land to cultural memory are extremely important for reaffirming family and community kinship ties and a sense of belonging. Overall, there is strong evidence that Indigenous student success within higher education is enhanced through land-based learning and Indigenous pedagogies, which lends further support for cultural resilience theory.

The TIPM yields additional insights regarding the effectiveness of land-based pedagogies. Dimension 3, which describes the utilization of land-based curricula, most closely mirrors our findings on cultural resilience. By raising consciousness in the classroom, instructors are directly challenging microaggressions and racism that often challenge Indigenous student success within university contexts. Dimension 4 of the TIPM, which focuses on cultural and social justice actions, most closely aligns with community resurgence theory, which emphasizes the move from transformation to direct action in order to make vital reconnections to land, culture, and community. Overall, the TIPM offers some linkages between our findings on cultural resilience and Dimension 3, which emphasizes transformative approaches, such as land-based learning. The actions detailed in Dimension 4 were not as evident in our findings but highlight the linkages between social justice action and everyday acts of resurgence.

As a barometer for Indigenous student success and to help locate where universities are situated on the four TIPM dimensions, we have developed several questions which will help Indigenous and non-Indigenous faculty to identify future indicators of the effectiveness of pedagogies and Indigenous student learning:

- What efforts are made by the institution to include Indigenous cultural activities that are relevant and meaningful to those students whose land bases may be outside of their band/nation territories?
- For universities that are located within and outside reservations, what efforts can be initiated to engage and re-engage students to the land?
- Does the university culture embrace co-existing cultures to promote the free exchange of ideas that lead to other ways of knowledge and learning?
- How can the past be respectfully addressed to include a focus on the resilience, resurgence, and strengths of Indigenous peoples?
- Are faculty trained in civil discourse simply defined as open-mindedness, compromise, and mutual respect (Leskes, 2013) and do class guidelines exist on how these methods can be respectfully employed?
- What avenues are available to assist the students in refocusing when confronted with more colonized approaches?

These sample questions can be used as a guide to assist in identifying areas that may not be consciously addressed in many institutions of higher education. In turn, a careful analysis of current organizational culture can be used to inform decisions that can help to minimize unintended consequences embedded in social and cultural injustices.

Overall, we find much potential in better understanding the overlap and explanatory power of the TIPM with cultural resilience, resurgence, and land-based learning. Understanding these dynamics is critical to the future success of Indigenous students so that future generations will thrive.

NOTES

1. When discussing land in this paper we also include water, and more-than-human relationships as part of the larger constellation of place-based relationships. We further draw on the description of land articulated by Styres et al. (2013, p. 37): "Land encompasses all water, earth, and air and is seen simultaneously to be an animate and spiritual being constantly in flux. It refers not only to geographic places and our relationships with urban Aboriginal landscapes but also gestures to the ways that discourses within places inform and are informed by our vision, pedagogies, and teaching practices."

REFERENCES

American Psychological Association (2014). *The road to resilience.*

Amy, K. V., Kennedy, D. M., Gladstone, J. S., & Birmingham, C. (2015). Native American cultural influences on career self-schemas and MBA fit. *Equality, Diversity and Inclusion: An International Journal, 34*(3), 201–213.

Bang, M., Curley, L., Kessel, A., Marin, A., Suzukovich, E. S., III, & Strack, G. (2014) Muskrat theories, tobacco in the streets, and living Chicago as Indigenous land. *Environmental Education Research, 20*(1), 37–55. doi:10.1080/13504622.2013.865113

Bartmes, N., & Shukla, S. (2020). Re-envisioning land-based pedagogies as a transformative third space: Perspectives from university academics, students, and Indigenous knowledge holders from Manitoba, Canada. *Diaspora, Indigenous, and Minority Education, 14*(3), 146–161. doi:10.1080/15595692.2020.1719062

Borrows, J. (2017). Outsider education: Indigenous law and land-based learning. *Yearbook of New Zealand Jurisprudence, 15*(45). doi:10.22329/wyaj.v33i1.4807

Bowra, A., Mashford-Pringle, A., & Poland, B. (2021). Indigenous learning on Turtle Island: A review of the literature on land-based learning. *The Canadian Geographer, 65,* 132–140. https://doi.org/10.1111/cag.12659

Burnette, C. E., Clark, C. B., and Rodning, C. B. (2018). "Living off the land": How subsistence promotes well-being and resilience among Indigenous peoples of the southeastern United States. *Social Service Review, 92*(3), 369–400.

Cajete, G. (2015). *Indigenous community: Rekindling the teachings of the seventh fire.* Living Justice Press.

Champagne, D. (2007). *Social change and cultural continuity among Native nations.* Altamira Press.

Corntassel, J. (2021) Life beyond the state: Regenerating Indigenous international relations and everyday challenges to settler colonialism. *Anarchist Developments in Cultural Studies, 2021*(1), 71–97. https://journals.uvic.ca/index.php/adcs/article/view/20172

Corntassel, J., & Hardbarger, T. (2019). Educate to perpetuate: Land-based pedagogies and community resurgence. *International Review of Education, 65*(1), 87–116. https://doi .org/10.1007/s11159-018-9759-1

Corntassel, J., Alfred, T., Goodyear–Kaʻōpua, N., Silva, N., Aikau, H., & Mucina, D. (Eds.). (2018). *Everyday acts of resurgence: People, places, practices.* Daykeeper Press.

Corntassel, J. (2012). "Re-envisioning resurgence: Indigenous pathways to decolonization and sustainable self-determination." *Decolonization: Indigeneity, Education and Society, 1*(1), 86–101.

Coulthard, G. (2014). *Red skin, white masks: Rejecting the colonial politics of recognition.* University of Minnesota Press.

Daigle, M. (2019). The spectacle of reconciliation: On (the) unsettling responsibilities to Indigenous peoples in the academy. *Environment and Planning D: Society and Space, 37*(4), 703–721. https://doi.org/10.1177/0263775818824342

Drywater-Whitekiller, V. (2010). Cultural resilience: Voices of Native American students in college retention. *The Canadian Journal of Native Studies, 30*(1), 1–19.

Drywater-Whitekiller, V. (2017). We belong to the land: Native Americans experiencing and coping with microaggressions. *The Canadian Journal of Native Studies, 37*(1).

Drywater-Whitekiller, V. (2019). *Indigenous cultural resilience supporting higher education pathways.* Submitted to Canada Fulbright Canadaas part of the fulfillment of 2018–2019 Fulbright Canada Research Chair in Aboriginal Studies.

Drywater-Whitekiller, V. (2020). First Nations, Metis, and Inuit university students share advice for college entry and retention. *Journal of Indigenous Research: Going Full Circle, 8*(2020), Article 6 . https://doi.org/10.26077/v9f8-cr37

Fellner, K. D. (2018). Embodying decoloniality: Indigenizing curriculum and pedagogy. *American Journal of Community Psychology, 62,* 283–293 doi:10.1002/ajcp.12286

Goodyear-Kaʻōpua, N. (2013). *The seeds we planted: Portraits of a Native Hawaiian charter school.* University of Minnesota Press.

Hawk, A. (2020). Understanding risk and protective factors influencing urban American Indian/Alaska Native youth graduation expectations. *American Indian and Alaska Native Mental Health Research (Online), 27*(1), 42–63. https://doi.org/10.5820/aian.2701.2020.42

Johnston-Goodstar, K., & Roholt, R. V. (2017). "Our kids aren't dropping out; They're being pushed out": Native American students and racial microaggressions in schools. *Journal of Ethnic & Cultural Diversity in Social Work, 26*(1-2), 30–47, doi:10.1080/15313204.2016.1263818

Kauanui, J. K. (2016). "A structure, not an event": Settler colonialism and enduring Indigeneity. *Lateral, 5*(1). https://csalateral.org/issue/5-1/forum-alt-humanities-settler-colonialism-enduring-indigeneity-kauanui/

Leskes, A. (2013). A plea for civil discourse: Needed, the academy's leadership. *Liberal Education, 99*(4).

Locklear, S., Harris, C., Yang, A., Liu, K., Ramsey, E., Adamson, T., Dominguez, A. & Echo-Lopez, J. D. (2018). Factors influencing American Indian and Alaska Native postsecondary persistence: A millennium falcon persistence model. *Research in Higher Education: Journal of the Association for Institutional Research, 59*(6), 792–811. https://doi.org/10.1007/s11162-017-9487-6

Lopez, J. D. (2018). Factors influencing American Indian and Alaska Native postsecondary persistence: AI/AN millennium falcon persistence model. *Research in Higher Education, 59*(6), 792–811.

Mark, E. (2016). International Indigenous youth cooperative (IIYC): Youth, cultural sustainability, resilience, and survivance. *Journal of American Indian Education, 55*(3), 111–133.

Mowatt, M., Finney, S. de, Cardinal, S. W., Mowatt, G., Tenning, J., Haiyupis, P., Gilpin, E., Harris, D., MacLeod, A., & XEMŦOLTW̱_Claxton, N. (2020). ȻENTOL TȽE TEṈEW̱_(Together with the land): Part 1: Indigenous land and water-based pedagogies. *International Journal of Child, Youth and Family Studies, 11*(3): 12–33, doi:10.18357/ijcyfs113202019696

O'Keefe, V., & Greenfield, B. (2019). Experiences of microaggressions among American Indian and Alaska Native students in two post-secondary contexts. *American Indian and Alaska Native Mental Health Research (Online), 26*(3), 58–78. https://doi.org/10.5820/aian.2603.2019.58

Pewewardy, C. D., Lees, A., & Clark-Shim, H. (2018). The Transformational Indigenous Praxis Model: Stages for developing critical consciousness in Indigenous education. *Wičazo Ša Review, 33*(1), 38–69. https://doi.org/10.5749/wicazosareview.33.1.0038

Rogin, M. P. (2017). *Fathers and children: Andrew Jackson and the subjugation of the American Indian in manifest destiny.* Routledge. https://doi.org/10.4324/9780203792056

Sakakibara, C. (2017). People of the whales: climate change and cultural resilience among Iñupiat of arctic Alaska. *Geographical Review, 107*(1), 159–184. https://doi.org/10.1111/j.1931-0846.2016.12219.x

Shotton, H. J. (2017). "I thought you'd call her white feather": Native women and racial microaggressions in doctoral education. *Journal of American Indian Education, 56*(1), 32–54.

Simpson, L. B. (2017). *As we have always done: Indigenous freedom through radical resistance.* University of Minnesota Press.

Smith, L. T. (2012). *Decolonizing methodologies: Research and Indigenous people.* Zed Book Ltd.

Styres, S., Haig-Brown, C., & Blimkie, M. (2013). Towards a pedagogy of land: The urban context. *Canadian Journal of Education, 36*(2), 34–67.

Sue, D. W., Capodilupo, C. M., Torino, G. C., Bucceri, J. M., Holder, A. M. B., Nadal, K. L., & Esquilin, M. (2007). Racial microaggressons in everyday life: Implications for clinical practice. *American Psychologist, 62*, 271–286. doi:10.1037/0003-066x.62.4.271

Thambinathan, V., & Kinsella, E. A. (2021). Decolonizing methodologies in qualitative research: Creating spaces for transformative praxis. *International Journal of Qualitative Methods.* https://doi.org/10.1177/16094069211014766

Truth and Reconciliation Commission of Canada. (2015). *Calls to action.* https://www2.gov .bc.ca/assets/gov/british-columbians-our-governments/indigenous-people/aboriginal -peoples-documents/calls_to_action_english2.pdf

Tuck, E., McKenzie, M., & McCoy, K. (2014). Land education: Indigenous, post-colonial, and decolonizing perspectives on place and environmental education research. *Environmental Education Research, 20*(1), 1–23. https://doi.org/10.1080/13504622.2013.877708

Walters, K. L., & Simoni, J. M. (2002). Reconceptualizing native women's health: an "indigenist" stress-coping model. *American Journal of Public Health, 92*(4), 520–524.

Wildcat, M., McDonald, M., Irlbacher-Fox, S., & Coulthard, G. (2014). Learning from the land: Indigenous land-based pedagogy and decolonization. *Decolonization: Indigeneity, Education & Society. 3*(3), I–XV.

Yerxa, J. R. (2014). Gii-kaapizigemin manoomin Neyaashing: A resurgence of Anishinaabeg nationhood. *Decolonization: Indigeneity, Education & Society, 3*(3), 159–166.

CHAPTER 10

Facilitating Wayfinding in Social Work Education

A Pinay Scholar Warrior of Kapu Aloha and
Mahalaya's Roles and Responsibilities

*Alma M. Ouanesisouk Trinidad (Pinay/Paoay, Ilocos Norte, Philippines;
Molokai, Kingdom of Hawai'i), Brenda Cruz Jaimes (Latina/Mexican),
Brandon Join Alik (Marshallese/Rilujennamu clan), Ann Jeline Manabat
(Asian with Filipino roots; Pacific Islander/Commonwealth of the Northern
Mariana Islands), Austin Delos Santos (Chamorro; Pacific Islander/
Commonwealth of the Northern Mariana Islands), Sherry Gobaleza
(Pinay/Buhay clan in the Philippines)*

I, Alma, began my professorship position at Portland State University (PSU) in 2009 and earned my tenure and my promotion to associate professor in 2016. Born and raised on the island of Molokai, Hawai'i and with roots from Ilocos Norte, Philippines, I never dreamt of such a career in higher education and the professoriate. Arriving at that point came with ongoing challenges, incidents of trauma, deep scars, and joys and passions, simultaneously.

My post-tenure review[1] was conducted recently, and I'm preparing to go up for full professorship soon. I am once again at a juncture of questioning the academy and the purpose and role of higher education, specifically social work education and its training of allied helping professions at a predominantly white institution in the Pacific Northwest. With threats of defunding integrated community-based partnership and collaboration in the academy and contradictory messages of racial justice, I am situated in a faculty position that unsettles me. The multiple pandemics in our communities—COVID-19; racial inequities and police brutalities among our BIPOCs (Black, Indigenous, People of Color); climate change; hate crimes— explicitly reveals disparities and gaps, and encourages us to facilitate change. With that, I am amazed by the strengths and survivance of the BIPOC communities I serve, come from, and stand in solidarity with. We are communities who historically have been minoritized, and currently face deep ongoing threats to our well-being and livelihoods. During these unprecedented times, I am once again re-examining my roles and responsibilities as a scholar activist.

I remember the contentious history of displacement, forced migration, and contemporary enslavement of my peoples. Being a descendant of the *Sakadas* (Filipinos imported for skilled labor by the sugar and pineapple industries to Hawaiʻi), having affiliation with the Laos refugee experience (through witnessing my life partner's families and communities), and having settled in Hawaiʻi and now in Oregon, as a social worker and social welfare scholar activist, I bear witness to the historical and contemporary trauma that permeates our communities. We are not meant to live well, and yet, we rise. It is in this role of a scholar, a *Pinay* (Filipina American) Scholar of *Kapu Aloha* (radical and sacred love, in Hawaiian) and *Mahalaya* (freedom and love, in Tagalog) that I serve the people, and elevate their/our voices (Trinidad, 2014; 2021). To integrate the needs of the people, their multiple ways of knowing, addressing the power struggles and disparities faced across systems, and facilitating change, equity, and healing are at the heart of my responsibilities and sense of accountability as a scholar. I strive to bring humility, deep care, a sense of high moral ground, and excellence into my work, individually and collectively. I cannot do this alone. It is the togetherness and collectivity that I seek to ground in our shared spaces.

Academia implicitly pushes us toward tendencies of individualistic, colonial, capitalistic ways of knowing and being. The processes of decolonizing, reclaiming our genealogies, and upholding cultural values and ways of knowing are ongoing. Since entering academia as a doctoral student in the early 2000s, it has been my ultimate goal and focus to do such for myself and with the people I engage with across the academic spheres—students, fellow colleagues, and community members.

The academy is a space of gatekeeping of careers and professions, and ultimately the workforce across sectors. It was not originally built for our communities to thrive. Being the first of a cohort of faculty in shared lines with a school of social work and general education program, I take this role seriously, and strive to break the cycle of trauma and abuse. I am at a unique position to bridge and link. In light of my upbringing, past community work, and ongoing community partnerships, I must reassess my roles and responsibilities in academia, especially at a predominantly white institution that may implicitly lack or face ongoing challenges of creating opportunities for authentic transformation. Is it *still* the place to practice and forge the work?

With such pondering questions, this chapter is a venue for me to pause and honor our overlapping, parallel, and sometimes converging voyages of wayfinding among former students. I suggest conceptualizing in this article that wayfinding is a process of navigating through systems of oppression and knowledge production with an ultimate aim of healing and transformation. With deep respect and care, we share these experiences to demonstrate ways we decolonize and challenge the status quo by resisting erasure of our histories, genealogies, ways of knowing, and being. We share how we, through wayfinding, find our paths in healing, not just ourselves, but our communities. Our paths and voyages interweave, arriving, meeting at a juncture, and then departing again but keeping parallel collectivity at the core. We demonstrate the complexities and points of critical awareness, in hopes to highlight knowledge and sources of wisdom bestowed in our work together.

CONCEPTUALIZING WAYFINDING THROUGH CRITICAL INDIGENOUS PEDAGOGY OF PLACE

Building upon the literature on Critical Indigenous Pedagogy of Place (CIPP), wayfinding can be a process to build the growing critique and resistance of settler-colonizer-capitalist mentality. CIPP builds upon the concept of place, and Indigenous and cultural studies (Trinidad, 2009; 2012). In CIPP, three processes exist in centering knowledge in place (Trinidad, 2018): analysis of power and privilege, and oppressive forces (decolonization); Indigenization and reinhabitation; and sociopolitical development through community (see Table 1, p. 108 in Trinidad, 2018).

A process missing in CIPP is the trans- and/or comparative analyses of movement and critically reclaiming of "home" in the context of ongoing U.S. imperialism, colonization, and global capitalism. Home is place, with and by carrying the values and ways of being and living with us through family ties. Family-like relationships are part of this process. Utilizing the metaphor of "wayfinding" (Thompson, n.d.) and integrating it in my teachings and facilitating of collective learning, I strive to ground collective, cooperative (done together as a community) processes in embarking and navigating through the "land" (place in which one settles for a time) and "ocean" (to and for movement) of deep knowledge and intense observation of ourselves and the sociopolitical economic context of the healing work we do (Trinidad, 2020). It is the processes of navigation that connect us from multiple backgrounds and lived experiences. It is also the critical awareness of oppressive forces that colonize, divide, and conquer our BIPOC, and impose barriers of healing across and within our communities. Most importantly, these processes aim toward solidarity work in realizing it is the same structural regime, white supremacy, that limits our collective transformation. In each milestone or "destination" within the academy, the coauthors share their deep reflections on the following prompts that link to wayfinding: critical self-reflexivity, analysis of the sociopolitical economic climate, and understanding of their roles and responsibilities.

THE PROCESSES OF WAYFINDING

By integrating wayfinding with CIPP, together, it can facilitate an explicit critique and resistance of settler-colonizer-capitalist mentality, and harness change on multiple pathways in higher education, specifically in social work. The processes embedded in the forthcoming case examples facilitate wayfinding in social work education, decolonize and challenge the status quo, reclaim and indigenize the helping professions, and instill responsibility and accountability for the people and places.

To this end, I reached out to a handful of former students I've had since achieving tenure. I invited them to reflect upon our relationship and time together in learning communities. I provide the following prompts to share their experiences we've had learning together about the field (e.g., social work, health, community psychology):

- *critical self-reflexivity:* What did you learn about yourself throughout our engagement (e.g., mentorship with research; facilitating one's learning in a course)? What did you learn about your strengths and values of being a [name the indigenous identities or any intersectional identities that matter to you]?
- *sociopolitical economic context:* What did you learn about your communities and/or the communities you serve throughout our engagement? Specifically, what are the sources of resistance and cultural strengths as the communities face oppressive factors? You may provide concrete examples.
- *your roles and responsibilities of healing work:* How has your understanding of your roles and responsibilities, individually and collectively, impacted the healing work of our/your communities throughout our engagement?

Each co-author responded to each prompt or free-wrote. In some instances, creative work done during the courses they took from me were used to enhance their reflections.

CASE EXAMPLES OF WAYFINDING IN SOCIAL WORK EDUCATION AND ALLIED PROFESSIONALIZATION

I provide four voyages of wayfinding through higher education. Each voyage de-scribes a specific pathway in higher education. I parcel these voyages in the fol-lowing way:

- Brenda: from undergraduate, general education program (freshman) to master's in social work
- Brandon: master's level, graduate of social work
- Ann Jeline and Austin: undergraduate research in the health sciences
- Sherry: PhD program in liberatory psychology

In each voyage, as an educator, I facilitated processes that encouraged students to bring their authentic selves, their cultural identities, and their strengths in finding their purpose, roles, and responsibilities in the field of healing.

From Freshman to Master's Level: Worthy of Knowledge

I begin with Brenda's voyage as an undergraduate in my general education course on race and social justice. She then completed the bachelor's and master's social work degrees. Her voyage sheds light to gaining insight of one's worthiness of knowledge and excellence. Brenda, who presently works as the associate director of diversity, equity, and inclusion initiatives at a local, private Catholic high school, has found voice in her way as a Latina social work scholar and practitioner. She began with a *Where I'm From* poem written in 2012:

> I am from a family who values hard work.
> I am from long nights of homework and early school days.
> I am from many hours spent on community service,
> from helping kids learn and taking care of those in need.
> I am from an ethnic group who is constantly discriminated against.
> I am from a community of students who have goals.
> I am from a group of dreamers who fight to overcome obstacles day by day.
> I am from a growing and thriving community, and I am proud to be from a Hispanic heritage.

Let's compare this poem to the poem she wrote in 2018 in the MSW graduate program (https://media.pdx.edu/media/Screen+Capture+-I+am+from+poem-+2018 +Jul+10+01A26A14/0_rlchjdsp). She notes her capability, intelligence, community who empowers each other with strong traditions and values rooted in family, and honoring of the la tierra de mis padres (the land of my parents).

Brenda's values, beliefs, cultural norms, and biases were made clear during her voyage. Her understanding of systemic oppression, privilege, intergenerational trauma, and the importance of representation and voice within academia were fostered. Brenda was able to engage with BIPOC-led work, and observed the investing in collective strength and action. This led to learning more about advocacy for diverse representation and voice in the educational system.

Brenda was able to learn how to find healing within and break the generational cycles that are not serving the community. She learned that individual and collective healing is possible by channeling contemporary and ancestral wisdom, meaning that relying on one's community and support systems is just as important in being able to engage in individual and collective healing.

A Descendent of Marshall Island

Brandon's voyage took place in my master's-level, graduate course on Societal, Community, and Organizational Structures and Processes, in the winter of 2020. Brandon was the *first* self-identified Pacific Islander enrolled in my graduate course. This engagement mutually challenged ways to integrate Pacific Island cultures and values in social work. Brandon shared his *Where I'm From* poem in inter 2020:

> I am from a small chain of atolls concealed from the naked eye, hidden from common knowledge deep in mid-pacific ocean. I am also from heavy traffic, heavy rain, heavy income taxes, and heavy forms of subtle racism.

I am from salty air and salty fries. I am from mangoes and juicy pandanus, but also from late night 7-11 snack runs and broken ice cream machines.
I am from family gatherings and a community, but I am also from cold harsh winds and ambiguous faces asking me where I am from.
I am from loud laughing and quiet classrooms, from legends about sharks and other ocean creatures, but also from police brutality and subtle forms of classism.
I am from coconut leaves and plates of seafood from the Marshall Islands, and policies of bans of plastic bags in Portland, Oregon. I am from sailors navigating through the dark skies and glimmering stars whose descendants survived World War 2. I am from a proud brown skin passed from my parents to me.

Brandon learned during his voyage that his ideas are true equality in health care and education with an emphasis towards human rights. He also examined how colonialism has had him and the Marshallese community internalize racism, ableism, and sexism, and how these forces pin Marshallese people against each other.

Brandon embraces his pride from remembering how his community is strong, especially when they are collectively fighting climate change. The resilience comes from the love and pride of the islands. Brandon has also found inspiration to be strong when he thinks about his parents who immigrated to the United States and worked really hard, even if the system was against them.

The Interwoven Voyage of a Canoe From the Commonwealth of Northern Mariana Islands

Ann Jeline and Austin's voyage involves my myntorship[2] with them as a group of undergraduate students. They are part of the university's health sciences' under-graduate research program. Although not all were interested in social work, they all identified as being interested in addressing health. They were the *first* of a crit-ical mass of students who transferred from the Commonwealth of the Northern Mariana Islands to PSU. These relationships encouraged us, together, to critically examine and reflect in our effort to make sense of our experiences on the U.S. mainland.

Ann Jeline: Redefine success, intergenerational voices. Ann Jeline found that having a Filipinx professor as a myntor allowed her to gain appreciation of our shared cultural experiences and how success may look like for our Indigenous peoples. Ann Jeline also was exposed to a cultural network and the experiences of intergenerational intersectionalities that occur among the Asian Pacific Islander (API) communities, specifically from the U.S. territories. By sharing each other's experiences of oppression and struggles of sense of belonging in higher educa-tion, Ann Jeline was able to work on a research project that captured the diverse experiences of moving to the U.S. mainland. She realized that her community was "marginalized within the margins," because the voices were often masked within the greater API groupings. She also found community strength through the values of *kapwa* (strong sense of unity), or *O le ala i le pule, o le tautua* (a pathway to leadership is through service). This brought an understanding that people carry their communities on their shoulders as they face adversity, while all the more reclaiming their API identity. Ann Jeline also realized that these stories also brought ways to heal from the turmoil of adjusting to a new environment, and staying true to the identities of one's own culture.

Austin: A Chamorro's way toward community-based work. Austin transferred to PSU from Saipan. As a first-generation college student, Austin was already a proud Pacific Islander-Chamorro from the Commonwealth of the Northern Mariana Islands (CMNI). He grew up in Section 8 Housing and was afraid of the things that limited his potential. The minimum wage in CMNI was $7.25/hour, while gas was $7.95/gallon. It taught him how to survive. He remembers living without electricity and water. He and his brothers would wake up at dawn to go fishing, hunting, and setting traps for whatever they could find in the jungles. This would be their food for the week. This cycle of struggle and depression among the many community members built resilience as we, as Chamorros, fought to live and survive. As I partnered with organizations and started working for a nonprofit agency that Dr. Alma linked me to, I realized that life provides opportunities for one to reach goals in life. Everything in life seems to be put in place, but it is up to us to open the doors, which reminded me of the Chamorro term, "Ina'fa Maolek," which means to live in harmony with the community. When one understands the social, political, and economic systems of a community, that knowledge can be used for positive growth.

As a scholar and an alum of PSU, Austin's goal is to apply the knowledge to assist his hometown. He seeks to work with organizations, public officials, and myntors to create better and sustainable food systems, land use, and transportation systems. He hopes to build a better place for the future generations. He plans to utilize his skills to advocate and develop initiatives that will change the systems to become a place of hope. He stands before my community as a beacon of resilience.

Sherry's Voyage of Kapwa and Decolonial Love in Research

Sherry, a self-identified Pinay PhD student, was enrolled in the inaugural course I taught on Indigenous Methodologies at Pacifica Graduate Institute. This engagement mutually elevated our interwoven concerns within our Filipino community and forced us to be in solidarity with other BIPOCs. Sherry wrote this poem:

> I come from an island once known as the pearl of Asia
> Where guava, tamarind, coconut and
> Pandan leaves lovingly woven into a mat laid on the floor, hands to hold me
> Who I am is 500 years of resistance

of blood, sweat, and tears of those who fought Magellan into pieces
Florez, Gobaleza, Buhay clan
lost, orphaned in the city of Manila
Lost in the storms like an avatar on the wind
Welcoming in the space of trouble and love
Born of the blood, sweat, and tears of my ancestors who fought
We are the Buhay clan
Grounded in love and memory
In the flowers I eat and the flowers I sow
Dominador Geli Florez Gobaleza
oldest of two boys and one girl
orphaned at 9 he raised our family
through orchids
and teachings
he lives in me and will never be forgotten

I was Sherry's first doctoral professor of Filipino background. It showed her that it is possible to not only survive academia day-to-day, but to significantly alter the learning space, which translates into a form of epistemic justice for Indigenous scholars. Sherry acknowledged that our warriorship has seen us through terrible violence of oppression against our people and land. We both were aware that our motherland of the Philippines is occupied by capitalist interests that silence and dominate Indigenous peoples. We were already aware of the forms of resistance that possess deep wisdom, warriorship, creativity, love, and the core value of *kapwa*. For Sherry, *kapwa* is the active embrace of our responsibility as living breathing beings to the world in which we live.

Sherry learned, as a crisis counselor, the importance of being rooted in the Ancestors, land, and *kapwa*. This offers a meaningful path for youth to resist the sociopolitical system. Our engagement together solidified Sherry's strength and inspiration, as a Pinay, to continue resisting the hegemony, and to center love in research, specifically, *decolonial love*—the love not just for one's own people, but for the humanity of all people (Maldonado-Torres, 2012; Sandoval, 2000). This helps in realizing our interdependency and Indigenous wisdom, and the voices of our Ancestors.

Discussion: Lessons Learned in Facilitating Wayfinding

The voyages shared are examples of how white supremacy in social work (and allied) education is interrupted, and center the student's Indigenous voices and lived experiences in their learning. They provide hope and invite us to forge a return to upholding Indigenous ways of knowing. Internalizing the critical reflections of former students, I am mindful of the impact I have on them and the decisions they made along the way. As a navigator, the power and privilege to be in a position to influence their thinking is immense. One must be able to foster authentic relationships by sharing both vulnerabilities and strengths in the experiences. Additionally, one must pull in communities and break through the walls of elitism that the academy imposes. When we come from minoritized communities, the internalized oppression and colonized mindset must be broken free to invite values like love and humility in, as demonstrated by the narratives above.

Wayfinding involves knowing the conditions of the land in which one settles and the water (migration movements), and being open to learning from and by your students and the community. These diverse perspectives can sharpen the analyses of sociopolitical economic climate. It also helps advance the critical mass of people to occupy positions of influence and change. This also may help in promoting and advancing collective leadership, and may alleviate compassion fatigue that comes in facilitating wayfinding in higher education.

Implications to Transformational Indigenous Praxis Model (TIPM)

The process of wayfinding can complement or overlap in the dimensions of TIPM. In multiple spaces in social work education and the training of allied professionals in the health sciences, students may arrive in higher education as recipients of the contributions and additive approaches of critical thinking. When they begin to engage with me, we explicitly share where we're from and our genealogies. We share our stories of how we have arrived to this place, including the academic major one has chosen. The process of gathering and deeply analyzing the sociopolitical economic context with a lens of seeing their communities being impacted helps facilitate transformative conscientization, the third dimension of TIPM, among everyone involved. Most importantly, the deep understanding of one's roles and responsibilities in wayfinding can promote movement in the final stage of the cultural and social justice action approach/transformational praxis of TIPM. It is at this juncture that one can reassess time and time again and recommit to values and action. As the narratives demonstrated prior, wayfinding can potentially promote healing at different developmental points and across multiple disciplines. As co-authors, we hope that our voyages collectively and individually can dialectically change academia and beyond. We are part of creating solutions together, and desire to facilitate empowerment, transformation, and healing for our peoples. It is our duty, as scholars and practitioners, to use our *mana* (power) to make things *pono* (righteous).

CONCLUSION

This chapter offers an example of pathway-making in higher education through the stance of a Pinay Scholar Warrior of *kapu aloha* (sacred radical love in Hawaiian) and *mahalaya* (freedom love in Tagalog). It provides case examples of the process of critical thinking and reflexivity in my roles and responsibilities of a social work/welfare scholar in teaching, myntoring (community-based practitioners and scholars), researching, and serving the community. Our effort was to demonstrate how the processes embedded in the case examples facilitate wayfinding in higher education through social work education, decolonize and challenge the status quo, reclaim and indigenize the helping professions, and instill responsibility and accountability for the people and places.

NOTES

1. This is a process in which a tenured faculty is reviewed by their peers for ongoing growth and professional development in the academy.

2. I use "myntorship" instead of "mentorship" as a way to decolonize and reclaim a criticalfeminist perspective on relationship building among those I engage with in a learning environment.

REFERENCES

Maldonado-Torres, N. (2012). Decoloniality at large: Towards a trans-Americas and global transmodern paradigm. *Transmodernity, 1*(3), 1–10. https://escholarship.org/content/qt58c 9c4wh/qt58c9c4wh_noSplash_dc443a300a46414dcf3a864de988aada.pdf?t=m6aapu

Sandoval, C. (2000). *Methodology of the oppressed.* University of Minnesota Press.

Thompson, N. (n.d.). *On wayfinding.* Hawaiian Voyaging Traditions. http://archive.hokulea.com /ike/hookele/on_wayfinding.html

Trinidad, A. (2009). Toward kuleana (responsibility): A case study of a contextually grounded intervention for Native Hawaiian youth and young adults. *Aggression and Violent Behavior, 14*(6), 488–498.

Trinidad, A. M. O. (2012). Critical Indigenous pedagogy of place: A framework to Indigenize a youth food justice movement. *Journal of Indigenous Social Development, 1*(1), 1–17.

Trinidad, A.M.O. (2014). The becoming of a Pinay scholar warrior of Aloha: A critical autoethnography of teaching, mentoring, and researching for social change. *Polymath: An Interdisciplinary Arts and Sciences Journal, 14*(2), 16–38. https://ojcs.siue.edu/ojs/index.php/ polymath/article/view/2935/994

Trinidad, A. M. O. (2018). Critical Indigenous pedagogy of place: Claiming place at multiple levels in sustainability and social work practice. In M. C. F. Powers & M. Rinkel (Eds.), *Social work promoting community and environmental sustainability: A workbook for global social workers and educators* (Volume 2, pp. 105–117). International Federation of Social Workers. https://www.ifsw.org/product/books/social-work-promoting-community-and -environmental-sustainability-volume-2/

Trinidad, A. M. O. (2020). Notes of a M.A./Ph.D. seminar on decolonizing and Indigenizing research and practice: We are ocean. In S. James & Creative Curator (Eds.), *Hearing voices* (pp. 39–40). Community, Liberation, Indigenous, & Eco-Psychologies, Pacifica Graduate Institute.

Trinidad, A. M. O. (2021). Navigating fierce love during the pandemic: Reflections of a Pinay scholar warrior. *Qualitative Social Work: Research and Practice, 20*(1-2), 256–263. https:// doi.org/10.1177/1473325020984151

CHAPTER 11

Transformational Praxis in Higher Education

Hyuny Clark-Shim (Korean Citizen)

INTRODUCTION

안녕하십니까? 심현정입니다. Hello, my name is Hyuny Clark-Shim. I am a Korean citizen who was born and raised in Paju-Si, Korea, a city whose footprint overlaps with a portion of the demilitarized zone (DMZ). Since my arrival in the United States in 2007, I have lived in the traditional homelands of Indigenous Peoples of the Columbia River.

This chapter travels through different dimensions of the Transformational Indigenous Praxis Model (TIPM) by sharing examples that draw upon scholarship in higher education within the United States and internationally. The journey begins by critically examining scholarly examples of historical denialism—rooted in the contributions approach—to push forward a colonialist agenda. The next example shows the additive approach, and comes from the Latin American Subaltern Studies Group; their scholarship reflects critical awareness, yet suffers limitations owing to a Eurocentric orientation. Reflecting paradigm shifts via the transformation approach, we then look at an example of scholarship that critically deconstructs Eurocentric epistemological hegemony and subjugation of Indigenous epistemologies, followed by scholarship examples that embrace Indigenous epistemological orientations. Reflecting the TIPM's cultural and social justice action approach, the last example is a dialogue about salmon and sea lions, and highlights Indigenous ways of being. The journey will conclude with the recognition of the need to embrace contextualized epistemologies in higher education to honor the sovereignty of Indigenous education.

CONTRIBUTIONS APPROACH IN ACADEMIA: HISTORICAL DENIALISM

This section introduces three academic journal articles that were written by university professors as examples of historical denialism pushing forward a colonialist, racist agenda while using the name of a university. These articles are about Japanese military "comfort women" during WWII, western colonialism, and the

Indigenous Peoples' movement. This section also discusses scholarship in resistance to this historical denialism.

HISTORICAL DENIALISM REGARDING
JAPANESE MILITARY "COMFORT WOMEN" DURING WWII

Mark Ramseyer, Mitsubishi Professor of Japanese Legal Studies at Harvard University, published "Contracting for Sex in the Pacific War" in 2021. In his article, using game theory as rationalization, Ramseyer claims that Korean women who were Japanese military "comfort women" (sexual slaves) were certified prostitutes who willingly worked based on "credible contracts" with recruiters. Yuji Hosaka (2021) points out the distortion of facts in Ramseyer's article by noting that a contract used to recruit women suggested their work was to serve drinks; however, the Japanese brothels where women were sent to work prohibited soldiers from drinking. According to Hosaka (2021), this deception was made by the Japanese government to avoid violation of the International Convention for the Suppression of the Traffic in Women and Children in 1925. Hosaka (2021) also rebuts Ramseyer's claim of recruiters having "no connection to the Japanese military" by pointing out that the "Japanese government selected the recruiters under strict confidentiality. . . . The licensed recruiters under the supervision of the Japanese government and military handled all related matters ranging from recruiting women to managing comfort stations" (p. 163). Based on the testimonies of surviving Japanese military's surgeons and soldiers, Hosaka (2021) signifies that Korean "comfort women," including both underage and adult women, were sex slaves who were deceived and kidnapped to Japanese military brothels. Ramseyer's article along with the next two articles illustrate historical denialists' attempts to negate and whitewash colonial crimes against humanity through academic publication.

Historical Denialism Regarding Western Colonialism

> Do you know why people like me are shy about being capitalists? Well, it's because we, for as long as we have known you, were capital.
>
> Jamaica Kincaid (1989), p. 37 cited in Gopal (2006)

Bruce Gilley, Professor of Political Science at Portland State University, published "The Case for Colonialism" in 2017. Using cost-benefit analysis as purported justification, Gilley argues for the benefits of western colonialism on "*subject peoples.*" Ndlovu-Gatsheni (2021) poignantly points out that Gilley was "whitewashing the sins of colonialism," including the enslavement of peoples under an argument of "moral evil, economic good." Klein (2018) also notes that Gilley's argument is not factual and "the notion that colonial rule was based on *universal values* is contradicted by the harshness of the conquest and its treatment of dissent" (p. 39).

For example, the Algerian population was estimated to have lost nearly half of its precolonial population of 4 million people in 1830 to the roughly 2 million in 1872 during French colonization (Brower, 2009). Around 825,000 Algerian lives were lost due to the violence of the first 45 years of French colonization; an equal number of Algerian lives were lost due to "famines and epidemics triggered . . . by the colonial-induced economic mutations"; and a further 350,000 Algerians fled colonial rule (Brower, 2009, p. 4). More loss of lives and casualties were suffered during the Algerian War of Independence, from 1954 to 1962.

Historical Denialism Regarding the Indigenous Peoples' Movement

In 2003, Adam Kuper, former professor in the Department of Human Sciences in Brunel University in the United Kingdom, published "The Return of the Native." In this article, Kuper (2003) vehemently attacked the Indigenous Peoples' movement by fictitiously arguing the proclamation of the United Nations (UN) on Indigenous Peoples is a restoration of "the ghostly category of 'primitive peoples' . . . seemed doomed to extinction," and equating the Indigenous Peoples' rights movement with European fascism, such as Nazis and apartheid (p. 389). Academic imperialism based on Eurocentrism and colonial racist paradigms "glorif(ies) western superiority" (Killsback, 2013, p. 86), implies Indigenous inferiority by dividing human societies into European and Other and juxtaposing "civilized" versus "primitive/savage," while it also distorts Indigenous peoples' histories and identities to bolster colonialist agendas and justify genocides and epistemicides of Indigenous peoples around the world (Grosfoguel, 2013). More importantly, Kuper's argument that Indigenous Peoples' rights movement and land claims are racial or ethnic problems does not reflect Indigenous Nations' sovereignty and self-determination. These articles based on historical denialism reflect the contributions approach in academic scholarship, reflecting colonized minds that are *dysconscious*[1] of colonialism and its crimes against humanity.

Resistance

The authors of the three articles discussed above distort colonial history and unethically defend "crimes against humanity," and were met with international criticism. For example, Ramseyer's article led to international criticism for lacking evidence and distorting facts (e.g., Gordon & Eckert, 2021; Hosaka, 2021; Korean Association of Harvard Law School Statement, 2021). It also ignited protests against historical denialism that unethically defends "crimes against humanity" since Japanese military "comfort women" were "a form of 'wartime sexual slavery,' constituting a war crime" (Cho, 2016, pp. 79–80 cited in Kim, 2017; Hosaka, 2021). Similarly, Gilley's notion of colonial rule based on "*universal values*" and his defense of crimes against humanity met with international outcries and criticism, such that Gilley's article was republished in 2018 with an editor's note reading: "[his article] provoked enormous controversy and generated two separate petitions signed by thousands of academics demanding that it be retracted" (p. 167).

On March 11, 2021, the Portland State University-AAUP (American Association of University Professors) released a statement condemning the "procolonialism" of Bruce Gilley.

Furthermore, Kuper's attack on the Indigenous Peoples' movement was faced with international criticism, including Kenrick and Lewis (2004) noting that Kuper's argument is based on "inaccurate analysis of the history of the indigenous peoples' rights movement" (p. 4) and calls for the need to understand Indigenous Peoples' struggles based on historical context. For example, it is impossible to understand Indigenous Peoples' struggles and movement in the United States without recognizing the impact of European colonization and consequential epistemic genocides that attempted to eradicate Indigenous cultures, illustrated for example by American Indian boarding schools and residential schools in Canada (Piccard, 2014). The Christian roots of colonization (e.g., the doctrine of discovery) posits Europeans as "mere products of circumstances, especially when suppressing Indigenous peoples" to "excuse" genocides and epistemicides caused by European colonization (Killsback, 2013; Kivel, 2013).

Colonialism "worked to steal the colonised people's history and to epistemically intervene in their psyche" (Ndlovu-Gatsheni, 2021). "Global coloniality," a term coined by Anibal Quijano, reflects "racial social stratification of the world population under Eurocentred world power" (Quijano, 2007, p. 171 cited in Ndlovu-Gatsheni, 2014). Even after the end of colonial administration, global coloniality continues to perpetuate Eurocentric racist, hierarchical power based on "theft of history" that imposes Eurocentric history, Eurocentrism, and colonization of space (conquest and settlement), time, being (racial social stratification), and nature (capitalistic approach to exploit "natural resources") (Ndlovu-Gatsheni, 2014). Moreover, the authors of these articles co-opt the names of their universities to disseminate historical denialist and negationist ideas beyond academic circles to push forward a colonialist, racist agenda (Rousso, 2006).

ADDITIVE APPROACH IN ACADEMIC SCHOLARSHIP

In such a hostile environment of higher education, a critical consciousness study group (CCSG) can be formed as a strategy to resist racist agendas. One such example involves collaborative efforts between the South Asian Subaltern Studies Group and the Latin American Subaltern Studies Group. This collaboration occurred in 1998 and was followed by publication of several issues of a dedicated journal (NEPANTLA) reflecting a burst of critical awareness; however, the collaboration dissolved recognizing the limitations of their scholarship under a generally Eurocentric epistemological orientation (Grosfoguel, 2007). The group recognized that their scholarship and "theory was still located in the North (USA) while the subjects to be studied are located in the South" such that the group still privileged western thinkers and primarily "produced studies *about* the subaltern rather than studies *with and from* a subaltern perspective" (Grosfoguel, 2007, p. 211). Recognizing the continuation of global coloniality, it is crucial to decolonize

Eurocentric epistemology in academia (Grosfoguel, 2007; Tshimpaka, 2018). Barnhardt and Kawagley (2005) also called for the need to recognize the coexistence of multiple epistemologies and understand multiple ways of being not only by Indigenous peoples but also non-Indigenous people.

TRANSFORMATION APPROACH: TOWARD LIBERATORY PEDAGOGY

Reflecting upon paradigm shifts via the transformation approach, the journey continues towards scholarship that critically deconstructs Eurocentric epistemological hegemony and subjugation of Indigenous epistemologies through a study analyzing media communication, followed by scholarship that embraces Indigenous epistemological orientations based on relational worldviews. The following academic scholarship helps its audience critically deconstruct and decolonize their minds by embracing Indigenous epistemologies and ontologies, thereby leading into paradigm shifts through conscientization.

Transformational Scholarship

Cynthia-Lou Coleman, Professor of Communication at Portland State University, examined the discourse of scientific controversies over "the Ancient One, who is popularly known as Kennewick Man" (Coleman, 2013, p. 65). The controversies over Kennewick Man are characterized by epistemological battles that juxtaposed Indigenous worldviews against Occidental science worldviews. Based on a critical analysis of media, academic and legal discourse, Coleman (2018) articulates the process of subjugating Indigenous knowledge systems through "sciencing"—"the act of conducting science"—which involves "Othering" that follows "scientific pursuits of the racialized Other, bolstered by scientific methods, enables 'us' to distinguish ourselves from 'them' . . . would necessarily leverage Occidental science over subjugated (Indigenous) knowledge systems" (p. 273). Based on her critical media analysis of Kennewick Man," Coleman (2013) deconstructs the discourse on Indigenous authenticity. Under NAGPRA (the Native American Graves Protection and Repatriation Act of 1990), local governmental officials contacted responsible officials in local Indigenous Nations, including the Confederated Tribes of Umatilla Reservation, who requested return of their Ancestor for proper ceremony and burial (Coleman, 2013). However, this request was met with opposition by James Chatters, freelance anthropologist, and his fellow anthropologists, which resulted in suing for the right to study this "gift" (Coleman, 2013).

The media portrayal and communication on this matter reflected Coleman's acute analysis (2018) in "sciencing" by juxtaposing anthropologists' claims as Occidental science as "scientific pursuits of the racialized Other" and framing Indigenous epistemologies as "beliefs, religion, ethics, or other perspectives that are characterized as *non-Science*" (p. 270). The media portrayal of Othering went as far as claiming the Ancient One that dates back thousands of years more resembled "Caucasian than Indian" by superimposing the image of actor Patrick

Stewart (as Captain Jean-Luc Picard) on the skull (Coleman, 2013, p. 73). The case study of the Ancient One by Coleman (2013; 2018) poignantly demonstrates the legal and social privileging of Eurocentric perspectives while devaluing Indigenous perspectives by imposing subjugated identity, epistemology, and ontology (way of being). This reflects Indigenous peoples' ongoing "struggles for sovereignty, indigenous rights, and dignity" (Killsback, 2013, p. 85). Furthermore, it is crucial to embrace Indigenous epistemological orientations and "cultural rationalities conjoin ethics within ontological relationships" such that Indigenous epistemologies "consider relationships with the universe as the basis for ethical behaviors offers a quite different perspective on ethics than does sciencing" (Coleman, 2018, p. 286). The next section discusses scholarship based on Indigenous epistemological orientations, illustrating a relational worldview that emphasizes interdependence.

Indigenous Ways of Knowing: Relational Worldview

The relational worldview reflected in Indigenous epistemologies "sees life as harmonious relationships" (Cross, 1997, p. 6) "both seen and unseen" and is "oriented toward understanding complex patterns, embracing complexity, and the pursuit of wisdom" (Cross et al., 2019, p. 103). In comparison to a Eurocentric approach focusing on categorization, Atran and Medin (2008) note a relationally oriented knowledge base in Indigenous Nations. For example, in Ross et al. (2003), examination of cultural and experiential differences between Indigenous (Menominee) children, rural majority children, and urban majority children, they find that only urban majority children showed early anthropocentrism, this being due to impoverished exposure to nature. Furthermore, Menominee children of all ages and older rural majority children demonstrated clear ecological reasoning, noting ecological relations among beings, such as "a bee might sting a bear" or "a bear will eat honey." Furthermore, "Menominee children did not differentially attribute properties from humans to higher versus lower animals" (p. 39). This may reflect a different sense of humans' relationships with animals compared to the hierarchical categorization of animals in a Eurocentric worldview.

By no means are Indigenous peoples the only ones that have relational worldviews and values. While a Eurocentric approach in education overemphasizes the need to educate children based on a categorization-based construction of nature, in many parts of the world people tend to understand nature relationally (e.g., Nisbett, 2003), such that many East Asians, when asked to group two of the following three items as belonging to each other—banana, apple, and monkey—an overwhelming majority responded that monkey and banana belong to one another by focusing on relations among beings rather than a categorization-based sorting of fruits and animals. Similarly, differences in values (axiology) between Euro-Americans and Africans are noted as Africans placing "highest value (is) in positive interpersonal relationships among people" based on cooperation, interdependence, spiritualism, and circularity while Euro-American place "highest value (is) in objects or acquisition of objects" (Myers, 1993, p. 97 cited in Carroll, 2008).

Indeed, this is one of the fundamental differences between European settlers and Indigenous peoples in their epistemological orientations and value systems.

CULTURAL AND SOCIAL JUSTICE ACTION APPROACH: KINCENTRICITY

Reflecting the TIPM's cultural and social justice action approach, the last example shared is the salmon and sea lion dialogue held in an academic setting that honors Indigenous ways of being—kincentric ecology—and highlights the moral and epistemological connection of Indigenous people's identity with the land and Indigenous ways of relating to others based on Indigenous Circle Methodology (Graveline, 2012). In sharing this example, my hope is to illustrate engaging transformational praxis in higher education through insurgent research that promotes understanding of the deep connection that Indigenous Peoples have with land and reconciliation of relationships.

Kincentricity

> We don't call a tree a resource, we don't call the fish a resource. We don't call the bison a resource. We call them our relatives, But the general population uses the term resources, so you want to be careful of that term—resources for just you?
>
> —Onondaga Elder Oren Lyons's remarks during 25th-anniversary Earth Day celebration in Washington, DC, cited in Deloria & Wildcat (2001, p. 94)

Salmón (2002) articulates kincentric ecology as follows: "Indigenous people view both themselves and nature as part of an extended ecological family that shares ancestry and origins" with an "awareness that life in any environment is viable only when humans view the life surrounding them as kin (or relatives)" (p. 1327) based on reciprocity. Similarly, Coulthard (2014) defines *grounded normativity* as "the modalities of Indigenous land-connected practices and longstanding experiential knowledge that inform and structure our ethical engagements with the world and our relationships with human and nonhuman others over time" and land as a "system of reciprocal relations and obligations" (p. 13). Salmón (2002) also recognizes the importance of Indigenous languages that capture "the concept of kincentric ecology in traditional terms" (p. 1328) such that Indigenous people's history, identity, and land is intricately connected and expressed in Indigenous language.

Dialogue Regarding the Salmon and Sea Lion Issue at Bonneville Dam

In the past decade, sea lions have gathered near the base of the Bonneville Dam to prey on large numbers of salmon (Schneider, 2013). Concerned with sea lion predation affecting the salmon population, government bodies have consulted with stakeholders and decided to remove and in some cases euthanize sea lions. However, objection to the euthanasia of sea lions led to conflicts among stakeholders and resulted in a court appeal (*Humane Society v Locke 2010* as cited in Carey et al., 2012).

For reconciliation of relationships among stakeholders, an initial half-day dialogue was held in 2010, and participants appreciated having an opportunity to be heard with respect and to meet each other as "humans" rather than "dehumanized others." They also expressed the need for a follow-up dialogue to seek further reconciliation and collaborative strategies to resolve the salmon and sea lion issue. The follow-up 2-day dialogue was organized in February 2011, and the participants included Indigenous leaders, commercial and sports fishing organization leaders, government agents, and environmental and animal advocacy organization leaders.

The dialogue gatherings were based on collaborative efforts between faculty in Indigenous Nations Studies (INS), United Indigenous Students in Higher Education (UISHE) at Portland State University, as well as both Indigenous and non-Indigenous community members. The dialogue exemplifies insurgent research in higher education that embraces Indigenous ways of knowing and relating through Indigenous Circle Methodology. Throughout dialogues, Indigenous Peoples shared their cultural knowledge and practices. Through the respectful interactions, non-Indigenous Peoples came to appreciate the kincentric ecology. Furthermore, people in conflict came to appreciate each other's perspectives and reconcile their relationships.

Both dialogues began with singing and drumming by Professor Cornel Pewewardy in INS. Jeff Goebel (an experienced dialogue mediator) helped participants engage in Indigenous Circle Methodology that promotes deep listening. Shulamit Urenia and Carol Becker along with other UISHE members helped connect with Indigenous community members and organizations as well as government agencies and animal advocates. They also prepared and shared food throughout dialogue gatherings. Indigenous Elders shared cultural ceremony and food (traditionally prepared sun-dried salmon) with everyone at the gatherings.

Dialogue based on the Indigenous Circle Methodology allowed participants to share and be heard with respect among stakeholders. Through these respectful interactions, people came to appreciate one another and reconcile their relationships. For example, after the two days of the dialogue, one of the participants approached me and shared their feelings that they initially wanted to leave the meeting because they were so upset to see one of the participants in the conflict, yet they later expressed how glad they felt after staying and engaging in the dialogue. They were very much appreciative of the opportunity to deepen their understanding of the other participant and reconcile the relationship.

During the second day of the dialogue, Jeff encouraged these two conflicting participants to share their stories and be heard based on "Third-Person Reappraisal": after one of them shared their story, other participants would rephrase what they heard so that the listener not only could hear what was shared by the conflicting participant, but also got to hear the recount of what was being shared by two other people. This process can help reduce the distortion of what might be heard by another person in a conflict because of previous history and negative interactions; in so doing, the third-person reappraisal can promote facilitation of deep and respectful listening. At the end of their dialogue through third-person reappraisal, the two conflicting participants came to the center of the circle, were honored with blankets, and greeted one another back-to-back. Jeff mentioned that this greeting may have represented their relationship moving forward since they may not see eye-to-eye on the topic but they would continue to greet and laugh in order to work together. Indeed, at the end of the dialogue, one of the two conflicting participants had a possibility of not being able to return home due to harsh weather conditions. The other participant invited them to their home to stay with their family in case the harsh weather continued. This moment of reconciliation illustrated the power of Indigenous ways of relating to one another that promote deep listening and building relationships.

Indigenous Circle Methodology promotes holistic understanding between people from different cultures. One of the amazing moments that I observed during dialogue was when Indigenous Elders voluntarily shared a song and blessings. At that moment, everyone in the dialogue voluntarily created a circle around the Indigenous Elders and listened with respect and expressed their appreciation. Engagement of deep listening and participation of cultural ceremonies allowed the rest of the participants to deepen their understanding of the connection that Indigenous Peoples have with land and nonhuman others, notably salmon and sea lions.

CONCLUSION

This travel through different dimensions of the TIPM helps us appreciate that education should create a space that embraces Indigenous perspectives with holistic understanding of the world through contextualized Indigenous epistemologies and ontologies (Barnhardt & Kawagley, 2005). Sovereignty and self-determination of Indigenous education "begins with attentiveness to the relations around us" (Deloria & Wildcat, 2001, p. 138).

Educators need to move beyond pluralism in multicultural education and appreciate Indigenous epistemology and ontology of kincentricity that connects Indigenous peoples' identity with land (nature) and interweaves "moral and epistemic prominence based on ancient and sustained relationships to land" (Marker, 2006, p. 486). Furthermore, the holistic approach in Indigenous epistemologies rests on "suspended judgement" instead of claiming "universalism" as in the Eurocentric approach (Deloria & Wildcat, 2001, p. 6). The TIPM can be guiding transformational praxis to promote creative and insurgent approaches that lead into collective commitment and action for decolonization of education.

NOTE

1. The term *dysconsciousness*, coined by Joyce King (1991), represents "an uncritical habit of mind" that lacks critical judgment and "accepts [social order] uncritically" (p. 135).

REFERENCES

Atran, S., & Medin, D. L. (2008). *The native mind and the cultural construction of nature* (p. 21). Cambridge, MA: mit Press.

Barnhardt, R., & Oscar Kawagley, A. (2005). Indigenous knowledge systems and Alaska Native ways of knowing. *Anthropology & Education Quarterly, 36*(1), 8–23. https://doi.org/10.1525/aeq.2005.36.1.008

Brower, B. C. (2009). *A desert named peace: the violence of France's empire in the Algerian Sahara, 1844–1902*. Columbia University Press.

Carey, M. P., Sanderson, B. L., Barnas, K. A., & Olden, J. D. (2012). Native invaders—challenges for science, management, policy, and society. *Frontiers in Ecology and the Environment, 10*(7), 373–381. https://doi.org/10.1890/110060

Carroll, K. K. (2008). *Africana studies and research methodology: Revisiting the centrality of the Afrikan worldview in Africana studies research and scholarship*. https://academicworks.cuny.edu/bb_pubs/1157/

Coleman, C. L. (2013). The extermination of Kennewick Man's authenticity through discourse. *Wičazo Ša Review, 28*(1), 65–76. https://muse.jhu.edu/article/506188

Coleman, C. L. (2018). How discourse illuminates the ruptures between scientific and cultural rationalities. In *Ethics and Practice in Science Communication* (pp. 270–290). University of Chicago Press. https://doi.org/10.7208/9780226497952-019

Coulthard, G. S. (2014). Red skin, white masks: Rejecting the colonial politics of recognition. University of Minnesota Press

Cross, T. (1997). Understanding the relational worldview in Indian families. *Pathways Practice Digest, 12*(4), 6–12.

Cross, T. L., Pewewardy, C., & Smith, A. T. (2019). Restorative education, reconciliation, and healing: Indigenous perspectives on decolonizing leadership education. *New Directions for Student Leadership, 2019*(163), 101–115. https://doi.org/10.1002/yd.20350

Deloria, V., Deloria Jr, V., & Wildcat, D. (2001). *Power and place: Indian education in America*. Fulcrum Publishing.

Gilley, B. (2018). The case for colonialism. *Academic Questions, 31*(2), 167–185. https://doi.org/10.1007/s12129-018-9696-2

Gopal, P. (2006). The "Moral Empire": Africa, globalisation and the politics of conscience. *New Formations*, (59), 81–98. https://link.gale.com/apps/doc/A155919839/AONE?u=oregon_sl&sid=AONE&xid=a14aa0b2

Gordon, A., & Eckert, C. (2021). Statement by Andrew Gordon and Carter Eckert concerning J. Mark Ramseyer, "Contracting for sex in the Pacific War." https://dash.harvard.edu/bitstream/handle/1/37366904/Eckert%20Gordon%20on%20Mark%20Ramseyer%20article%20for%20public%20release%20final.pdf?sequence=1

Graveline, F. J. (2000). Circle as methodology: Enacting an Aboriginal paradigm. *International Journal of Qualitative Studies in Education, 13*(4), 361–370. https://doi.org/10.1080/095183900413304

Grosfoguel, R. (2007). The epistemic decolonial turn: Beyond political-economy paradigms. *Cultural studies, 21*(2-3), 211–223. https://doi.org/10.1080/09502380601162514

Grosfoguel, R. (2013). The structure of knowledge in westernized universities: Epistemic racism/sexism and the four genocides/epistemicides of the long 16th century. *Human Architecture, 11*(1), 73. https://www.niwrc.org/sites/default/files/images/resource/2%20The%20Structure%20of%20Knowledge%20in%20Westernized%20Universities_%20Epistemic.pdf

Hosaka, Y. (2021). Contracting for sex? "True story" of the so-called "comfort women" during World War II. *Journal of East Asia & International Law*, *14*(1), 161–178. http://dx.doi .org/10.14330/jeail.2021.14.1.09

Kenrick, J., & Lewis, J. (2004). Indigenous peoples' rights and the politics of the term 'Indigenous'. *Anthropology today*, *20*(2), 4–9. https://doi.org/10.1111/j.0268-540X.2004.00256.x

Killsback, L. (2013). Indigenous perceptions of time: Decolonizing theory, world history, and the fates of human societies. *American Indian Culture and Research Journal*, *37*(4), 85–114. https://doi.org/10.17953/aicr.37.4.86k2lh8101521j66

Kim, M. (2017). Dilemma of historical reflection in East Asia and the issue of Japanese military "comfort women": Continuing colonialism and politics of denial. 통일인문학, *3*(1), 43–68. https://www.snkh.org/include/download_files/v3/1_43-68.pdf

King, J. E. (1991). Dysconscious racism: Ideology, identity, and the miseducation of teachers. *The Journal of Negro Education*, *60*(2), 133–146. http://www.jstor.org/stable/2295605

Kivel, P. (2013). *Living in the shadow of the cross: Understanding and resisting the power and privilege of Christian hegemony*. New Society Publishers.

Klein, M. A. (2018). A critique of colonial rule: a response to Bruce Gilley. *Australasian Review of African Studies*,*39*(1), 39. https://doi.org/10.22160/22035184/ARAS-2018-39-1/39-52

Korean Association of Harvard Law School. (2021). *KAHLS statement in response to Professor J. Mark Ramseyer's article "Contracting for sex in the Pacific War"*. https://orgs.law.harvard. edu/kahls/statements/

Kuper, A. (2003). The return of the native. *Current Anthropology*, *44*(3), 389–402.

Marker, M. (2006). After the Makah whale hunt: Indigenous knowledge and limits to multicultural discourse. *Urban Education*, *41*(5), 482–505. https://doi.org/10.1177/0042085906291923

Ndlovu-Gatsheni, S. J. (2021, February 26). *Moral evil, economic good: Whitewashing the sins of colonialism*. Aljazeera. https://www.aljazeera.com/opinions/2021/2/26/colonialism-in -africa-empire-was-not-ethical

Ndlovu-Gatsheni, S. J. (2014). Global coloniality and the challenges of creating African futures. *The Strategic Review for Southern Africa*, *36*(2). https://upjournals.up.ac.za/index.php /strategic_review/article/download/189/141

Nisbett, R. (2004). *The geography of thought: How Asians and Westerners think differently . . . and why*. Simon and Schuster.

Piccard, A. (2014). Death by boarding school: "The last acceptable racism" and the United States' genocide of Native Americans. *Gonzaga Law Review*, *49*(1), 137–185. https:// gonzagalawreview.com/article/10117-death-by-boarding-school-the-last-acceptable -racism-and-the-united-states-genocide-of-native-americans

Ramseyer, J. M. (2021). Contracting for sex in the Pacific War. *International Review of Law and Economics*, *65*, 105971. https://doi.org/10.1016/j.irle.2020.105971

Ross, N., Medin, D., Coley, J. D., & Atran, S. (2003). Cultural and experiential differences in the development of folkbiological induction. *Cognitive Development*, *18*(1), 25–47. https://doi. org/10.1016/S0885-2014(02)00142-9

Rousso, H. (2006). The political and cultural roots of negationism in France. *South Central Review*, *23*(1), 67–88. https://doi.org/10.1353/scr.2006.0014

Salmón, E. (2000). Kincentric ecology: Indigenous perceptions of the human–nature relationship. *Ecological Applications*, *10*(5), 1327–1332. https://doi.org/10.1890/1051-0761(2000)0 10[1327:KEIPOT]2.0.CO;2

Schneider, L. (2013). "There's something in the water": Salmon runs and settler colonialism on the Columbia River. *American Indian Culture and Research Journal*, *37*(2), 149–164. https:// doi.org/10.17953/aicr.37.2.0426145lx4v602u4

Tshimpaka, L. M. (2018). Curbing inequality through decolonising knowledge production in higher education in South Africa. *The Australasian Review of African Studies*, *39*(1), 53–80. https://afsaap.org.au/assets/vol39no1june2018_tshimpaka_53-80.pdf

Part IV

EDUCATIONAL LEADERSHIP

CHAPTER 12

Learning With Each Other

A Relational Indigenous Leadership Philosophy

Dawn Hardison-Stevens (Omushkeg Cree-Metis,
Ojibway, Cowlitz, Steilacoom)

Plants and animals are our relatives who speak to us. We can hear them if we listen. Respect all living things and they will respect us.

—Arapaho Proverb

Waterways connect each community like bridges, weaving between the aged Trees encircling the Native communities nestled in diverse forests of the Pacific Northwest. Bare branches invite the autumn sun to warm reflections of the welcoming windows. Leaves calmly rest around their former hosts' mighty trunks on the forest floor where the wind placed them in a swirling fanfare of color, marking one season's end and another's arrival. Each step yields a soft crunch that echoes in the still air, calmly announcing my arrival. This experience circles toward the Transformational Indigenous Praxis Model (TIPM) and other chapters in this book sharing connections with nature, showing the land as an integral aspect of teaching and learning. My story connects with two Native Nations for conversations with a Tribal education director and a Native teacher, both former Tribal council leaders.

Upon entering the building, the Tribal education director sits comfortably with college pennants hung high around the room, inspiring students to follow an academic path. The seeds of such dreams are planted here to motivate and prepare Indigenous learners for higher education and workplace success. The goals reach beyond their communities so learners can bring an enhanced knowledge, honed perspectives, and resources home to benefit their Native communities' self-governance and sovereignty—and themselves as role models for future generations. "If Native communities are preparing these younger generations to go out and get that college experience, have that advanced degree, that real-world experience, work in corporate America or academic America, those folks need to come back to the community," the education director says.

Today's western education systems still rely heavily on single-subject textbooks that do not make connections or establish relevance with other content areas—and most assessments of academic understanding and achievement rely on rote memorization of this material with little or no connection to the real life around them (Brayboy & Lomawaima, 2018; Pewewardy, 1992). Native knowledge systems with TIPM teach a relatedness of life, teaching, learning, and leadership.

Native people have used a traditional means of knowledge that is demonstrative, with applied hands-on and experiential learning (Demmert & Towner, 2003). The research on Native student learning styles, in conjunction with students failing in the current school systems identified in numerous studies, suggests failure is based on a lack of culturally relevant content (Brayboy & Lomawaima, 2018; Demmert & Towner, 2003; Hankes et al., 2011; Sabzalian, 2019). TIPM identifies the need to bridge different worlds of education, to build understanding between conventional western and traditional Native ways of knowing and learning.

How can Native educational leaders prepare students for academic success in western-style environments while still helping foster their development of Native value systems and familial/communal connections that both guide their desire for higher education and motivate them to use the fruits of it to strengthen their communities?

There is no single answer to this question, but rather a series of connected solutions—practices Native educational leaders can employ to engage and teach Native learners, as well as learn from them. TIPM addresses the positive views, knowing we are all teachers and learners. These practices compose an Indigenous Leadership Philosophy we will explore in this chapter.

THE INDIGENOUS LEADERSHIP PHILOSOPHY

Native knowledge is understanding that everyone is unique, like everything that grows in a diverse forest. As Warner and Grint (2006) write:

> [Native] traditions tend to be more related to the requirements of the community, to be much more dispersed throughout that community, and to be rooted in situations rather than individuals. Thus, one could argue that American Indian traditions of leadership are more akin to heterarchies than hierarchies: flexible and changing patterns of authority rather than rigidly embedded in a fixed and formal bureaucracy. (p. 227)

As TIPM identifies, Indigenous leadership styles encompass an educational balance of all people relative to the natural world with an emphasis on equality (Belgarde et al., 2002; Pewewardy et al., 2018). Minthorn (2014) states, "Indigenous knowledge at its core is relational. Knowledge generated, in how we know what we know, is shared with all creation and thus becomes relational knowledge" (p. 5). The orientation of traditional Indigenous methods of education encompasses an awareness of how the learning process is relevant for the learner's innate life path within their natural environments. The traditional European style of rote memorization within a textbook education and a reward system fails Indigenous students because of its disregard for Native ways of holistic learning (Belgarde et al., 2002; Brayboy & Lomawaima, 2018; Demmert & Towner, 2003). In Native knowledge, education must be more experiential and accordingly transformational for each Indigenous student.

Seven key philosophies were identified as a focus of leadership that, when combined, can expand a Native learner's volition. See Figure 12.1 The Relational Indigenous Leadership Philosophy.

Sensory Awareness

In many situations or contexts, Native people do not speak due to custom, lack of confidence, or lack of opportunity, but rather engage the six senses to feel the energies surrounding them. The first step toward achieving sensory awareness is to become receptive by taking the action to be silent. Utilizing the senses, such as listening, allows effective Indigenous leadership of recognition in listening to others' words, thus building an understanding to engage meaning. Fixico (2003) states, "Listening as a part of oral tradition is essential for understanding relationships and their multiple meanings. . . . Silence is the test for patience" (p. 5). If open to the phenomenological perspective, education is found everywhere, and everyone can be an absorbent lifelong learner and absorb our being "related" with nature and reflective in our knowledge (Cajete, 2000).

Figure 12.1. The Relational Indigenous Leadership Philosophy[1]

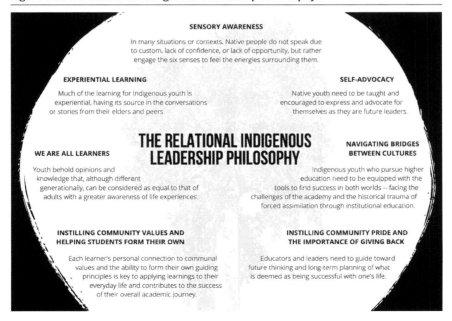

Experiential Learning

Leadership styles within most cultures adapt based on leaders learning from experiences, good and bad, then establishing the necessary change to offer individual and group growth toward successful outcomes.

Historical trauma is a factor experienced by Native peoples that affects leadership (Minthorn, 2014). Stories abound of the injustices in educational institutions like boarding schools to assimilate Native youth into a culture of Eurocentric dominance. Effective experiences engage the sensory factors of touching, seeing, hearing, smelling, speaking/tasting, and intuition.

Much of the learning for Indigenous youth—and many non-Indigenous youth—is experiential, having its source in the conversations or stories from their Elders and peers. Place- and Land-based education teaches students out in the environment. The hands-on, sensory learning stays with the learner more than just book learning from chapter to chapter and beyond testing. Students need relevance, since phenomenological involvements or "direct experiences" take hold based on individual perspectives. "What we term progressive education today," the education director says, "is just a return to the roots of how people had always been." Land and nature are educators and considered our first teachers (Calderón, 2014; Tuck et al., 2014).

We Are All Learners

Many researchers, administrators, and community members often forget or neglect to ask the young people their perspectives. In understanding TIPM, youth have opinions and knowledge that, although different generationally, can be considered as equal to that of adults with a greater awareness of life experiences.

In addition to learning *from* their students, it is critical for educational leaders to learn *about* them. What are their individual passions, dreams, and talents? Being aware of students' personal interests enables leaders to help guide them along the paths they are choosing for themselves, to help them engage with and see real value in their education, their educators, and themselves. "The people of each generation have a responsibility," the education director says. "If you are a weaver, then you have to look amongst the children of that next generation and find those who have the talent for weaving. If you are a carver, then you must find those carvers. If you are a storyteller, then you must find storytellers."

Instilling community values—and helping students form their own. Communal values are key to establishing any successful relationship between educators and their students. A leader will build trust, patience, respect, honesty, humor and will honor differences and similarities, whether based on perspectives, ideals, interests, and values promoting support. Verbos and Humphries (2014) share how "one should live a good life" through the "Seven Grandfather Teachings, an ancient sacred story of Potawatomi and Ojibwe peoples. These teachings state that human beings are responsible for acting with wisdom, respect, love, honesty, humility, bravery, and truth toward each other and all creation" (p. 1). Cajete (2000) mentions by "relational values we mean a way of being, knowing, understanding, feeling, and acting in relationship to other humans, plants, animals, and the natural world, as interrelated and spirit-filled" (p. 2).

Even experiential learning, discussed earlier, is crucial to Native learners, which "enforces traditional Native values such as respect for the individual, development of an internal locus of control, sharing, and harmony" (Little Soldier, 1989). This respect for the individual can enable learners not only to internalize communal values, but also begin to develop their own. Each learner's personal connection to communal values and the ability to form their own guiding principles is key to applying learnings to their everyday life and toward success along their broader academic journey. A guided "success" leads toward a good life through balanced emotional, social, physical, and spiritual heart in the connectedness of their passionate interests.

Instilling community pride—and the importance of giving back. As TIPM identifies, positive messaging is necessary when discussing Native communities and people. The education director shared many stories about instances of long-standing *negative* messages, such as those casting Native peoples as relics of long ago:

> [We] were doing some work with the Blackfeet and staying in a little hotel in East Glacier, Montana. There are not a whole lot of places to go for breakfast or lunch, so we pull into this little restaurant; it is a really, really, old log facility. You can see that it is really, really, old. I am reading the back of the menu and there is this history of the person that originally built this structure, and they are saying that this person was one of the early explorers of this area known as Glacier National Park today.
>
> And there was a time, years ago, when I would have thought, "Wow, that is so cool." But as my eyes are a little more open, I realized: How could it be an early explorer if there were already people living there? There is a lot of that kind of thinking when you get into your other questions, that it has just kind of been ingrained into us over time, that we must open our eyes and see beyond.

The education director mentions the "long and well documented history of discrimiNation and oppression has been experienced by many different Native peoples in many different ways" through colonization practices. They mentioned the differing perceptions of individuals when identifying colonialism, noting many believe the attitude was from the past and do not see its effects today. Educators and leaders need to guide toward future thinking and long-term planning of what is deemed as being successful with one's life.

We are starting to see more Native students go on to college and Native communities are thinking about what happens once they graduate. As Native students obtain degrees, their shared experiences encourage others to complete formal education. The education director commented on the educated ones coming back to their communities and taking over important positions:

> These students bring back with them a broader perspective, reaching out to widen the spectrum, especially through entrepreneurships. Now that we have more students going off and receiving a higher education, we must plan for them to return to the reservation. And for that to take place, we need bigger buildings, we need to house them, we need to have them working within each of our departments depending on their chosen areas of expertise. Tribes supporting their people's secondary and postsecondary educational opportunities find value as it becomes necessary to grow the community's infrastructure to fit the goals of the educated people.

Navigating Bridges Between Cultures

Many Indigenous people who pursue higher education have commented on "living in two worlds," whereas the education director stated, "You have that Native community you are growing up in and being a part of and you have that other world outside of your Native community that you are trying to be a part of." In addition, the director has "actually seen Native people who talk about that experience as not walking in two worlds because they're not successful in both of those worlds," and instead feel like they are "stuck somewhere in between."

The education director discussed examples of having members who understand grant writing, noting a recurring theme in the experiences of Native people in so many different programmatic areas. Federal and philanthropic programs offer grants, but they "want evidence-based programs that are going to guide where your program is going to go," the director says. "Well, when they say evidence-based programs, they are literally saying, 'Who has a PhD and has done the research to say this works?' Well, there are no Native PhDs who have the research behind them to show that the traditional practices worked."

Even Native learners who feel drawn to postsecondary education opportunities beyond their community may still feel held back or discouraged by Elders' own deference or negative experiences with outside education. The director shared:

> There was a beautiful and highly intelligent Native student who was beyond her years. This girl passed college exams in her sophomore year of high school. She lived on one of the reservations and was awfully close to her family. For many high school students, that is not the case as they rebel against parents. One day, this female student shared that her grandmother needed 24-hour care and insisted that she be the caregiver. There were futile attempts to discuss the situation with the grandmother as she claimed, "I did not get a high school diploma and was successful in life, so my granddaughter does not need a high school diploma." And one does not argue with an Elder, so the granddaughter chose to abandon education.

Like many other students in this generation, the grandmothers, grandfathers, aunties, and uncles are products of being forced to assimilate in a dominating culture's boarding-school era. The education director mentioned the history of boarding schools on and off the reservations with administrators recommending to "Kill the Indian, Save the Man," with Indigenous students removed from their homes and communities. These schools were established with military standards. In 1865, Indigenous boarding schools were located on the reservations, whereas the director shared:

> My wife wound up being raised much of her growing years by her grandmother. Her grandmother was born in 1899, so we are only talking 10 years after Washington statehood. We are not talking about modern Washington. In that period the practice is when you turn eight years old, you get sent off to boarding school. So, at eight years old—we are talking 1907— she was sent to a boarding school in Montana.
>
> She is one of nine siblings that were sent to five different boarding schools. So not only are you disconnecting them from their community but from each other. There are far too many horror stories of what conditions Native youth experienced in those situations. Kids were being abused, beaten, killed; kids were running away. Today, generations of Native people who survived through those experiences—many of them have come away from that with the view not necessarily that the boarding school was bad but with the emotional baggage that says the education was bad. That is what they are passing down through their families.

There also exists a second fear in the community for those Native learners who do branch out and pursue their academic dreams—that they will not return. The education director tells the fear of youth not returning to their community, noting more than 70% of Native people do not reside on the reservations:

> Even if the tribe steps up and says we are going to support these kids . . . through their four-year degree; when these kids get that four-year degree, then what choice is facing them? Because until the last 10–20 years, when they get that college degree, they turn around and look at the community they come from and there is nothing for them to come back to and use that degree for. In so many cases, that means if you are a community that can teach this kid how to be successful in a modern world, you are also telling them goodbye.

Therefore, it's important for Native students to stay connected to their own values and those of their communities while they live and study elsewhere. The director continued:

> We can't go there and lose sight of who we are and where we came from because otherwise there is not a reason for us to come back . . . we [become]

an orphan of identity. We have lost that sense of who we are and now we are wandering around the world trying to find somebody else's culture to latch onto, so they feel a part of something. . . . [It is a] discouraging, frightening place to be because that means we have just lost another one of the people. We have to make sure our young people—all of our people—understand what it means to be one of us, encouraging them to go into the world to get that formalized education.

In traditional ways, we are communal people working together.

When listening to one Native teacher speak of the lessons a grandmother taught about life's psychology and sociology regarding living in "two worlds," they shared:

I asked her about that when I was about 14 years old. I had a psychology book that talked about it. I took it to my grandmother and asked her about if she believed in the two worlds [theory]. It was beautiful: I could still see her; she was a tiny thing. She sat and she put her head down and she looked up and she looked around and then she looked at me and she said, "No, Grandchild; there aren't two worlds. There is only one. That World is right here," patting the chest over the heart. "If you can accept and acknowledge this World here," again patting the chest, "you can go visit any world you choose because you can always come home. Because you know where it is."

Self-advocacy. In encompassing TIPM, many students' "learning style" consists of observation and listening while engaging all the senses. Numerous secondary and postsecondary educators are unaware of cultural traditions when working with Native communities and students. Traditions call for Native students applying their cultural knowledge of respect and preferring to "blend in" and not "stand out" in social circles and classrooms. One non-Native administrator commented, "It is ironic but in higher education, Native students are the last ones to ask questions. Sometimes it is hard to get students to be candid because they have spent a lifetime learning how to be respectful. Sometimes candor can feel like disrespect even when it is what you want."

Native people need to become educators for teachers and administrators biased by these paradigms. Education teaches a bias eliminating culture from the non-Native lens. As the Native educator recounted from his youth:

I had a professor who got up and did a five-minute monologue on men who wore earrings. I am sitting in class there with my earrings. There were two other Natives and a Black gentleman, and the rest were white/European whatever. Two friends looked at me, and everybody was laughing because this teacher was questioning if we were men or not. I was sitting there as he went on and on, and I was watching the class. I was not offended because I know why I wear earrings. I know that creation started from my childhood and why the earrings came to be.

The next day I write this three-page, legal-sized letter to the professor. My Sioux friend said, "Why didn't you say something?" I hand the document to him and say, "I want you to read this." He reads it and says, "What are you going to do with this?" I said I was going to hand it to the professor. He said, "Now if you do that, you know how they work around here; they will have you out of school in no time!" I look at him and say, "What are we going to tell our children and our grandchildren? If the same thing happens to them in the same classroom and the same campus, you and I look at them and say 'Well, that happened to us back in 1982.'" I said, "What are we going to say when our children and our grandchildren look at us and ask, 'What did you do, Grandpa?' What are you going to say when you say, 'I didn't do anything'?"

I took the letter, and went down to the program secretary, and said, "May I?" She said, "I will take this." I said, "No, I want to take it in myself." So, I walked in the professor's office, handed the letter to him, and I walked out.

The next week in class the teacher says, "I was given a letter. With the author's permission, I would like to read it verbatim." He looks over at me, I just nod my head, and even when I called him "ignorant" in the letter, he read it word for word. When he finished, he looked down and he said, "Mr. [interviewee's name], would you please stand up?" I stood up and he said, "To you, and to your people, all people who have a story, and understanding of why they wear what they wear, I apologize."

Well bless his heart, he was the only one I had any respect for out of all the professors I had down there.

State and local educational leaders need to mandate the need for teacher and administrative professional development that enables learning from those voicing and initiating change by engaging Native peoples and Native communities, like Washington State's passed legislation. In addition, Native youth need to be taught and encouraged to express and advocate for themselves as they are our future leaders.

CONCLUSION

Engaging students in learning from two worlds of perspectives, Native and non-Native, will build understanding among educators and leadership of how the learning disciplines work together from a traditional big picture. Moving the theory into practice within an educational setting, the technique can bring together a community as traditional and conventional educators work together to teach everyone in a culturally suitable learning style.

Many students who go on to college have had one or more parents either attend or graduate from college, whereas most youth of color are first-time college students. Cultivating confidence and offering guidance to students assists Native communities in encouraging their learners to further their college education.

In an interview with Native alumni, one participant commented on how college readiness programs "motivated me to become a college student while in high school. The teachers acted and treated you just like a college student" and "had more respect for the students than what the high school teachers demonstrated." When communities come together academically, cohorts form. Peer cohort groups should be established for educational purposes, which act as a student support system. Another area in need of discussion is the preparation model to foster Indigenous leadership beginning in high school.

Each positive connection forged between and within Native learners is like a seed being planted, an energy, with educational leaders as the cultivators. These tenets of the Relational Indigenous Leadership Philosophy—these balanced "nourishing" techniques—have the potential to reap Lands that feed untold numbers of Native descendants and their communities.

As one Native education leader tells it, this type of cultivation is a most selfless act, since we won't be here to witness much of its yield. But we can begin the process, and guide its development, sharing, "I may not know what that change is in my lifetime. That may be something that 100 years from now may change into something beautiful, but I will not be there to see it. I helped them to plant the seed and I hope that it grows."

Similar to TIPM's analogy of the energies of ocean wave actions, life continues to move and feed the balance of diversity in relational ways. Indigenizing educational systems and knowledge requires that all learners must not be marginalized by who they are but identifies the relationality in their learning journey where experiential sensory consciousness guarantees the innate gifts, which brings us onto our own unique life paths.

NOTE

1. There are seven key philosophies represented in the figure and, through the circular representation, each has a connection to the creation of an Indigenous leadership philosophy. The headers demonstrate the relationship amongst them.

REFERENCES

Belgarde, M. J., Mitchell, R. D., & Arquero, A. (2002). What do we have to do to create culturally responsive programs? The challenge of transforming American Indian teacher education. *Action in Teacher Education, 24*(2), 42–54.

Brayboy, B. M. J., & Lomawaima, K. T. (2018). Why don't more Indians do better in school? The battle between US schooling & American Indian/Alaska Native education. *Daedalus, 147*(2), 82–94.

Cajete, G. (2000). *Native science: Natural laws of interdependence.* Clear Light Books.

Calderón, D. (2014). Speaking back to manifest destinies: A land education-based approach to critical curriculum inquiry. *Environmental Education Research, 20*(1), 24–36.

Demmert, W. G., & Towner, J. C. (2003). *A review of the research literature on the influences of culturally based education on the academic performance of Native American students.* Northwest Regional Educational Laboratory.

Fixico, D. L. (2003). *The American Indian mind in a linear world: American Indian studies and traditional knowledge.* Routledge.

Hankes, J., Skoning, S., Fast, G., Mason-Williams, L., Beam, J., & Mickelson, W. (2011). Closing the mathematics achievement gap of Native American students. *Voices of Native American Educators: Integrating History, Culture, and Language to Improve Learning Outcomes for Native American Students*, 211.

Little Soldier, L. (1989). Cooperative learning and the Native American student. *The Phi Delta Kappan, 71*(2), 161–163.

Minthorn, R. (2014). Perspectives and values of leadership for Native American college students in non-Native colleges and universities. *Journal of Leadership Education, 13*(2), 67–95.

Pewewardy, C. D. (1992). *"Practice into theory" Journey to the year 2000: Culturally responsible pedagogy in action . . . The American Indian Magnet School.* ERIC Document Reproduction Service. https://files.eric.ed.gov/fulltext/ED355079.pdf

Pewewardy, C. D., Lees, A., & Clark-Shim, H. (2018). The Transformational Indigenous Praxis Model: Stages for developing critical consciousness in Indigenous education. *Wíčazo Ša Review, 33*(1), 38–69. https://doi.org/10.5749/wicazosareview.33.1.0038

Sabzalian, L. (2019). *Indigenous children's survivance in public schools.* Routledge.

Tuck, E., McKenzie, M., & McCoy, K. (2014). *Land education: Indigenous, post-colonial, and decolonizing perspectives on place and environmental education research. Environmental Education Research, 20*(1), 1–23.

Verbos, A. K., & Humphries, M. (2014). A Native American relational ethic: An indigenous perspective on teaching human responsibility. *Journal of Business Ethics, 123*(1), 1–9.

Warner, L. S., & Grint, K. (2006). American Indian ways of leading and knowing. *Leadership, 2*(2), 225–244.

CHAPTER 13

Resistance and Survivance for Indigenous Educational Leadership

Applying the Transformational Indigenous Praxis Model to Support Educational Self-Determination

Hollie J. Mackey (Northern Cheyenne), Sashay Schettler (Three Affiliated Tribes), and Melissa Cournia (Settler)

Indigenous communities' relationship with educational systems designed for and maintaining coloniality are marked by continuing ideological and practical tensions between Indigenous educational self-determination, that is, Native Nations' ability to exercise their sovereign rights to establish the educational prerogatives affecting their citizens, and western institutional systems and structures. Educational leadership preparation programs perpetuate the notion that "leadership" is designated to specific individuals, thereby creating educational structures within school communities that "continue to uphold efforts of assimilation" by ignoring broader community, family, and student leadership contributions (Pewewardy et al., 2018, p. 41). We sought to disrupt the traditional model of leadership preparation by engaging in story work (Archibald, 2008; Mackey et al., forthcoming) and micro-dosed[1] professional development as a means of identifying problems of practice central to advancing Indian education initiatives in an urbanized school district serving students from various Tribal Nations in the North Dakota region. Through the story work process, we located points where our interests as scholars and practitioners intersected. We then carved out a pathway to generate a professional development opportunity that was conducted on a regular interval for shorter periods of time for non-Native educators to draw meaningful connections between the school and Indigenous students. In this way, we sought to advance participants through the Transformational Indigenous Praxis model to better serve Indigenous students within the school district (Pewewardy et al., 2018).

STORY WORK TO ADVANCE INDIGENOUS
EDUCATIONAL LEADERSHIP[2]

The story of this work begins long before professional goals entered our minds. Being born Indigenous children situates us, as community members and educators, within a story that began before us, includes us while we are here, and continues long after we have completed our walk in this world. Sashay Schettler, an enrolled member of the Three Affiliated Tribes in North Dakota, shares her story:

In my childhood I remember loving and celebrating all parts of my culture. My mother always reminded me to be proud of who I was, my people, and where we came from. As I reflect now, she was trying to help me build my self-worth and establish a strong sense of identity. I view this now as a shield, one woven from infancy into adulthood.

When I was in elementary school, there were only two times that Indigenous peoples were emphasized in the state standards and therefore the curriculum in BPS. I cannot remember the content taught, but I do remember my mixed feelings associated with the lessons. Pride and shame collided as we went through the subjects. During the times that these lessons were prevalent I would speak up and assert my Indigenous identity. I remember my classmates being astounded that I was an "Indian." Many times, this assertion was met with questions. They would question my appearance, "But you don't look like an Indian!," or they would ask me to speak "Indian."

The first time that I can explicitly remember that I felt ashamed to be Indigenous was in the 4th grade. We had taken a field trip to the United Tribes International Powwow. I was excited to see the familiar cultural displays and hear the music that I associated with my mother. I proudly asserted that I was Native. Some of my classmates jumped at the opportunity to ask me to dance and sing "Indian." These requests came as they simultaneously jumped around and did fake war cries. The questions, demands, expectations from my peers were riddled with ignorance, resulting in a lack of connection to my peers, and a feeling of shame to be "Indian." An "Indian" only existed in two contexts, the romanticized "Indian brave" of Hollywood or the "Indian" plagued with problems created by their own devices. Some of the students in my class were excited by the experiences, others in my class mocked and jeered the dancers and singers.

These experiences created a fire within me. When I took my first Indigenous studies class from the University of North Dakota, I began to feel empowered by my identity and the opportunity that education provided me to make a difference. When I came back to Bismarck Public Schools as a Cultural Responsive Coordinator, the need for work around culturally responsive practices and representation was still very prevalent.

This story is familiar to many Indigenous students and educators striving to maintain cultural identity within institutions designed to reward assimilative educational outcomes. The "fire" Sashay cites being started within her is similar to the experience Hollie Mackey, enrolled member of the Northern Cheyenne nation, shares:

> Similar to Sashay, schooling was never a comfortable fit for me. I quickly learned to mask my Indigenous identity as a way of avoiding uncomfortable interactions with administrators, teachers, and peers— always experiencing the gnawing feeling of being a fraud and traitor for not being more vocal about what was happening. I am what is often described as "ambiguously ethnic" leaning towards white passing, allowing me to blend in to spaces without standing out too much. We moved around a lot, so I was always confused by each state and school district's ability to teach around American Indians without actually teaching me anything about what it meant to be Native. This became more prevalent to me when my family moved back to my home state—Montana—to a town located approximately 90 miles from my reservation. It wasn't until I enrolled in my first Native American Studies course at Montana State University-Billings that I learned about the many Tribal Nations existing within the borders of the state. It made me angry that I had taken Montana and U.S. history classes but was never exposed to this knowledge. I was left wondering why the teachers and school leaders I'd been told I could trust had access to this knowledge and chose not to share it. Now, having worked with teachers and administrators seeking advanced educational leadership degrees, I've learned that they were also likely unaware of the Indigenous communities across the state.
>
> My "fire" was sparked when I took a teaching position on my home reservation and I realized the degree to which the school was able to incorporate culture and language without compromising other academic subjects. It was liberating to see Indigenous children not have to mask who they are between 8:00–3:00. I also gained a better understanding about the ways applying an Indigenous lens to teacher and leadership preparation benefitted all practitioners whether they taught in a Native school or in an urban area serving a small percentage of Indigenous students. I pursued my doctorate to gain entry into the world of academia to teach about and conduct research to advance the efforts of many before me who have fought to strengthen Indian education. Now that I am established in my career, I seek out ways to bring the next generation of educators into the conversation about how to continue the work. This is how my story became joined with Sashay's story. Melissa, our third author, is not an Indigenous person, however she was introduced to Indian education through her professional connection to Sashay with culturally responsive teaching work and later as my doctoral student at North Dakota State University. Now we have formed a formidable team working to redefine what it means to be an educational leader serving students and families from Tribal Nations.

Our stories provide the foundation for how we understand the responsibility to prepare educators to engage in leadership that both benefits and advances Indigenous self-determination in education. The next section will discuss how these stories are contextualized within our professional spaces where the bulk of our work takes place.

CONTEXTUALIZING STORY WORK IN SPACE AND PLACE

Educational leaders are faced with increased pressure to improve educational outcomes for all students. Improving educational equity to advance self-determination for Indigenous students presents unique multifaceted challenges related to Indigenous education. Public education institutions situated outside Indian Country (1949) largely render Indigenous school community members invisible, complicating the sense of awareness and urgency (National Congress of American Indians [NCAI], 2019), yet 90% of Indigenous students attend public schools (Rafa, 2016). Many of these students attend schools in urban centers with varying proximity to Tribal lands (NCAI, 2019), further complicating the ways school leaders can access authentic resources to support Indigenous students' learning.

This invisibility within our professional working contexts at an urban, predominantly non-Indigneous school district and a predominantly white institution of higher education in the state of North Dakota creates challenges for designing and implementing professional development directly related to advancing the interests of Indigenous families and communities. In North Dakota, Indigenous students make up 10% of the student population compared to 1% of the nation's student population (Rafa, 2016). In Bismarck Public Schools (BPS), 10% of students are Indigenous, and at Bismarck High School (BHS), 14% of students are Indigenous. BHS is considered a "low-density public school" (Rafa, 2016, p. 2) with less than 25% of students being Indigenous. BHS data confirms the disparity between our Indigenous students and other demographics: graduation rates, academic proficiency, discipline, representation in advanced classes versus remedial classes, chronic absenteeism, grade point average, credit loss, participation in extracurriculars, graduating college-ready, and participation in career and technical classes. Anecdotal evidence from BHS further exemplifies this: the lack of laughter and joy on Indigenous students' faces, especially in the classroom and when interacting with teachers and administrators, and one student's essay on *To Kill a Mockingbird* commenting on the need to "be white" and "act civilized" when he enters the classroom. Within a national context of standardization and accountability (Mackey, 2017), BHS will need to be deliberate in disrupting these inequities in service of Indigenous self-determination.

RESISTANCE AND SURVIVANCE

Historically, policies developed under federal Indian law frameworks served to eradicate or assimilate Indigenous peoples. Although "Indigenous education existed prior to European contact" (Pewewardy et al., 2018, p. 38), early treaties called for the U.S. government to provide for Indian education. Over time, this federal trust responsibility resulted in the U.S. government establishing boarding schools. The aim of these boarding schools was to erase culture and language through acculturation, assimilation, and removal from family and community (Bureau of Indian Education [BIE], n.d.; Meza, 2015). Most significantly, "Indian children faced a different form of segregation—a segregation from themselves" (Baca, 2004, p. 1166). The Indian Reorganization Act (1934) shifted the assimilation model to reflect self-determination as the greater purpose for Native schooling (BIE, n.d.). It also established the formal responsibility for states to provide public education for Indigenous students (Mackey, 2017). The Indian Self-Determination and Assistance in Education Act of 1975 further strengthened the role of public schools to better meet the cultural needs of Indigenous students (Mackey, 2017). Although there has been movement away from a blatant acculturation and assimilation model for Indian Education, the past century of educational experiences enacted through federal policy have historically been a weapon against Indigenous youth and communities (Mackey, 2017).

Movement from assimilation to self-determination in the form of resistance and survivance can be framed through Tribal Critical Race Theory (TribalCrit). Brayboy (2005) constructed TribalCrit theory on the foundation of Critical Race Theory. Critical Race Theory applies the role of race, its social construction, and its persistence by "recognizing the experiential knowledge of people of color" (Pewewardy et al., 2018, p. 48). Central to TribalCrit is the influence of colonization in shaping the relationship between dominant U.S. society and Indigenous peoples (Mackey, 2017). Indigenous Postcolonial Theory extends TribalCrit to include "decolonizing the mind" and "consciousness-raising" (Pewewardy et al., 2018, p. 47). This then "provides us the opportunity to question our understanding of power, knowledge, and truth" (Mackey, 2017, p. 790) and "moves toward a postcolonial future that is not yet known or understood" (Pewewardy et al., 2018, p. 47). This is where possibility and hope move us into action to do better by our Indigenous students than we have for the past centuries.

PROFESSIONAL LEARNING FOR INDIGENOUS STUDENT SUCCESS

At Bismarck High School, we are working to improve educational equity for self-determination of Indigenous students through our Indigenous Student Success Cohort. The need for the cohort arises from the disparity in educational outcomes and the unique cultural needs of our Indigenous students. Since "72% of Americans rarely encounter or receive information about Native Americans" (NCAI, 2019, p. 8), the latter is highly likely for BHS educators serving Indigenous youth. This then further perpetuates the invisibility of Indigenous peoples, affecting both Indigenous and non-Indigenous students and communities.

As educational leaders designing professional learning of this cohort, we recognize that the work of disrupting inequities is multifaceted in addressing deep rooted practices, beliefs, relationships, and school cultures that stem from the historical purpose of acculturation and assimilation of Indigenous students. For this reason, the cohort was comprised of more than 20 BHS educators, including teachers from every discipline, specialists, two social workers, school psychologist, family liaison, aides, district Indian Education director, counselor, instructional coach, and every administrator. Of the 33 participants, 11 identified as Indigenous while 22 identified as non-Indigenous. The educators invited to this cohort were intentionally selected based on both our Indigenous students' perceptions of them and these educators' previous advocacy. We chose to make participation invitational instead of voluntary because we recognize that this work required educators to engage in self-examination and reflection related to issues of race, colonialism, and equity. The cohort was a space for like-minded educators to come together in a safe space as a critically conscious study group seeking to "grow and develop one's consciousness" (Pewewardy et al., 2018, p. 61).

One part of the cohort's work is to better understand our district's mission—"empower every learner to thrive"—in relation to our Indigenous students. Because of the *unique obligation* BHS has to the self-determination of our Indigenous students and communities, *thrive* cannot mean acculturate and assimilate. We need to learn from Indigenous students and families what they want thriving and self-determination to look like as a result of a BHS education. The first question we asked ourselves was, "Is Bismarck High School worthy of our families' trust?"

To build trust, we had to first do our own self-examination and reflection related to our beliefs, biases, and behaviors, so when we collaborate in the future with students and families we can show up to listen and learn because "theory [is]derived from their stories [and] must be connected [to practice] in deep and explicit ways" (Brayboy, 2005, p. 430). The first part—self-examination—and the second part—listening—will require us to recognize and critically examine the systemic racism, colonialism, and white supremacy perpetuated by our school system (Pewewardy et al., 2018).

Another part of the cohort's work was to examine our collective and individual pedagogy. Educators too often do not consider the education of Indigenous youth prior to colonization, but we can move toward a more Indigenized pedagogy grounded in self-determination by utilizing an historical Indian education framework of holistic, social, relational, and experiential learning centered on an individual responsibility to the good of the community (Pewewardy et al., 2018).

As our cohort addressed how we teach, we also addressed what we teach. Bringing in Indigenous culture is a priority for Tribal communities. North Dakota legislation and the Native American Essential Understandings framework developed in partnership with the North Dakota Department of Public Instruction (n.d.) and Elders from North Dakota tribes contain no requirements to teach any content not already included in the North Dakota history standards. This makes it highly likely that Indigenous history, contemporary issues, and accomplishments are invisible in our curriculum and the curriculum of earlier schooling. In studies of other states with policy in place that allowed Indigenous students to see themselves in the curriculum, "students were able to transcend expectations by making connections from their heritage to the lessons in their textbook" (Meza, 2015, p. 364). Building a pedagogy on "collective engagement, critical thinking, healing, and cultural restoration" (Pewewardy et al., 2018, p. 38) can foster self-determination and engage Indigenous students in their own processes of decolonization.

As an educator, raising the visibility of a people who have been historically marginalized will require vulnerable self-examination and reflection because "efforts of decolonization seek a reality that does not yet exist, and educators must experiment within the current colonial system to dream a better future" (Pewewardy et al., 2018, p. 85). Our cohort was largely in the additive stage of Indigenous Transformational Praxis, which is framed upon Indigenous Postcolonial Theory. In the additive stage, we are working to decolonize ourselves but not yet enacting deep changes in pedagogy (Pewewardy et al., 2018). As this cohort, in collaboration with Indigenous students and families, dreams a better future and enacts a holistic and liberatory pedagogy, our hope is to expand our work and mentor other BHS and BPS educators in this work of centering students' and families' voices, increasing our own critical reflection, and creating an empowering pedagogy that fosters the self-determination for Indigenous students to thrive in service of Tribal sovereignty.

REFLECTION FROM THE COHORT EXPERIENCE

Increased state-level control over Indian education has placed increased responsibility on local school districts to engage in work intended to advance educational outcomes for Native students. "Educational leaders in schools serving American Indian and Alaska Native students have good reason to concern themselves with Tribal self-determination and implication for shifts in authority over Indian education" (Mackey, 2017, p. 784) due to state legislatures affirming time and again their reluctance to mandate meaningful reform to state educational standards. This has become evident with the 2021 North Dakota Legislature recently passing S.B. 2304 (2021), a bill that, while mandating schools teach about North Dakota Tribal histories, is largely symbolic due to the existing 4th- and 8th-grade social studies standards already including North Dakota history. In essence, school districts already meet the minimum threshold for compliance without changing content or pedagogy. The complex hierarchy between federal, state, local, and Tribal education departments does not necessarily privilege Indigenous visions for education. Too often experiences and stories of Indigenous peoples are not deemed as valuable data sources to drive theory and change (Brayboy, 2005). When reflecting about co-leading the Indigenous Student Success Cohort, Melissa shared:

> My spark was knowing the data at Bismarck High School and the disparities between different demographics, but I think there was a really interesting combination of things that led finally to taking action to better serve our Indigenous students: Sashay, now our Indian Education Director, and her colleague had presented to our staff a month before the pandemic shutdown; a few of us were on the Bismarck-Mandan Team of Champions for the

North Dakota Native American Essential Understandings; we had started an English Learners team to better serve our English Learners; and we had a strong grasp on how to foster collective teacher efficacy for schoolwide improvement efforts. So, during our fall data review, a counselor asked the perfect question: "Why don't we have a team like the EL team but for our Indigenous students?" This led to my collaboration with Sashay to create a team, our Indigenous Student Success Cohort, that would learn together, become leaders together, and grow schoolwide the passion, understanding, and capacity to do better for Indigenous students. Ultimately, I think we felt hope and saw clarity with how to actually approach this work.

I've heard that 1 hour of professional learning requires 2 hours of preparation; that's nowhere near the amount of preparation Sashay and I have had to do together. There's no tidy list to capture our preparation and collaboration, but it consists of two parts. First, it's a big mind-dump that is responsive to student evidence, previous cohort sessions, all the pieces of this complex work, and what she and I are currently learning. From this, we find the next step for this cohort and plan how to facilitate it. We're intentional about the space we wanted to create—a safe-enough space, a brave space—and how to create it. When we facilitate, we determine who will take which parts and why, who will walk the room, or who needs to be in a certain conversation. We've also just begun doing immediate writing and reflection sessions. All of this has to also be communicated to and supported by our school and district leadership, so Sashay and I navigate those conversations, pulling each other in as needed.

In our partnership, Sashay and I offer two complementary lenses. We're both passionate about equity, so we both bring different things we're learning to the table. With this Sashay also brings the lens of the lived experience and her area of scholarship, and I bring the lens of the educational system. Sashay then brings the unique expertise of Indigenous cultures, Indigenous students and families, Indigenous ways of knowing, Indigenous values, and current issues Indigenous students face in Bismarck and across the state. I bring the Bismarck High School lens—what I know about my educators to make this professional learning effective, and the instructional coach lens— what I know about adult learning and professional collaboration to make this time together work for us. I don't know if this work would be as effective as it currently is if it weren't for our unique lenses and shared passionate commitment.

The Indigenous Student Success Cohort provided all participants the opportunity to familiarize themselves with the various responsibilities associated with implementing a state law designed to increase Indigenous representation within district curricula. The structure and design of the cohort provides space to co-create meaningful professional development between Indigenous and non-Indigenous leaders and participants that prioritizes Indigenous voices, leading to tangible changes within the school district.

CONCLUSION: CONNECTING INDIGENOUS STORIES TO LIBERATION

The space we created is one of the strongest components of this project. We cannot move equity work forward with predominantly white teachers, administrators, counselors, and other school staff if we are not also engaging each other in the vulnerable internal work of checking our biases, understanding our identities and the privileges it might afford us, recognizing the colonizing white supremacist educational systems, and thus BHS, are built on and perpetuate. Change needs to happen at three different levels: participants' beliefs level, the relationships and power dynamics between leaders, teachers, and staff, and the very concrete level of behaviors, resources, and policy.

If given the opportunity to go back to the start of this cohort, there are first a few small, concrete revisions we would make. We would be more intentional with setting regular dates for this group to meet. We began with formal monthly meetings for the large group and engaged in debriefing with one another on a weekly basis. The next round would benefit from weekly discussions with participants as well. We would also include the BHS family liaison in more of the planning sessions. Similarly, we would seek out administration feedback on a regular basis—we need to grow our leaders as much as everyone else. For some of the larger revisions, we would be more intentional about including students' and families' voices to inform this work; we need to be very mindful and deliberate in the best way to build that partnership, yet we cannot move further ahead without incorporating their direct input.

In planning the professional learning of this cohort, we recognized that the work of disrupting inequities is multifaceted in addressing deep-rooted practices, beliefs, relationships, and school culture that stem from the historical purpose of acculturation and assimilation of Indigenous students. For this reason, the cohort was comprised of more than 30 educators across different roles in BPS: teachers from every discipline, specialists, social workers, school psychologist, family liaisons from our school and our feeder middle school, aides, district Indian Education director, counselor, instructional coach, and every administrator. It was important that every Indigenous educator in the building was invited, and this has since grown to include district cultural liaisons. As a result, Indigenous students at BHS now have a cohort of educators and administrators who are far more familiar with the needs of Indigenous families, strengthening the relationships and providing a foundation for trust.

Adult learning theory needs to make space for Indigenous epistemology, so educators can begin to experience how learning might shift as a result. Learning is relational and experiential, so we made space for sharing stories. Learning is cyclical, so we made this learning happen regularly to continually expand on previous learning. Learning is spiritual, so we brought in prayer, quotes about community, and reflection on the self as indomitable. There is a reciprocity in relationships, so we shared how we were right there with them as learners co-constructing meaning. Knowledge is not finite and concrete, so we talked about this journey we are all on, the inner work of understanding our current world and how to disrupt the power, oppressions, colonization, injustices, and harm systemic to our society.

NOTES

1. *Micro-dose* is the term we coined to denote professional development that is short in duration, limited in focus, and occurring on frequent bases to sustain momentum over the course of an academic school year.

2. This chapter begins with the stories of two Indigenous authors then closes with the story of the non-Indigenous author to offer perspective on the ways TIPM works from a non-Indigenous perspective.

REFERENCES

Archibald, J. (2008). *Indigenous storywork: Educating the heart, mind, body, and spirit.* UBC Press.

Baca, L. R. (2005). *Meyers v. Board of Education*: The *Brown v. Board* of Indian Country. *University of Illinois Law Review, 2004,* 1155–1180. https://www.illinoislawreview.org/wp-content/ilr-content/articles/2004/5/Baca.pdf

Bismarck Public Schools. (n.d.). *Indian Education.* Retrieved from https://www.bismarckschools.org/Page/431

Brayboy, B. (2005). Toward a Tribal Critical Race Theory in education. *The Urban Review, 37*(5), 425–446. https://doi.org/10.1007/s11256-005-0018-y

Bureau of Indian Education. (n.d.). *Bureau of Indian Education (BIE) tribally controlled schools.* Retrieved from https://www.bie.edu/topic-page/tribally-controlled-schools

Every Student Succeeds Act, 20 U.S.C. § 6301 (2015).

Indian Country, 18 U.S.C. § 1151 and 40 C.F.R. § 171 (1949).

Indian Reorganization Act, Pub. L 73-383 (1934).

Indian Self-Determination and Assistance in Education Act, Pub. L. 93-638 (1975).

Mackey, H. (2017). The ESSA in Indian Country: Problematizing self-determination through the relationships between federal, state, and tribal governments. *Educational Administration Quarterly, 53*(5), 782–808. https://doi.org/10.1177/0013161X17735870

Mackey, H. J., Luecke, D., Robinson, J., Biggane, E., & Rino, R. (2021). Partnership through story: Promising practices for meaningful research. *Tribal College Journal, 33*(2). https://tribalcollegejournal.org/partnership-through-story-promising-practices-for-meaningful-research/

Meza, N. (2015). Indian education: Maintaining Tribal sovereignty through Native American from culture and language preservation. *Brigham Young University Education and Law Journal, 2015*(1), 353–366. https://digitalcommons.law.byu.edu/elj/vol2015/iss1/12

National Congress of American Indians. (2019). *Becoming visible: A landscape analysis of state efforts to provide Native American education for all.* https://www.ncai.org/policy-research-center/research-data/prc-publications/NCAI-Becoming_Visible_Report-Digital_FINAL_10_2019.pdf

North Dakota Department of Public Instruction. (n.d.). *Teachings of our elders.* https://teachingsofourelders.org/

Pewewardy, C. D., Lees, A., & Clark-Shim, H. (2018). The Transformational Indigenous Praxis Model: Stages for developing critical consciousness in Indigenous education. *Wíčazo Ša Review, 33*(1), 38–69. https://doi.org/10.5749/wicazosareview.33.1.0038

Rafa, A. (2016). State and federal policy: Native American youth [Policy brief]. Education Commission of the States. https://www.ecs.org/wp-content/uploads/State_and_Federal_Policy_for_Native_American_Youth.pdf

S.B. 2304, 77th Legislative Assembly, 2021 Reg. Sess. (N.D. 2021). https://www.legis.nd.gov/assembly/67-2021/documents/21-1054-03000.pdf

CHAPTER 14

Set the Prairie on Fire

Confronting Colonial Entanglements Through
Autoethnographic Ribbon Work

Alex RedCorn (ꜧʌꝫʌꝫɑ /Osage)

INTRODUCTION

Here I am, an Osage teacher who became an education leadership academic, reflecting back on my time in the classroom as a teacher before going back to graduate school.

I felt

disconnected.

I was a social studies teacher in the 'burbs. I enjoyed my job. I loved working with high school students, and I loved education as a field of study and profession.

I still do.

But I just felt

disconnected.

I was doing the work I felt was important—education, trying to make the world a better place—but I felt like my job was actually pulling me further away. It was like I was on some sort of assimilationist moving sidewalk powered by status quos put in motion long ago, headed in a linear path away from Osage Elders and knowledges.

I wanted off.

Upon entering academia, I was looking to strengthen my connection as a professional to my Indigeneity, a shift from social studies curriculum and instruction towards better understanding Indigenous perspectives in our educational systems through the lens of educational leadership. At the time, I thought I was "walking in two worlds"—at least those were the words I used when applying to my Educational Leadership doctoral program. On that application I also emphasized how "sometimes when looking through both lenses at the same time, things don't make sense." So, I entered that doctoral program looking for answers, at a land grant university on the prairies of Kansas; land that was founded using wealth accrued from the removal of the Kaw (Lee & Ahtone, 2020)—Dhegiha Siouan relatives of the 𐓷𐓘𐓻𐓘𐓻𐓟 (Osage). A settler-colonial entanglement, indeed, although at the time I didn't have the critical lexicon to name and explain my context. Regardless, my professional world as a social studies educator wasn't in line with my 𐓷𐓘𐓻𐓘𐓻𐓟 sensibilities.

I needed something more, and I knew I needed to better understand

what Eurocentric schools

had failed to teach me.

Yet, there I was, grasping for the elusive understanding of my own socio-cultural positionality as an educator, applying to said land grant institution hoping to repair something, or maybe find something.

Although, still,

I wasn't sure exactly what.

Thankfully, what I found in that program were critical scholar allies who connected me to an Indigenous academic network which would provide me with a tool kit to name and explain that moving sidewalk—phrases such as whitestream institutions, assimilationist education, settler colonialism, cognitive imperialism, dysconscious racism, Red Pedagogy (Grande, 2008), decolonizing and Indigenous methodologies (Kovach, 2010; Smith, 1999), and of course, Transformational Indigenous Praxis (Pewewardy et al., 2018). I was under no illusion when I applied to this predominantly white institution (PWI); I didn't expect to find Native professors or experts in American Indian education—I always figured I'd have to find those academic Elders, aunts, and uncles outside of the program. Or rather, outside of the status quo I'd experienced to that point in my career. But I felt I needed the institution, regardless, if I was to put myself in a position to lead positive change. Mostly I was after the credentials along with the intellectual challenge and personal growth, and the space and time to explore. I also recognized that having "Dr." in front of my name opens up opportunities in our systems, and pursuing principalship was also a possibility as I entered the program. But academia opened up some new opportunities and career pathways to work with Native educators—I couldn't resist.

In all of my academic meanderings, however, a key paragraph from Osage anthropologist Jean Dennison became a spark that eventually turned into a raging prairie fire in my mind—tearing through my dissonant and entangled experiences—making way for change and regrowth in my thinking. It was a restoration of balance. I've cited this passage many times before (Hayman et al., 2018; RedCorn, 2016, 2017, 2019), but it was such a significant moment in my learning that it's worth bringing forward again for others to see in full context. In writing about the Osage constitutional reform process from 2004 to 2006, Dennison (2012) wrote:

> For their part the Osage and all American Indian nations have long understood the colonial process as at once devastating and full of potential. Osage ribbon work, born out of eighteenth-century trade with the French, is perhaps the ideal metaphor of colonial entanglement. Using the raw material and tools obtained from the French, Osage artists began by tearing the rayon taffeta into strips and then cutting, folding, and sowing [sic] it back together to form something both beautiful and uniquely Osage. In picking up the pieces, both those shattered by and created through the colonial process, and weaving them into their own original patterns, Osage artists formed the tangled pieces of colonialism into their own statements of Osage sovereignty. Osage ribbon work reminds us that it is possible to create new and powerful forms out of an ongoing colonial process. (p. 6)

These words burned through my mind. They moved through the entangled overgrowth of my lived experiences as a student and teacher moving across both Osage and settler systems of learning. The regrowth that followed restored balance among the competing knowledge ecosystems embedded into my worldview through educational systems.

charred soil.
from the
emerged

Clarity

I have worn Osage ribbon work my entire life in our ᑕᒪᏬᎦᏂᎷ, so this passage resonated with me the same way the drum grabbed ahold of my soul as a young boy in our dance. When I was a short blonde-haired and blue-eyed kid moving around that drum, surrounded by tall Osage men who look more like the Indians I'd seen in the movies, I was short enough that all of the men's ribbon work suits were close to eye level. As the drum carried hundreds of dancers in that counter-clockwise kaleidoscope of collective cultural synchronicity, I had the privileged opportunity to study the various ribbon work patterns, colors, and variations.

This was my place of Osage education.

Year,   To watch.
   after   Listen.
     year.   Learn.
       With the drum,
           carrying all of us
               forward.

While there are many forms of ribbon work found across Indigenous communities (see Figure 14.1), Osage ribbon work has a certain place in my heart, as it does with other Osages. To be honest, we can be a bit Osage-centric in our opinions about ribbon work, but I see that as a form of pride, in a good way. Osage ribbon work is found on ceremonial clothing and blankets, but it is also found on Osage Nation letterheads, murals, and sculptures in the community, along with tattoos and other personal expressions of art and Osage existence. I even doodled ribbon work designs on the margins of my notebooks and the straps of my backpack in school, while passively listening to Eurocentric lessons from non-Native teachers. Furthermore, Osage ribbon work has a distinct look to it, and there's a commitment to quality amongst Osage artists, yet, there is not a single "correct" way to do it (Powell, 2018). It's up to the artist, and only bound by their imagination in color choices and patterns. This is where the clarity began, as an educational leadership academic fumbling through the dissertation process in search of credentials but finding something much more valuable.

Figure 14.1 Osage Ribbon work on Men's Straight Dance Suit

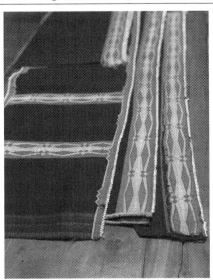

A broadcloth men's straight dance suit (leggings, tail piece, breechcloth) with Osage ribbon work, lying on a cedar chest. This was passed down to me from my grandparents, and while I don't know where they acquired it, it was approximately 30-40 years old when I used it as a teenager and young adult in the ᏁᎶᏍᎭᎯ. As seen in the image, the ribbons are in need of repair from extended use over decades

THE VALUE OF RIBBON WORK IN EDUCATIONAL LEADERSHIP
AND AUTOETHNOGRAPHY

First, given that leaders in training are often implored to engage in systems level thinking, Dennison's words immediately gave me the tools to articulate ribbon work as a framework for examining educational systems. Given that the phrase "Indian Education" in the United States represents a highly complex system of overlapping sovereignties and jurisdictional gray areas, many of which rest on Eurocentric foundations (see RedCorn et al., 2019), there is value in seeing these various bureaucratic systems as various ribbons to be creatively manipulated, analyzed, or reformed as new statements of intellectual sovereignty (Warrior, 1995), as well as political sovereignty.

While I didn't draw a direct connection to ribbon work in my effort to build a working capacity building model for Native Nations in education (see RedCorn, 2020), there is value in merging these two concepts. In that model, I emphasize a broad and dynamic systems thinking approach to leadership that is centered on a Native Nation's cultural and governance systems. After (re)centering, I urge leaders to invoke their intellectual sovereignty by "a) assessing the educational landscape and identifying community assets, b) fostering professional growth across systems, and c) engaging in ongoing systems development and alignment advocacy" (p. 1). If one were to juxtapose ribbon work with this model, the leader's job then is to creatively lead in and across educational systems in a way that reshapes and reforms those systems to meet the intellectual needs of our Native students, families, communities, and nations. This can be done by advocating for change in curricular systems, professional development and educator training programs, law, policy, and more. This form of systems alignment would be a form of *ribbon work leadership* in education, and as a form of leadership "reminds us that it is possible to create new and powerful forms out of an ongoing colonial process" (Dennison, 2012, p. 6).

Second, on a more personal level I was able to see the various threads of my previously compartmentalized lived experiences as autoethnographic ribbons that could be cut, sewn, folded, and stitched back together to represent the narratives of my entangled life. This then becomes a form of narrative inquiry I frame as *ethnographic ribbon work,* which in this specific case is *autoethnographic ribbon work*—exhibited here in this chapter. But in my case as an Osage academic, this simultaneously works as a *prairie fire autoethnography*, with ribbon work serving as the initial spark that allowed me to confront my colonial entanglements.

But with this new clarity, I found myself with a handful of ribbons, and a vision for what I might do with them, but little practice in the art of autoethnographic ribbon work—a process of cutting, sewing, and weaving my own entangled lived experiences with existing literature in educational leadership, Indigenous studies, Indigenous education, and other relevant subfields. In this manner, autoethnographic ribbon work is both the process of stitching these seemingly entangled stories into a coherent discernable pattern, and simultaneously the process of stitching these unique sociocultural and intersectional Indigenous perspectives into the literature. It's an act of pushing back against pan-Indianism and honoring Indigenous diversity and acknowledging the entangled lived realities Indigenous peoples have inherited and making those stories visible. In a way, it's another form of storying Indigenous survivance (Sabzalian, 2019; Vizenor et al., 2014), and making our stories of settler-colonial entanglement visible in the literature.

To this aim, I began the practice of autoethnographically working through these entanglements using writing as method (Richardson & St. Pierre, 2005). As a graduate student, it was like I was a novice attempting to make actual Osage ribbon work for my ᏁᏓᏍᎦᎵ dance clothes, but I was using cheap ribbons, and my pattern was out of balance. My early manuscripts looked like ribbon work I'd be proud of my kids for trying to make, but god bless 'em, I probably wouldn't wear it into our dance, especially on a Saturday night or Sunday. As I tried to make sense of things, I read and re-read Indigenous academics, feeling both excited and over-whelmed, returning to the computer to stitch the words together. Writing feedback ensued—with red markings through track changes in my word processor making my manuscript look like it was some form of digital butcher paper for a buffalo slaughter—blood all over the page, delivering stress and insecurity to my mind. But what I came to realize eventually was that the process was just as important as the product, and that the dissertation was just one more cycle of learning—an ongoing prairie fire—that made it possible for a new cycle to begin.

So, through the anxiety of the dissertation, I eventually came back to the Osage concept of ᏏᎦᏍᎧᎵ, which has been translated to me by Elders as "doing your part and doing the best you can with what you have," and that "nobody can ask anything else of you." I eventually submitted my academic ribbon work, a prairie fire, and prepared for the next cycle of learning—even if from my current vantage point I'd like to lay out some fresh butcher paper and take a red pen to many parts of it.

ARTICULATING PRAIRIE FIRE AUTOETHNOGRAPHIES

When discussing Indigenous Leadership, Pewewardy (2015), who has been a long-time mentor of mine while navigating predominantly white academic spaces, writes, "I believe the first step in becoming self-determined is examining the 'sovereign self'" (p. 71). This is a central component of prairie fire autoethnography, which is a methodological tool for engaging the self using various critical frameworks such as Transformational Indigenous Praxis, and it is a form of Indigenous autoethnography by which I confront(ed) my colonial entanglements in educational systems through the dissertation (RedCorn, 2017). The dissertation became the canvas where I merged process and product through critically reflexive writing, and simultaneously found my critical voice as an educator and novice scholar.

While autoethnography has become a firmly established methodology in the field of qualitative inquiry (see Boylorn & Orbe, 2013; Chang, 2009; Ellis et al., 2011; Holman Jones et al., 2013, among others), there is a more specific group of scholars who are focused on Indigenous forms of autoethnography (Bainbridge,

2007; Bishop, 2020a, 2020b; Francis & Munson, 2017; Houston, 2007; Iosefo, 2018; McIvor, 2010; RedCorn, 2017; Whitinui, 2014). From a Māori perspective, Whitinui (2014) describes how autoethnography is a "culturally informed research practice that is not only explicit to Māori ways of knowing but can be legitimated as an authentic 'Native' method of inquiry" (p. 456). Whitinui explains how Indigenous autoethnography is "grounded within a resistance based discourse," which "aims to address issues of social justice and to develop social change by engaging Indigenous researchers in rediscovering their own voices as 'culturally liberating human-beings'"(p. 1). Bishop (2020b) also emphasizes that "Indigenous autoethnographies cannot and will not be defined or reduced to a checklist. They operate from a different axiology and ontology that does not seek to categorise, classify, or simplify; instead, Indigenous autoethnographies strive to increase complexity" (p. 2). Furthermore, Bishop (2020b) describes how "cultural agency is asserted; bound by obligations to family, communities, Country, Knowledges— 'where storytelling can spiral into a bigger pattern, an interconnectedness that recognises and links together infinite experiences across time and space'" (p. 3, internal citation from Bishop, 2020a). It is within this emerging field of Indigenous autoethnography that I position ribbon work and prairie fire autoethnographies.

Considering the purpose of this kind of work, I look to my major professor Kakali Bhattacharya's (2015) explanation of how she is compelled to "dissolve dualities," and how "external separation of colonized and colonizer reflects the internal division in [her] being" (p. 5). She further explains how the de/colonization project is a form of healing and transformation, and as we take a deep dive into our own consciousness, "such 'home work' is critically necessary before any 'field work' can be accomplished for any social justice agenda; without it, we will only feed and amplify our pain, defeating our transformative desires" (p. 5).

With Bhattacharya's words intersecting with Pewewardy's emphasis on finding the sovereign self—two mentor scholars of mine—I believe Indigenous autoethnography is a tool which can provide clarity for leaders in training, particularly for those pursuing advanced degrees in non-Native institutions. For these emerging Indigenous leaders, knowing that they'll be obtaining shiny graduate degrees and credentials from universities built on stolen Indigenous lands—like I did—it is essential that we set the prairie on fire in our cognitive understandings so that we might make way for a new cycle of growth or change. This is the work of reestablishing balance and health in our world. In other words, we must confront our personal colonial entanglements to better understand our positionality within them, so we will be better prepared to lead in and across the various institutions influencing what, and how, Indigenous students learn. This was my own personal form of Transformational Indigenous Praxis.

My use of prairie fire here is also not intended to forward some overromanticized stereotype of being one with nature, and there is a need to be cognizant of this while engaging in this kind of work. Prairie fire in this context is simply a tool to help us deepen conversations about change, critical thinking, and personal growth cycles. Indigenous students and academics should lean into those core ideas, and feel inspired to take these concepts out of a prairie-specific context and move it to something more relevant to their own place-based contexts and/or metaphors. Also, I'm not forwarding a traditional Osage philosophy passed down to me, but more so working to engage creatively with what Cajete (1994) might call an ecologically informed consciousness. Through this form of ecological thinking, the following are the core components for how I conceptualize prairie fire autoethnographies.

Prairie fire autoethnography is first and foremost an *interrogation of the self*, and a confrontation of colonial entanglements. It is a deep dive into the tensions and confusion we experience as Indigenous peoples living in a modern existence— many of whom simultaneously descend from white settlers, or at minimum, were born into a life where we inherit and negotiate settler-colonial status quo's on a daily basis. Call it a theoretical framework or a methodology, or call it a mindset. It doesn't matter as long as you use it as an organizational tool to give order, purpose, and tone to your dissertation, thesis, or publication in a manner that allows you to also gain a better understanding of the self before acquiring a graduate degree and becoming credentialed for expertise and leadership in settler-colonial systems.

With this in mind, the fire represents critical thinking and reflexive writing through difficult internal tensions and understandings. As the fire spreads through the writing and reflection processes, it can become a powerful force for change and (re)growth of Indigenous ways of thinking and knowing. It is about the process as much as it is about the product. Ultimately, as Indigenous graduate students and academics become leaders in their field through systems of higher education built around settler-colonial ideologies, we then become agents within those systems with various degrees of power and influence. That power and influence can be used in several ways to Indigenize systems of higher education as we explore ways to rework the academy (or work outside of it) to more appropriately serve Native peoples and nations. However, that power and influence can also be naively used to replicate systems of assimilation and continue to cause harm to Native peoples and nations. Indigenous academics who haven't confronted their personal entanglements with settler colonialism run the risk of doing harm with the intent of trying to do something good. This is why prairie fire autoethnographies prioritize the interrogation of the self, in hopes of finding Pewewardy's notion of the sovereign self, most often rooted in knowledge and experiences found outside of settler-colonial systems of education.

Second, prairie fire autoethnographies *commit to the work of unpacking the complexity of Indigenous lived experiences while entangled in settler-colonial realities*. In other words, there must be attention given to nuanced sociocultural complexity. The prairie's deep-rooted ecosystem represents the diversity of knowledge, ideas, and understanding that feed our thinking and actions—while the tallgrass from afar can appear to represent homogeneity, a closer look and examination reveals nuanced diversity, movement, and connectedness among the various parts of an ecosystem. With some species of tallgrass prairie, the roots go 8–14 feet deep into the soil, which prompts me to reflect on the knowledge passed down through our Ancestors. However, we must consider how all of the biodiversity in any ecosystem has an element of competition for sun, water, nutrients in the soil, and so forth, and that competing knowledges are always present in our ongoing learning. But this reminds us that what is deep beneath the soil is still part of that system, even when we can't see what's going on in the subsoil without deep excavation of some kind. Indigenous autoethnography, in some ways, is exploring the whole knowledge ecosystem in which you reside—and all of its diversity—and sometimes that requires a deeper excavation of some parts more than others. Through the process of excavating personal and communal stories, memories, data, and artifacts through reflexive writing and analysis, we may not know exactly what we're looking for or what we will find. It might simply be that we are looking for clarity to some degree—but it is the process of confrontation by reflexively writing and analyzing those nuances that allows us to restore balance through an improved understanding of the self.

This is why the third component of prairie fire autoethnographies is focused on *restoration of balance*. Like any ecosystem, there are ways that it can become imbalanced, and invasive species can threaten the health of that system. For the prairie, fire is a tool for maintaining that balance; sometimes this happens through natural causes, sometimes through a prescribed burn for ongoing maintenance. For the purposes of prairie fire autoethnographies, balance can be restored by finding some degree of clarity, as clarity represents a new cycle of (re)growth after the fire burns through. Writing through one's entanglements then represents a form of replenishment to our personal ecosystems of knowledge and understanding.

CONCLUSION: LEADING THROUGH CHANGE

As leaders in Indigenous education, we must recognize that we have all inherited an entangled settler-colonial reality, and the process of creating positive change for our Indigenous students is a lifelong endeavor in Transformational Indigenous Praxis. It will never end, at least not in our lifetimes. However, we must also recognize that if we cannot confront these personal entanglements, particularly in educational systems, and better understand how they manifest in our lived experiences

then how can we expect to lead through these entanglements
for our relatives?
So they might
experience growth

For a new cycle of learning.

REFERENCES

Bainbridge, R. (2007). Autoethnography in Indigenous research contexts: The value of inner knowing. *Journal of Australian Indigenous Issues, 10*(2), 54–64.

Bhattacharya, K. (2015). Diving deep into oppositional beliefs: Healing the wounded transnational, de/colonizing warrior within. *Cultural Studies ↔ Critical Methodologies, 15*(6), 492–500. https://doi.org/10.1177/1532708615614019

Bishop, M. (2020a). Epistemological violence and Indigenous autoethnographies. In P. Stanley (Ed.), *Critical Autoethnography and Intercultural Learning: Emerging Voices* (p. 192). Routledge. https://doi.org/10.4324/9780429280016-2

Bishop, M. (2020b). "Don't tell me what to do" encountering colonialism in the academy and pushing back with Indigenous autoethnography. *International Journal of Qualitative Studies in Education, 34*(5), 367–378. https://doi.org/10.1080/09518398.2020.1761475

Boylorn, R. M., & Orbe, M. P. (2013). *Critical autoethnography: Intersecting cultural identities in everyday life*. Left Coast Press.

Cajete, G. (1994). *Look to the mountain: An ecology of Indigenous education* (1st ed.). Kivaki Press.

Chang, H. (2009). *Autoethnography as method*. Left Coast Press.

Dennison, J. (2012). *Colonial entanglement: Constituting a twenty-first century Osage Nation*. University of North Carolina Press.

Ellis, C., Adams, T. E., & Bochner, A. P. (2011). Autoethnography: An overview. *Forum Qualitative Sozialforschung / Forum: Qualitative Social Research, 12*(1). http://www.qualitative-research.net/index.php/fqs/article/view/1589

Francis, L. I., & Munson, M. M. (2017). We help each other up: Indigenous scholarship, survivance, tribalography, and sovereign activism. *International Journal of Qualitative Studies in Education, 30*(1), 48–57. https://doi.org/10.1080/09518398.2016.1242807

Grande, S. (2008). Red pedagogy: The un-methodology. In Norman K. Denzin, Y. S. Lincoln, & L. T. Smith (Eds.), *Handbook of critical and Indigenous methodologies* (pp. 233–254). Sage.

Hayman, J., RedCorn, A., & Zacharakis, J. (2018). New horizons in the Osage Nation: Agricultural education and leadership development. *Journal of Research in Rural Education, 34*(5), 1–10.

Holman Jones, S., Adams, T. E., & Ellis, C. (Eds.). (2013). *Handbook of autoethnography*. Routledge.

Houston, J. (2007). Indigenous autoethnography: Formulating our knowledge our way. *The Australian Journal of Indigenous Education, 36*(S1), 45–50. https://doi.org/10.1017/S1326011100004695

Iosefo, F. (2018). Scene, seen, unseen. In P. Stanley & G. Vass (Eds.), *Questions of culture in autoethnography* (pp. 56–64). Routledge.

Kovach, M. (2010). *Indigenous methodologies: Characteristics, conversations, and contexts* (Reprint edition). University of Toronto Press, Scholarly Publishing Division.

Lee, R., & Ahtone, T. (2020, March 30). Land-grab universities. *High Country News*. https://www.hcn.org/issues/52.4/indigenous-affairs-education-land-grab-universities

McIvor, O. (2010). I am my subject: Blending Indigenous research methodology and autoethnography through integrity-based, spirit based research. *Canadian Journal of Native Education, 33*(1), 137.

Pewewardy, C. D. (2015). Indigenous leadership. In *Indigenous leadership in higher education* (pp. 70–79). Routledge.

Pewewardy, C. D., Lees, A., & Clark-Shim, H. (2018). The Transformational Indigenous Praxis Model: Stages for developing critical consciousness in Indigenous education. *Wíčazo Ša Review, 33*(1), 38–69. https://doi.org/10.5749/wicazosareview.33.1.0038

Powell, Jami. (2018). *Creating an Osage future: Art, resistance, and self-representation* [Doctoral Dissertation, University of North Carolina at Chapel Hill]. https://cdr.lib.unc.edu/concern/dissertations/t148fh339

RedCorn, A. (2016). Stitching a new pattern in educational leadership: Reinterpreting a university partnership academy model for Native Nations. *Educational Considerations, 43*(4), 60–69.

RedCorn, A. (2019). Considerations for building a prosperous and self-determining Osage Nation through education. *Journal of Cases in Educational Leadership*. https://doi .org/10.1177/1555458919831339

RedCorn, A., McCoy, M., & Mackey, H. J. (2019). Indian country. In D. C. Thompson, R. C. Wood, S. C. Neuenswander, J. M. Heim, & R. D. Watson (Eds.), *Funding public schools in the United States and Indian country* (pp. 211–247). Information Age Publishing.

RedCorn, S. A. (2017). *Set the prairie on fire: An autoethnographic confrontation of colonial entanglements* [Doctoral Dissertation, Kansas State University]. https://krex.k-state.edu/dspace /handle/2097/36214

Richardson, L., & St. Pierre, E. A. (2005). Writing: A method of inquiry. In N. K. Denzin & Y. S. Lincoln (Eds.), *The Sage handbook of qualitative research* (3rd ed., pp. 959–978). Sage Publications.

Sabzalian, L. (2019). *Indigenous children's survivance in public schools*. Routledge. https:// www.routledge.com/Indigenous-Childrens-Survivance-in-Public-Schools/Sabzalian/p /book/9781138384507

Smith, L. T. (1999). *Decolonizing methodologies: Research and indigenous peoples*. Zed Books; Dunedin, NZ.

Vizenor, G., Tuck, E., & Yang, K. W. (2014). Resistance in the blood. In E. Tuck & K. W. Yang (Eds.), *Youth resistance research and theories of change* (pp. 107–117). Routledge.

Warrior, R. Allen. (1995). *Tribal secrets: Recovering American Indian intellectual traditions*. University of Minnesota Press.

Whitinui, P. (2014). Indigenous autoethnography exploring, engaging, and experiencing "self" as a Native method of inquiry. *Journal of Contemporary Ethnography, 43*(4), 456–487. https:// doi.org/10.1177/0891241613508148

Native Educational Sovereignty in Teaching and Leadership (NESTL)

The Transformation of Leadership Utilizing a Holistic Corn Pollen Model to Serve All Students at a Research University

Shawn Secatero (Canoncito Band of Navajo)

INTRODUCTION

Yaa'at'eeh Shi Dine', Shi ei Dr. Shawn Secatero dashijini'. Tohajiileehedi' naasha'. Tabaaha' nishlo' doo' Naakai'i Dine'e ba' shishchiin. Da' shi chei' ei Ashiihi' nili, doo shinali' eiya' Tlaashchiihi nili'. Tohajiileehe' aldo kedahwaht'i.

Greetings my people. I am Dr. Shawn Secatero and I am from Tohajiileehe', New Mexico. I am a member of the Water's Edge people and born for the Latino people. My grandfather belongs to the Salt clan and my maternal grandmother belongs to the Red Bottom Canyon people. They also reside in Tohajiileehe'.

In this chapter, I will provide a personal narrative of my own leadership path and my continued work with the highly successful POLLEN (Promoting Our Leadership, Learning and Empowering our Nations) cohort at the University of New Mexico that prepares advanced Indigenous teachers to pursue school administrative licensure with an educational specialist certificate. Furthermore, an objective of this chapter is to describe my journey of establishing transformational leadership and social action by creating a leadership center entitled the Native Educational Sovereignty in Teaching and Leadership (NESTL) Center at the University of New Mexico's College of Education and Human Sciences.

I will delve further into my analysis by honoring and integrating the Transformational Indigenous Praxis Model (TIPM) approach by Pewewardy et al. (2018). This chapter will align each of the model dimensions of creating the NESTL center including the contributions, additive, transformation, and social action approaches. Furthermore, I will provide additional implications and promising leadership practices from our Indigenous-based POLLEN program, which incorporates holistic-based Native educational leadership concepts into curriculum, internship, and coursework while fulfilling university, state, and national leadership competencies.

The key factors in addressing the purpose of creating the UNM Native Educational Sovereignty in Teaching and Leadership (NESTL) serve as our research-inquiry questions in our university and in our Tribal Nations:

1. Why are there a limited number of Native teachers pursuing educational leadership programs to become principals?
2. Are university-based school administrator programs recruiting potential Native teachers to become school leaders through pathway programs?
3. How can we effectively transform our Native leadership programs through the Transformational Indigenous Praxis Model (TIPM) or other holistic based models that address decolonization and Indigenization practices?

These questions also serve as my own vision to aspire toward along my journey of becoming a well-respected holistic leader and educator in my community, tribe, and nation.

MY LEADERSHIP PERSPECTIVE AND EXPERIENCE

As a Navajo student attending a Bureau of Indian Affairs (BIA) school, I often wondered why there were no Navajo school administrators or principals employed in our school system. Upon reflecting on my primary-school experience, I wanted to do more for my students and community so I went back to school to earn my master's degree in secondary education.

Eventually, I gained acceptance into the University of New Mexico's Educational Leadership Licensure program and earned an educational specialist degree to become a licensed school principal. The leadership curriculum focused on state competencies and intensive leadership research; there was limited content in Indigenous based leadership practices. There were no Indigenous instructors in the leadership program. I did complete the program but felt unprepared to lead a Native-serving school, especially in regards to fulfilling Bureau of Indian Education policies and standards. As part of my leadership path, I was able to secure leadership positions as a director of Bilingual Education and School-to-Work programs in my own Tribal school and Albuquerque Public Schools Indian Education Unit. After reflecting upon these valuable work experiences, I felt the need to continue my education and pursued doctoral studies at the University of New Mexico's College of Education in 1997 and finished my dissertation study, "Beneath Our Sacred Minds, Hands and Hearts: Stories of Persistence and Success among American Indian Graduate Students" (Secatero, 2009). My dissertation study inspired me to develop the Corn Pollen Model to help future school leaders and principals as an Indigenized framework for leadership and to incorporate the TIPM to advance social justice in our schools.

As I reflect on my current position as tenured associate professor, I envision transformational change in preparing Indigenous school leaders and administrators by using the Transformational Indigenous Praxis Model (Pewewardy et al., 2018) which addresses my knowledge base and growth as an educator through the various approaches of the contributions, additive, transformation, and social action approaches.

PURPOSE

Native American school leaders and administrators serve as essential transformational change agents in the lives of our Native American children and Tribal communities by providing effective teaching, learning, and leading for their students and staff members. The well-prepared Native school principal sets the overall leadership environment of the school and effectively collaborates with all education agencies and Tribal entities to ensure that Native students are receiving an equitable education. I was dismayed with the small numbers of Native American licensed principals in our state and decided to delve further into addressing this shortage.

In my research of identifying the latest statistics for Native American principals working in Bureau of Indian Education schools and state-funded public schools, few demographics exist, especially in federally funded schools. According to New Mexico Public Education Department (NMPED) statistics, Native American principals leading our public school districts account for less than 2%, as compared to the overall Native American population that represents 12% of our state population (NMPED, 2019).

In terms of nationwide statistics, the National Center for Education Statistics (NCES) reports that Native American principals constitute less than 1% in serving public schools (Taie & Goldring, 2019). Currently, the NCES reports that there are 90,900 school principals, of which 46% identify as male and 54% identify as female. Educational attainment of school principals varies at different educational levels as 62% possess a master's degree, 26% have earned an educational specialist certificate, and 11% have earned doctorate degrees. Furthermore, the NCES identifies the ethnic background of school principals as 78% white, 11% African American, 8% Hispanic, and 1% as Asian or Native American.

Faircloth and Tippeconnic (2015) conducted studies in regards to the historical background of Native school administrator training programs, which began to evolve during the 1970s with several university training programs such as Pennsylvania State University, Arizona State, Harvard, and the University of Minnesota. Faircloth and Tippeconnic (2015) posit that school leadership training programs were based on historical authoritative school leadership-style training of principals such as "Planning, maximizing, and controlling" (p. 128) all aspects of school operations including staffing, curriculum, and budgets. They further suggest that university-based leadership programs offer Indigenous-based knowledge, research, and other leadership paradigms to counteract colonial thinking for rising school leaders and principals. These transformational leadership practices are much needed in today's Native-serving schools, as I will explain within the context of my own praxis and research through the TIPM that embarks on the contributions, additive, transformational, and social action approaches.

Contributions Phase

Pewewardy et al. suggest in their TIPM, "The initial dimension of the TIPM portrays experiences of educators who have not yet developed their consciousness to critically examine school structure and curriculum content" (p. 4, this volume). My research, teaching, and service as an Assistant Professor was just beginning to evolve to challenge mainstream leadership practices and ideologies. The majority of my educational leadership graduate students never experienced the teachings of an Indigenous professor, which correlates to a new style of pedagogy that encapsulates a holistic approach toward leadership. When I began to teach my first doctorate-level class, I did face incidents of resistance from a few non-Indigenous students who did not fully understand the concepts of holistic leadership and its connections to spiritual, mental, physical, and social well-being attributes. According to Cross (1997), "The linear worldview is rooted in European and mainstream American thought. It's very temporal, and it is firmly rooted in the logic that says cause has to come before effect. In contrast, the relational worldview sees life as harmonious relationships where health is achieved by maintaining balance between the many interrelating factors in one's circle of life" (p. 6). The majority of my students were not accustomed to thinking about the various connections of leadership and learning through a holistic lens. Dhiman (2019) posits holistic leadership as, "A voyage of inner discovery which begins with self-knowledge and culminates in living one's deepest values at the personal, team, and organizational level and effective leaders holistically engage the mind, body, heart, soul, and spirit of those whom they lead" (p. 6).

As an untenured professor, I utilized mainstream leadership anthologies that highlighted exemplary Anglo male biographies of leadership practices. Many of my graduate students were accustomed to reading mainstream society books about successful white male leaders. However, I wanted to take a new Indigenized approach to teaching, rather than utilizing mainstream colonization reading and learning materials. As part of my leadership pedagogy, I embraced self-reflection and reflexivity in praxis and had my students learn about themselves through purpose, critical thinking, self-care, and creating professional relationships. The UNM Educational Leadership Program faculty provided a W.K. Kellogg grant to increase the number of Native School principals in New Mexico, which provided the opportunity to create a cohort-based teacher to school leader pathway program entitled, "Promoting Our Leadership, Learning, and Empowering our Nations" (POLLEN) in 2016, which embeds Indigenous leadership curriculum into administrative licensure courses. We accepted our first cohort of 13 teachers, who all completed their studies in an accelerated hybrid model of coursework. Through active collaborative efforts with colleagues, I created an Indigenized leadership curriculum guide referred to as the Corn Pollen Model, or "Naadaa' Baa Hane." The components of this holistic model are inspired through the teachings of my Navajo Elders to examine and practice the essential elements of spiritual, mental, physical, and social well-being attributes (Secatero, 2009; see Figure 15.1).

Corn Pollen Model. The planting of the Corn Pollen model began in 1997 as my doctoral student journey of discovery at the University of New Mexico. I conducted brief interviews with my local traditional Elders on Navajo epistemology and well-being. Their valuable contributions focused on the symbolic nature of corn and its connections to the spiritual, mental, physical, and social well-being pillars. In my research quest, I was limited in finding Native American based educational leadership models or research articles to finish my dissertation study. I could only find a few articles and research studies that began my qualitative research study. I strengthened my study as 23 Native American participants shared their graduate success stories to highlight their pathway of persistence and success. I also integrated the four main pillars of the Corn Pollen Model to guide my dissertation study and it continues to guide me presently (see Figure 15.2).

Figure 15.1. Corn Pollen Model With Four Main Well-Being Pillars

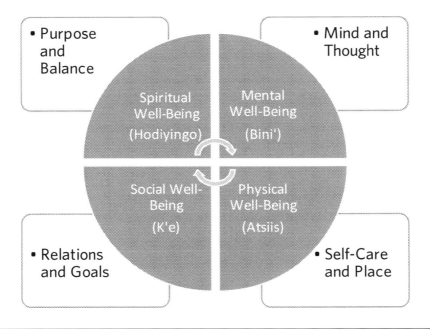

Source: Reprinted with permission from Secatero (2009).

Figure 15.2. Corn Pollen Model Developmental Stages

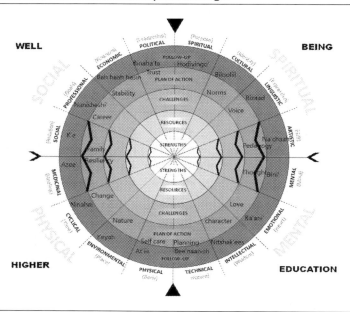

Source: Reprinted with permission from Secatero (in press).

The sacred symbol of corn in Navajo cultural lifeways serves as a holistic symbol of success for all students in education, well-being, and leadership. The symbolic roots of the corn, also called Naadaa' bi'keloo, serve as our spiritual connections to the earth through cultural, linguistic, and artistic well-being. The corn leaves, also referred to as naa'daa' bit'aa, represent our knowledge systems, which correlate to mental well-being. Furthermore, the embedded pillars of emotional, intellectual, and technical well-being pillars further promote the concepts of mindfulness and thinking processes. The corn stalk, also called Naa'daa' Bikaaz, represents our third quadrant, which refers to physical well-being, which relates to self-care and health. This bonding strength of physical well-being refers to additional subpillars, which include environmental, cyclical, and medicinal well-being. Finally, the corn tassel called Naadaa' bi'zool serves as a symbol of our social, professional, economic, and political well-being pillars. These examples of relationships, professional well-being, economics, and political attributes represents a holistic pathway to honoring leadership and education (Secatero et al., 2022).

Additive Approach

The second phase of TIPM concerns the additive approach, which Pewewardy describes as depicting educators "with initial curiosity around settler-colonial educational structures with beginning steps toward change through 'bursts of critical awareness'" (p. 5, this volume). I began to transform my inquiry into leadership and educational studies, which resulted in the birth of the POLLEN (Promoting our Leadership, Learning, and Empowering our Nations) Program, which serves as a highly successful Indigenous-based leadership program at the University of New Mexico. This cohort-based program recognizes the importance of pathways to community and educational leadership, and is designed to increase the number of licensed school administrators serving Native American students throughout the state of New Mexico. The required coursework is specifically designed to prepare future principals to be responsive to the needs of Native communities throughout our state and the Navajo Nation, which spans into Arizona and Utah. Courses are delivered in a blended online/face-to-face format to ensure access to communities throughout the state, and center on Native American leadership, vision, epistemology, and culture in addressing current issues in Native American education.

As an example of connecting the Corn Pollen model to spiritual leadership, I assigned my students to create their own personal definition of leadership along with a mission statement that embraces holistic leadership to praxis. These concepts further involve critical bridging of their cultural, linguistic, and artistic well-being strengths. Another task for my students was to create a leadership symbol for themselves so they too could draw on their strengths, resources, challenges, plan of action, and follow up (see Figure 15.3).

Figure 15.3. Well-Being in Higher Education Model

Ataa'didiin (Corn Pollen/Spiritual)
Hodiyingo'

PROFESSIONAL WELL-BEING
(Goals & Success) Nanish 'ishi

INTELLECTUAL WELL-BEING
(Wisdom) Nitsahak'ees

ARTISTIC WELL-BEING
(Gift or Expression) Na'ach'aah

CYCLICAL WELL-BEING
(Time) Ninahahai

EMOTIONAL WELL-BEING
(Heart) Ba'ani'

LINGUISTIC WELL-BEING
(Voice/Language) Bizaad

PHYSICAL WELL-BEING
(Body or Cornstalk) Hatsiis

POLITICAL WELL-BEING
(Leadership) Binahat'a'

TECHNICAL WELL-BEING
(Future and Planning) Bee'nanish

MEDICINAL WELL-BEING
(Healing) Azee'

FINANCIAL WELL-BEING
(Stability) Baah haah hasin

ENVIRONMENTAL WELL-BEING
(Place) Keyah

CULTURAL WELL-BEING (Identity)
Bi'ilooliil

MENTAL WELL-BEING
(Mind/Thinking) Bini'

SOCIAL WELL BEING
(Relation or Roots) K'e

SPIRITUAL WELL BEING
(Seed or Purpose in life)
Hodiyingo'

Source: Reprinted with permission from Secatero (2015).

After assigning this activity, one comment from a non-Indigenous student indicated that my Native materials and research were not scholarly enough for teaching doctoral students, which relates to the concept of James Youngblood Henderson's (2000) Eurocentric diffusionism that channels colonized thinking and cognitive imperialism. Indigenous holistic leadership models such as TIPM are arising as mainstream universities can benefit from Indigenous leadership and ways of knowing.

As an Indigenous professor in a research university, I focused much of my teaching to incorporate Mental Well-Being in my own practice to survive and receive tenure. Mental well-being involves a variety of different pillars including the emotional or "heart work," intellectual or "wisdom", and technical well-being or "future planning" pillars. I continued to learn through my own transformational approach in helping our Native-serving schools and my tenure process.

Transformation Approach

The transformation approach of the TIPM developed by Pewewardy et al. (2018) is described as, "Educators demonstrate their practices toward social transformation and have a deep awareness of how settler-colonial policies impact Indigenous children and children of color. They recognize the need for decolonizing and critical pedagogies in the curriculum and experiment with implementing such approaches." This transformational approach embodies physical well-being that infuses environmental pillars or sense of place, cyclical, "time and change" and medicinal "healing and resiliency" concepts. The Corn Model continued to grow and flourish through these pillars of strength and success factors.

When I co-established the POLLEN program here in my educational leadership program, I collaborated with our faculty and instructors about incorporating Indigenous leadership concepts into the curriculum and supporting Native teachers working in Native-serving schools. Our POLLEN cohort members provided meaningful feedback through external evaluations, course feedback, and ongoing collaboration from faculty members. Our current and unique POLLEN program offers tuition assistance, mentorship, and student support for cohort members. We also have a 97% on-time completion rate, a 96% licensure test pass rate, an 87% placement in leadership position, and an 87.5 % retention as a principal or assistant principal.

Cultural and Social Justice Approach

The cultural and social justice approach described by Pewewardy et al. (2018) in the TIPM is reflected in our successful findings and lessons learned from the three previous cohorts of the POLLEN program. The following recommendations are part of the social well-being process that encapsulates relationships, goals, stability, and leadership pillars for ongoing improvement and development. I share the following promises practices of our NESTL Program:

***Lesson One: Redesign curriculum, pedagogy, and assessments around cultur-
ally relevant professional development.*** Faculty and community members who
represent the candidates' races and ethnicities play key roles in the design and
delivery of degree programs and hiring practices. One POLLEN cohort member
indicated the following: "I know offhand [that] 1 in 2,500 will have a master's degree that are Native American, 1 in 7,000 will earn their doctorate degree. . . . We
can relay . . . to our students that 'You guys can do it—we need to make these statistics a lot better'" (POLLEN Alumni quoted in McREL International, 2016, p. 42).

***Lesson Two: Establish professional networks to help candidates develop their
leadership knowledge and skills and support their career aspirations.*** Expand
networks with partners who know, value, and enact the local community's culture and practices. A POLLEN cohort member commented, "I think for us,
bringing in that cultural relevance [is important] . . . because that also is another
component that we have to be mindful of when we go back to our communities,
and also being respectful to people who practice those traditions and culture
more so than we might [ourselves]" (POLLEN Alumni, McREL International
2016, p. 42).

***Lesson Three: Mentoring: Widen the mentoring circle with intensive coaching
and mentoring by diverse scholars and practitioners during the preparation program, internship, and throughout the professional journey.*** POLLEN candidates
noted the following recommendations from external evaluation interviews: (1)
Focus on bringing a problem-based approach to implementing professional leadership standards in Indian Country, (2) Use multicultural assessment tools involv-
ing video, print, and visual artifacts, (3) Provide a choice to develop one's own
"real" scenarios and receive recommendations from peers and mentors, and (4)
Extend learning opportunities to co-present with faculty at external seminars and
conferences (Williams et al., 2018).

Lesson Four: Center content in a social and relational context. Aspiring teachers who plan on becoming school administrators and leaders need to establish
their purpose, identity, and expression as it relates to the 16 pillars of the holistic
Corn Pollen Model. One cohort member commented,

> This program [POLLEN Program] will move mountains in relation to supporting stu-
> dent success. Knowing where you come from as an Indigenous educator within the
> community, you know exactly the demographic perception, achievement, and process
> data that you are working with. Adding the mixture of the 16 pillars of well-being in
> regard to student's well-being, you know the walk of life they come from. This program
> has reignited my flame to stand up, speak for, and push for equality for education for
> ALL of our students, for they are our future and most treasured profession. (POLLEN
> Alumni, McREL International 2016, p. 43)

Lesson Five: Link content to spiritual and cultural roots. Several POLLEN participants described the importance of modeling community customs-from morning blessings to shared leadership-in the school setting. Praying each morning for all living things including your school, community, and tribe. "In my culture, they say the children are sacred; that they still speak like a spirit. If we're going to say that children are sacred, then we need to show them that they are, living it and showing it in a school. I call it the story of justice. So, in the story of justice, students and principals don't have to deal with non-negotiable(s). You help them by asking, "What is going on with that child? What is going on in the whole family? How is this classroom disrupted? How are we going to get back into balance?" That's helped me a lot to bring our culture back with leadership" (POLLEN Alumni, McREL International, 2016, p. 43).

Lesson Six: Assure content is in harmony with Indigenous wisdom. As Pewewardy (2002) wisely noted, educators must be prepared so western paradigms can coexist with Native worldviews about life's complex interconnections among peoples and with nature. As one POLLEN alumni stated:

> This program has really made us reflect and dig deep within ourselves to realize and discover what our Indigenous values are. We grew up with them in our culture, we were taught them, but they were kind of tucked away because the way that western education is kind of drilled into your mind. So, by enrolling in this program, it really allowed me to realize that these [values] are my strengths, that this is where I'm grounded, this is where I'm from. (McREL International, 2016. p. 43)

Lesson Seven: Ground the program in place and well-being. POLLEN faculty stressed forms of connectedness and networking in the coursework to strategically poise aspiring leaders for the work ahead. Some POLLEN participants identified district reorganization and "turmoil" as a barrier to career advancement. Others explained that they enrolled in POLLEN to overcome barriers such as the "glass ceiling," an invisible barrier that has traditionally prevented American Indians from becoming school leaders (McREL International 2016, pp. 44). "The good thing about our professors is they're keeping in mind that we're from Native schools and servicing Native populations, so that helps us directly when we go back to our schools after we achieve licensure" (POLLEN Alumni, McREL International, 2016, pp. 45).

Lesson Eight: Recruitment and Intensive application screening process for POLLEN candidates. This application process includes (1) submitting a research paper on their Indigenous Educational philosophy, (2) a letter of intent demonstrating commitment to leading in Native-serving schools, (3) a Zoom technology–based interview with faculty with questions geared toward Indigenous education and leadership, and (4) consensus among faculty to admit the best and brightest teachers and aspiring leaders.

The cultural and social justice approaches for the POLLEN program have created a foundation for Indigenized leadership through research, teaching, and service. Furthermore, the creation of a proposed national center for Indigenous leadership called Native Educational Sovereignty in Teaching and Leadership (NESTL) is currently being established here at UNM to incorporate the Corn Pollen Model Framework into the curriculum through the following:

1. Native American Leadership in Education (NALE): Three Native cohorts with 21 students who are currently enrolled in our Educational Leadership Educational Doctorate (EdD) Program; we graduated our first EdD recipient in Spring 2021 and have 5 dissertation defense candidates.
2. Promoting Our Learning, Leadership, and Empowering our Nations (POLLEN) program, which has graduated 31 aspiring school principals and leaders in 3 successive cohorts funded under the Kellogg Foundation. POLLEN graduates have earned an educational specialist certificate with administrative licensure. We have another rising POLLEN 4 Cohort and another two successive cohorts funded by the New Mexico State legislature's "Grow Your Own Teacher" initiative.
3. Striking Eagle Native American Invitational (SENAI) is one of the largest high school basketball tournaments in the country, which is designed to combine athletics, leadership, and academics during the winter break at UNM. Over 3,000 student athletes, 30,000 spectators, and 495 volunteers have been involved with SENAI since its inception in 2011.
4. Striking Eagle Academy is comprised of educational workshops to inspire junior and senior high school students during our SENAI event to learn how to balance spiritual, mental, physical, and social well-being attributes as part of the Corn Pollen Model.
5. Rising Eagles Dual Enrollment Initiative (REDE) is a partnership between NESTL and New Mexico State University Grants to promote dual enrollment-based leadership and teaching courses for high school and undergraduate students.
6. Society of Native American Graduate Students (SNAGS) is a chartered UNM student organization that sponsors activities designed to support education, mentoring, service learning, and leadership initiatives for both undergraduate and graduate students.
7. NESTL Advisory Council is a group of distinguished professional Elders, educators, and alumni who provide leadership guidance and assist in the overall delivery of the initiatives.

CONCLUSION

The NESTL program has recently updated the Corn Pollen Model (Secatero, in press), which connects education and leadership through spiritual, mental, physical, and social well-being attributes. The Corn Pollen Model consists of four main

Figure 15.4. Corn Pollen Model in Native-Serving Schools and Communities Framework

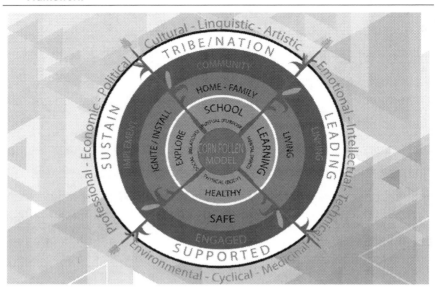

Source: Reprinted with permission from Secatero (in press).

quadrants that include the roots of our being, which provide purpose or spiritual well-being; the corn leaves of knowledge to connect our learnings; the cornstalk, which upholds stability to support the pillars; and the corn tassels to signify our growth for success and persistence (see Figure 15.4).

In the spiritual quadrant, we embrace our sense of purpose by honoring school, home, family, community, and Tribal Nations. These attributes include cultural, linguistic, and artistic well-being pillars. As part of embracing our mental well-being, we connect learning with living, linking, and leading well-being pillars. These connections are supported through emotional, intellectual, and technical well-being pillars. In terms of physical well-being, we must ensure that we provide healthy lifestyles, which are channeled through safety, engagement, and supportive practices. This quadrant envelops living a healthy, safe, engaged, and supportive lifestyle through environmental, cyclical, and medicinal well-being pillars. In the social well-being quadrant, we value the importance of relationships, which posits exploring, igniting, implementing, and sustaining our way of life through professional, economic, and political well-being pillars. As we continue to grow as leaders, we must embody the wisdom of our Elders to continue to serve in this work. I conclude with the following words, which I have shared with POLLEN cohort members:

> You are created as a seed which was planted in our sacred mother earth to honor your purpose, mind, body, and relations. Honor your roots, grow

your leaves of knowledge, stand strong as a cornstalk, and sprout your beautiful tassels for your people. Always remember who you are, where you are from, and where you are going in life. Create and continue your legacy by following the corn pollen path through education, well-being, and leadership.

REFERENCES

Cross, T. (1997). Understanding the relational worldview in Indian families. *Pathways, 12*(4), 6–7.

Dhiman, S. (2017). *Holistic leadership: A new paradigm for today's leaders.* Palgrave MacMillan.

Faircloth, S., & Tippeconnic, J. III. (2015). Leadership development for schools serving American Indian students: Implication for research, policy and practice. *Journal of American Indian Education, 54*(1), 127–129.

McREL International. (2016, July). *University of New Mexico Transformative Action Group: Promoting our leadership and learning and empowering our Nations.* McREL International, Mid-Continent Regional Education Laboratory.

New Mexico Public Education Department. (2015). *New Mexico educator equity plan.* https://files.eric.ed.gov/fulltext/ED572846.pdf

Pewewardy, C. D. (2002). Learning styles of American Indian/Alaska Native students: A review of the literature and implications for practice. *Journal of American Indian Education, 41*(3), 22–55.

Pewewardy, C. D., Lees, A., & Clark-Shim, H. (2018). The Transformational Indigenous Praxis Model: Stages for developing critical consciousness in Indigenous education. *Wíčazo Ša Review, 33*(1), 38–69. https://doi.org/10.5749/wicazosareview.33.1.0038

POLLEN (Promoting Our Leadership, Learning, and Empowering our Nations) Cohort: UNM College of Education and Human Sciences website: https://coehs.unm.edu/departments-programs/teelp/education-leadership-program/pollen-cohort.html

Secatero, S. L. (2009). *Beneath our sacred minds, hands and hearts: Stories of persistence and success among American Indian graduate and professional students* (Unpublished doctoral dissertation). University of New Mexico, Albuquerque.

Secatero, S. L. (in press). *The corn pollen model: A holistic pathway to leadership, education, and well-being.* University of Arizona Press.

Secatero, S. L. (2015). The leadership tree: Our roots of Indigenous leadership and well-being in higher education. In R. Minthorn & A. F. Chavez (Eds.), *Indigenous leadership in higher education* (pp. 114–127). Routledge.

Secatero, S., Williams, S., & Romans, R. (2022). A pathway to leadership for diverse cadres of school leaders: Honoring Indigenous values in a principal preparation program in New Mexico. *Leadership and Policy in Schools, 21*(1), 81–94. https://doi.org/10.1080/15700763.2021.2022705

Taie, S., & Goldring, R. (2019). *Characteristics of public and private elementary and secondary school principals in the United States: Results from the 2017–18 National Teacher and Principal Survey first look* (NCES 2019-141). National Center for Education Statistics. https://nces.ed.gov/pubsearch/pubsinfo.asp?pubid=2019141

Williams, S., Secatero, S., & Perrone, F. (2018). Preparing and developing leaders for Indigenous-serving schools via the holistic blessing of POLLEN's leadership tree. *The Journal of American Indian Education (JAIE), 57*(3), 27–50.

Youngblood Henderson, J. (2000). Postcolonial ghost dancing. In M. Battiste (Ed.), *Reclaiming Indigenous voice and vision* (pp. 57–76). UBC Press.

CHAPTER 16

Indigenizing Doctoral Programs

Embodying Indigenous Community Ways of Being

Robin Zape-tah-hol-ah Minthorn (Kiowa Citizen and Descendant of the Apache/Umatilla/Nez Perce/Assiniboine Nations)

INTRODUCTION

Before I begin this chapter, I want to acknowledge that space, place, and our Ancestors are sacred to who we are as Indigenous people and scholars. I acknowledge that I am writing today from the Ancestral lands of the Puyallup Tribe of Indians. I am a citizen of the Kiowa Tribe of Oklahoma with descendancy to the Apache, Umatilla (and Cayuse), Nez Perce, and Assiniboine tribes. I acknowledge that I was born in Pendleton, Oregon, and grew up in Lawton, Oklahoma. My Ancestors from my Umatilla (and Cayuse) and Nez Perce Ancestors traversed the imposed state boundaries of Washington. I acknowledge that I am responsible to this land, to tell a story that will bring honor to our Ancestors, other Indigenous scholars, and those who may come behind us.

Let us begin.

THIS IS WHERE WE BEGIN

This chapter will provide a deeper understanding on how to engage and work with Tribal Nations and Indigenous education sites to create meaningful connections to educational leadership programs. This will be done through sharing the creation story of NALE (Native American Leadership in Education) and how it was intentionally created. It will provide an example of how we move to Dimension 4: cultural and social justice action in the Transformational Indigenous Praxis Model (TIPM) in our heartwork as Indigenous scholars and require colleges and universities to decolonize their approaches to academic programs. At the center of this heartwork is to embed an Indigenous storywork approach in honoring Indigenous students' whole selves. At the crux of this manifestation in these relationalities are honoring Indigenous knowledge and epistemology that incorporates intellectual, spiritual, emotional, and physical ways of being throughout their experience in this doctoral cohort program (Archibald, 2008). This heartwork (Minthorn, 2018) has led to another Indigenous-community grounded journey in co-creating a Tribally based doctoral cohort with the Muckleshoot Indian Tribe[1] at the University of Washington Tacoma. Both of these efforts in building and creating Indigenous based doctoral programs serve as a piece of our (Indigenous higher education) story to honor who we are as Indigenous peoples.

ANCESTRAL KNOWLEDGE

The framing of this heartwork highlights two Indigenous focused ways of constructing and connecting place and Ancestral knowledge. The first is the Transformational Indigenous Praxis Model (TIPM), and the second is Indigenous storywork. It was essential to utilize these two frameworks that conceptualize educational systems to the deep process of honoring all that is Indigenous in framing learning.

Transformational Indigenous Praxis Model

The Transformational Indigenous Praxis Model provides a framework for Indigenous educators and non-Indigenous educators to begin conceptualizing where we find ourselves in educational systems and curriculum building with Indigenous students and communities. There is a recognition to be responsive to Tribes and Indigenous communities to co-create systems and curriculum that represents their knowledge and culture. This framework is not meant to be pathologized or prescriptive, but it is meant to be a starting point to Indigenizing and decolonizing educational systems.

Indigenous Storywork

Indigenous storywork is articulated by Archibald (2008) as a way of weaving our teachings and cultural beliefs through stories that are translated through oral and written ways. Indigenous Storywork includes seven principles that provide a foundation for how to utilize and integrate stories in our heartwork. These principles are respect, responsibility, reverence, reciprocity, holism, inter-relatedness, and synergy. Indigenous storywork provides space in academic and western spaces and verifies their need and use in the places we navigate.

GENEALOGICAL CONNECTIONS TO COMMUNITY WAYS OF BEING

It is important to honor the Ancestors[2] who have created space and sustained us for who we are today. I would like to take this time to honor and acknowledge heartwork from Indigenous scholars that impacts how Indigenous education is situated between Tribal sovereignty and reclamation of land and culture. First,

(Deloria & Wildcat, 2010) break down our connection to place and the power that is intertwined when we acknowledge this as humans and our connection to the non-human. As we migrate into centering Indigenous perspectives in pedagogy and learning spaces we must acknowledge (Grande, 2015) Red Pedagogy. It honors the intersection between dominant modes of critical educational theory and the sociopolitical landscape of American Indian education. McCoy, Tuck, and McKenzie (2016) offer a book, *Land Education*, that provides a critical analysis of the pathways toward centering education on Indigenous land. They provide decolonial perspectives in our understandings of land-based education that is mostly situated in Indigenous land paradigms and knowledge. In *Indigenous Community: Rekindling the Teachings of the Seventh Fire* (2015), Cajete calls for the revitalization and sustainment of our sense for community. He provides a framework in creating an Indigenous leadership community studies curriculum.

Christman, Pepion, Bowman, and Dixon (2015, p. 136) provide a list of recommendations for Native leadership programs. The recommendations include areas of mentorship, supporting and respecting cultural knowledge, addressing program challenges, peer support processes, authentic professional development, and incorporating a balance of praxis/theory-oriented literature. In *Indigenous Innovations in Higher Education* (2017), Sumida Huaman and Brayboy provide a first text that discusses a collaborative project of an Indigenous graduate program partnering with Tribal institution partnership. This text provides examples of the Indigenous graduate student's contributions of knowledge, theory, and praxis tied back to their Tribal communities. Finally, Faircloth and Minthorn (2018) provide a timeline of Indigenous education and policy that has impacted the evolution of these programs and share examples of Indigenous-based doctoral programs with recommendations for the future evolution of programs. In the next section, I share the creation stories of two Indigenous doctoral cohort programs.

CREATION STORIES

Creation stories for Tribal Nations and communities are the foundational stories of who each of us are as a people. Many of our stories are not tied to humans or are intertwined with the non-human and spiritual aspects. For many, we revisit our creation stories to share with our children and grandchildren so we will never forget who we are and where we came from. In this section, I honor the beginnings of the two Indigenous-based doctoral programs I have connections to.[3]

NALE (Native American Leadership in Education) Doctoral Cohort

This is the story of how the Native American Leadership in Education (NALE) cohort came into existence. In spring 2014, a community-grounded journey to Indigenizing doctoral education began. This journey included feedback on the delivery, curriculum, outcomes, and whether to highlight strengths of the community. This approach included over 18 in-person meetings and 42 survey meetings with Tribal leaders, Tribal education directors, and Indigenous education entities that ended with a NALE forum to report back what was found. The community connections remained with the establishment of an advisory board and regular updates to the community. There was also the creation of a summer workshop that maintained connections to these Tribal communities and Indigenous education community sites by physically going to visit them and the community deciding what they wanted to highlight within their Indigenous education areas. This also created ties and built relationships between current doctoral students and the Tribes and Indigenous communities that built the program through their input (Minthorn, 2020). This is how our story began.

Muckleshoot Doctoral Cohort

This is the story of how the Muckleshoot Doctoral cohort came into existence. In September 2019, a Muckleshoot Tribal College (MTC) staff member, Amy Maharaj, reached out to me. I met with Amy and Dr. Denise Bill, and this first meeting became one of many meetings (there were 18 meetings between MTC and UW Tacoma School of Education) over the course of 6 months. A Memorandum of Agreement was signed in February 2020 and recruitment and admissions processes would take place over the next few months[4]. The first Muckleshoot doctoral cohort includes a group of 14 women who are mostly Indigenous and all work within a context of supporting Tribal/Indigenous communities. The uniqueness of this cohort is that it is Tribally based and if not for the pandemic all classes would be held on Muckleshoot Tribal lands. The inception began with a Muckleshoot canoe journey song and a prayer to start us off in a good way. As we began our second quarter, we held a collective prayer. All of the classes are grounded and situated in Indigenous scholarship and taught by Indigenous faculty. The focus of the EdD curriculum has been Indigenized through the scholarship, assignments, and within the class discussions of the course. There are other ways in which the intention of the Muckleshoot cohort is being Indigenized through the creation of a commissioned Muckleshoot Tribal design to engage the Tribal community and to represent the Tribal Nation whose land we are connected to through the cohort. This is how our story began.

DECOLONIZING APPROACHES TO ACADEMIC PROGRAMS

Decolonizing approaches to academic programs means doing some intentional reflexivity as a college/school/institution both internally and individually. We have to understand how our relationships would be described by Indigenous and Tribal communities in the state or territories we are located. In this section, I carve out space to build out praxis that has been built and created within institutions and Indigenous/Tribal communities connected to community consciousness, Indigenous/Tribal input in academic programs, and approaches to decolonizing and Indigenizing academic programs. I start each section with a question followed by subsections that include additional questions and suggestions for ways to begin addressing some approaches to decolonizing academic programs.

How Do We Infuse a Community Consciousness?

Acknowledging Place and Building Land Reflection into Praxis

The first step in building community consciousness is to understand how colonial violence has impacted Indigenous communities. How did the university occupy or acquire the lands that the institution sits on? Who were the original caretakers of the land? How is this acknowledged and situated in the institutional history? Once this is found out, how does the institution rectify and verbalize this in land acknowledgments both oral and written, and how does institutional history and memory reflect this? Next, as individuals, we must begin to reflect how we are each benefiting by the occupation of these lands. How do we become caretakers in ensuring that the Indigenous/Tribal memory is centered in building future initiatives and academic programs?

Praxis. In the Muckleshoot cohort and all of the EdD courses we include a land acknowledgment in the syllabus. We also ensure our courses are community centered and that we understand and acknowledge how colonization has impacted the surrounding Tribes in the area. This is done through discussions and assignments and incorporating a decolonial approach in the curriculum. It is also about creating space for each person to do a land reflection not only within the courses but within the School of Education as a whole.

Responsibility to and Reciprocity With Community

How do we build responsibility to and reciprocity with the community? Our responsibility as individuals and institutions is not to assume because we have relationships with the community that we can speak for them. We have to build in layers of consultation and opportunities for co-construction. Even if we belong to a Tribal community it doesn't mean we know everything about our own communities. Sometimes, we have to be reminded how to listen to our Elders,[5] the youth, and to those most vulnerable within our communities. This mindset and consciousness will create an inherent sense of responsibility and create opportunities for reciprocity.

Praxis. In the NALE cohort this responsibility was in creating a NALE advisory board that was open to any Tribal/Indigenous communities to provide input as we developed the Indigenous-based doctoral cohort. There were continuous efforts to provide updates to the 23 Tribes and school districts through updates in a letter, copies of brochures, and newsletters. With the Muckleshoot cohort this responsibility and reciprocity is being carried out through the Muckleshoot

Partnership Education Committee, where we have equal representation of committee members represented from the Tribe and from the UW system.

How Do We Include Indigenous/Tribal Community Input in Our Academic Programs?

Including All Voices and Building Connections Across Generations

When institutions think of getting feedback and input in what they are doing they often think of the Tribal Leaders who have been elected or appointed to be in those positions to represent the people. This is a wonderful beginning, but if an institution wants to deepen their understanding, we have to start thinking about the multitude of voices that are represented within a Tribal/Indigenous community. Meaning, how do we include the Elders, the youth, the Tribal schools, the businesses, the language and cultural preservation departments in our building of academic programs?

Praxis. When we started that process of seeking input for the NALE cohort, we reached out to Tribal leaders of each Tribe to seek their input, but we also were open to their suggestions of who to talk to within the Tribe, whether that be their education department or another entity. We also were intentional to include Indigenous education entities including Tribal colleges, Tribal schools, and Native charter schools in the state. It was important to be extensive in receiving input, listening, and going to these places to meet Tribal leaders, education, and community voices to intentionally include their voices.

Needs and Strengths Assessment with Tribal Nations and Indigenous Communities

We must consider how we will better understand the lived realities and needs as articulated by the various voices within Tribal Nations and Indigenous communities. We also must consider our positionality and desire for understanding in order to meet a need. We should do so from a strengths-based perspective rather than a savior mentality. We also need to understand the strengths of the communities and the people who comprise these communities. As institutions and colleges/schools, we must see ourselves as part of the community but never better than it. We are responsible to the community.

Praxis. As part of the input process with Tribal communities and Indigenous education entities for NALE, I asked questions about curriculum needs, outcomes, and strengths they would highlight about their community around Indigenous education. It was important to understand where the needs lie within the community and what they would like to see Tribal citizens come away with from receiving their doctoral degree. Once the input process was complete, we held a NALE forum and shared the themes of what we found from the input we received. We made accessible the feedback from each community. One way of honoring the strengths of the community shared was to create a summer workshop that took the cohort out to the communities to connect with the Tribes and Indigenous education entities I had interacted with to create it. This created inter-Tribal and intergenerational interactions that would bridge knowledge and praxis.

How Do We Decolonize and Indigenize Our Academic Programs?

Indigenize Recruitment and Admissions Process

We have to re-frame how we approach recruitment as we want to bring Native students to campus knowing we are responsible for them when they arrive. We also have to be intentional to express this responsibility and commitment when we talk to families of students. In the admissions process we also have to consider the gatekeeping mechanisms that might prevent Native students from applying and how we help connect families in understanding the institutional process for admission and how to access funding.

Praxis. When I began recruiting for the NALE cohort it often began in un-traditional ways with community events where I would share about this new Indigenous doctoral cohort and they would be interested. What ended up emerging with the many interactions with prospective Indigenous doctoral students was alleviating their fears and encouraging them. For many prospective Indigenous doctoral students, we are first generation graduates and would be the first to receive a doctoral degree in our extended families. What has been found with the prospective students is that they are interested in finding programs that are Indigenous-based and centered. Across both the NALE and Muckleshoot doctoral programs, I would estimate my colleagues or myself have spoken to at least 100 prospective Indigenous doctoral students.

Honoring Family and a Ceremonial Beginning

Bringing in family as part of the recruitment and admissions process is essential. This also means being more intentional in how we honor family as students start their higher education or continue it if they are in graduate degrees. We know for most Native students we are nothing without our families and/or community. So, we must think of ways that we can honor families from the beginning through campus welcome days to creating ceremonies that honor the students and their families.

Praxis. In the first NALE cohort, we began our orientation with a Diné prayer from a Diné faculty member. I asked the cohort to invite their families to be a part of an induction ceremony. All seven cohort members had their family there with intergenerational representations. We had each student introduce their families to everyone. Later, we would end up having a NALE family potluck each semester where many of the same family members would attend. As we began the Muckleshoot doctoral cohort for our virtual orientation (due to the pandemic), we started it in a good way with prayer and a Muckleshoot canoe journey song. In the midst of a pandemic we still tried to bring in the parts of honoring our families and having students share pictures and introduce them via discussion boards.

Indigenize Curriculum and Teachings

When we are building or refreshing academic programs, we have to consider how language and suppositions of terminology affirm colonial language and create harm. It is important when we are considering Indigenizing curriculum that we include feedback from the community and Native faculty on campus. As we build these academic programs, we also must do our best to assert the need for more Native faculty and/or Native adjunct instructors to be brought in to center Indigenous perspectives. When this is not the case, we also must create training and professional development for non-Indigenous faculty who will teach Native students, with the goals being to help non-Indigenous faculty to understand their biases and learn about Tribal sovereignty and contemporary realities of Indigenous communities.

Praxis. In the NALE cohort there were intentional efforts for Indigenous-identifying faculty to teach most of the courses. When there was no Indigenous faculty teaching, there were efforts to encourage non-Indigenous faculty to include Indigenous scholarship and speakers in the classes. For the Muckleshoot cohort all of the instructors will be Indigenous except for one and that person will be mentored to include Indigenous scholarship and perspectives in the classroom. A deepening of the Indigenous faculty perspectives for the Muckleshoot cohort is to host Indigenous pedagogies meetings with UW Native faculty across the system to provide input on the current efforts to Indigenize curriculum and provide recommendations on Native faculty to teach future courses.

Indigenize Student Support and Center Holistic Approaches

When we think of student support, we often think of how to help students navigate their journeys. But we often don't do so from a holistic perspective. Especially when we are considering Indigenous students, how are we intentional to create frameworks and approaches to support students that are holistic and representative of the student's needs? Holistic approaches must always be mindful of the academic, social, cultural, mental, and spiritual levels. How are we creating spaces and opportunities for students to connect at all of these levels and remain connected to "home" and what that means for each student? Native students carry with them their Ancestors' legacy and memories along with the prayers that have been said by community and family. We have a responsibility to be intentional in how we Indigenize student support from the undergraduate to graduate levels.

Praxis. The NALE cohort attempted to bring in and honor various aspects for students. This included starting their journey with prayer, centering family at the beginning of each semester of the program, connecting them with the community through the summer workshops, providing professional development opportunities through conference presentations, and publishing. The Muckleshoot doctoral cohort interactions have had to be modified and intentional. The ways we have been intentional in this cohort have been through the beginning of the cohort starting in prayer and the intentional efforts to incorporate feedback from the students. Indigenous based doctoral cohorts/programs will not be perfect, but they can be carried out through centering Indigenous values and approaches in the curriculum and in support of the students.

CALLS FOR RECIPROCITY AND COMMUNITY BUILDING

As we start to see more intentional efforts by academia to include Tribal/Indigenous community voices in understanding how to support and serve Native American students, we must also move to create academic programs and curriculum that centers Indigenous voices, as well. This includes being intentional in Tribal/Indigenous communities in the university and college level strategic planning and visioning, building reciprocal relationships, honoring community voices, and also finding opportunities for co-creation.

Including Tribal/Indigenous Communities in Strategic Planning and Visioning

When institutions of higher education start revisiting their old strategic plans and re-envisioning how their universities or colleges can transform, it's important that they intentionally include Tribal/Indigenous communities in this process. That means going out to these communities and asking for them to share what they need for their Tribal citizens or where there is a gap in representation for professional fields. Universities and colleges have to be intentional to envision Tribal/Indigenous communities as the backbone and foundation to maintaining and creating academic programs and disciplines. Indigenous knowledge and wisdom have always been in these spaces and once there are reciprocal relationships in place there is no excuse for exclusion.

Building Reciprocal Relationships and Honoring Community Voice

Building reciprocal relationships takes time. Universities and colleges have to remember that there are scars in many Tribal communities in which universities and colleges have either been occupying their land that they have been the caretakers of since time immemorial, or that there have been various instances in which university faculty/administrators/staff have violated trust within these communities. We have to be able to take responsibility for these injustices, even if we weren't the person who committed them; we have to also find ways to reconcile and co-create a pathway to reciprocal relationships. There is a long pathway to build longlasting reciprocal relationships and the heartwork will never be done, it is continuous, as people leave the college and university the Tribal/Indigenous communities will remain there.

Opportunities for Co-creation

As the building of reciprocal relationships becomes stronger between Tribal/ Indigenous communities, the opportunity for co-creation happens. Co-creation isn't a one-time meeting; it is an opportunity to understand their vision and needs and find ways to see the fit within academic programs. It also means creating ways for accountability and feedback between the Tribe(s) and the university/college. Co-creation is an ongoing process and there may be opportunities for evolution into other colleges and academic programs. This then requires those working on previous heartwork to ensure university and college colleagues understand the protocol and expectations of building with Tribal communities. It takes much heartwork and labor, but it is creating pathways to higher education for Tribal citizens that might have not been there otherwise.

COMING FULL CIRCLE: CONNECTING TO TIPM

In this chapter, I share two stories and examples of praxis that connect to Dimension 4: cultural and social justice action in the Transformational Indigenous Praxis Model (TIPM). I provide examples of praxis that situate and ground this heartwork to the Ancestral knowledges they seek to honor. The TIPM is a way of processing through the resistance, reverberation, and wave- jumping that happens when we strive for equity and social justice as it lives and breathes in Indigenous communities. I acknowledge that for both of the stories shared they are living within the confines of western academy and curriculum while being tethered and umbilically connected to Tribal Nations and communities. In all of this, it affirms the process of moving between and back and forth across stages as we move between energy and time. We are rising and moving with the beings who make up the stories and join us on these journeys. TIPM gives us a way of conceptualizing our heartwork to understand, broaden, and shift the pathways that will impact future generations.

CONCLUSION: LEAVING IT IN A GOOD WAY

What has been shared are two stories of Indigenous (and Tribally) based doctoral cohort programs in the southwest and northwest parts of the United States. These were formed by the feedback of Tribal/Indigenous communities and are guided by their needs and input through reciprocal relationships. There are very few academic programs at the doctoral level that have been intentional to include Tribal/Indigenous perspectives and voices in academia. There shouldn't be two of a handful out there; these stories and praxis shared aim to encourage other universities and colleges to be intentional to include Tribal/Indigenous community in their building of programs and envisioning of new futures. When we center and include Tribal/Indigenous communities through building reciprocal relationships, something powerful happens and Tribal citizens envision themselves as part of the living history that ties their Ancestors' stories to their contributions of building for future generations.

NOTES

1. Tribe, Tribal, and Tribal Nation will be capitalized throughout this chapter to honor the sovereignty and Nationhood of each Tribal community.

2. Ancestors and Ancestral are being capitalized to honor the role that they have played in our continuation as Indigenous peoples and their legacy we live to uphold.

3. I want to acknowledge all the names or places that have contributed to these creation stories may not be shared but I want to acknowledge that each person and place has contributed to their existence.

4. This Tribal–university partnership within such a short time frame is acknowledged to have taken place because of those within the Muckleshoot Tribe and at UW who had established relationships before, and also because I had the previous experience with NALE and connecting with Tribal communities. It seemed to be the right timing to come together.

5. Elders is being capitalized to honor the regard and respect we have for them in our Tribal communities.

REFERENCES

Archibald, J. (2008). *Indigenous storywork: Educating the heart, mind, body, and spirit.* UBC Press.
Cajete, G. (2015). *Indigenous community: Rekindling the teachings of the seventh fire.* Living Justice Press.
Christman, D., Pepion, D., Bowman, C., & Dixon, B. (2015). Native American doctoral students: Establishing legitimacy in higher education. In D. Aguilera-Black Bear & J. Tippeconnic (Eds.), *Voices of resistance and renewal: Indigenous leadership in education* (pp. 116–141). University of Oklahoma Press.
Deloria, V., & Wildcat, D. (2001). *Power and place.* Fulcrum Resources.
Grande, S. (2015). *Red pedagogy: Native American social and political thought* (10th anniversary ed.). Rowman & Littlefield.
Faircloth, S., & Minthorn, R. Z. (2018). The evolution of Native education leadership programs: Learning from the past leading for the future. In S. Waterman, S. C. Lowe, & H. J. Shotton (Eds.), *Beyond access: Indigenizing programs for Native American student success.* Stylus Publishing.
McCoy, K., Tuck, E., & McKenzie, M. (2016). *Land education: Rethinking pedagogies of place from Indigenous, postcolonial, and decolonizing perspectives.* Routledge.
Minthorn, R. (2018). Being BRAVE in the ivory towers as "Zape-tah-hol-ah" (Sticks with bow). In M.C. Whitaker & E.A. Grollman (Eds.), *Counternarratives from women of color academics: bravery, vulnerability, and resistance.* Routledge.
Sumida Huaman, E., & Brayboy, B. (2017). *Indigenous innovations in higher education: Local knowledge and critical research.* Sense.

CHAPTER 17

Intergenerational Connections Through Cheyenne and Arapaho Female Leadership Experiences

Carrie F. Whitlow (Cheyenne and Arapaho, Kiowa, Creek)

CONCHO, OKLAHOMA

Concho. Where the Cheyenne and Arapaho School (Concho Indian School) was located and where my grandmother worked as a dorm matron and teacher aide.

Concho. Where my mother was raised along with her three brothers by my late grandmother and grandfather. Where my mother got in trouble for playing in the tunnels underneath the Concho Indian School.

Concho. Where the Cheyenne and Arapaho Tribes Department of Education is located. I sit in an office every day where my grandma used to work and took care of Cheyenne and Arapaho students.

Located in western Oklahoma, Concho is now home to the Cheyenne and Arapaho Tribes' government headquarters, Lucky Star Casino, which employs over 500 Tribal employees. The city and schools are one of 13 Tribal communities within the Cheyenne and Arapaho service area. Concho is located within the former reservation territory. The educational landscapes of our Tribal communities are entangled with deeply rooted structures of the settler-colonial consciousness that privileges Eurocentric public-school curriculum (Grande, 2015), yet many of our connections to our Cheyenne and Arapaho ways remain intact and vibrant. As a female who grew up in the area and who has moved in and out of these entangled learning environments, I have now been in Concho for the past 15 years working in various leadership capacities, most recently as the Executive Director of the Cheyenne and Arapaho Department of Education.

This chapter will provide an understanding of the effect of settler-colonial education in western Oklahoma through intergenerational Cheyenne and Arapaho female leadership experiences. Through stories and lived experiences, a grandmother, mother, and daughter remain connected by educational systems that continue to exclude Cheyenne and Arapaho ways of knowing and thinking. The stories provide informal lessons about the power dynamics lurking behind everyday experiences in school, lessons about race, power, and my sociocultural positionality.

"She Doesn't Love Me"

"No, Kay Kay, don't touch that! Sit down Kay Kay! Someone come get her! Make her behave. She's ornery and doesn't listen. I'm not riding in a car with her, I'll just stay home."

I was always in trouble. My grandma and mom were always correcting me before, after, or during altercations I got myself into. I believe they knew I was going to be the most difficult, therefore, they showed me the most tough love. It was so tough I used to always tell my mom, "Grandma doesn't even love me, she's always mad at me." Not realizing that was my own doing, not hers. It is often said by my mother that the reason my grandma and I did not get along very well was because we were just alike.

Before we attended a ceremony, powwow, or family function together, my grandma would remind my sister and I about her expectations of us. "Shake hands, say hello to people." If we were dancing, she would say, "You're here to dance, not walk around. Don't chew gum or act silly while you're dancing." Our grandma was teaching us how to be respectful young women. Those rules and expectations have now carried us into our lives as mothers and now we are teaching our daughters the same. Her tough love continues to guide me as a mother, auntie, daughter, niece, leader, advocate, educator, and scholar.

"I Work for White People!"

"You can't do that Kay Kay, I work for white people! You can't act like that, go sit in the van!"

My mom always tells this story: "We would be somewhere, and we would hear a kid cry, your grandma and I would look at each other and say, I hope Kay Kay didn't do it." Most of the time it was me and most of the time I was in trouble. My mother did not hesitate to discipline me in front of our friends and family. But worst of all, she would send me to sit in the van.

Of course, my mother would get hired at the school my siblings and I attended. She began as a teacher aide in 1990 and continues to work for Darlington Public Schools as the Director of Indian Education. She was there every day; for every basketball game, teacher parent conference, homecoming dance, fundraiser, and most importantly when I got in trouble. Punishment began with the teacher, the principal, and then came my mom. Honestly, I was the most afraid of my mom. It never failed, I would sit in class acting as if nothing happened and then came the knock on the door, "Carrie, it's your mom." She always reminded me, "I work for white people, and you can't continue to get in trouble like this. I have higher expectations for you." Those reminders and comments from my mother made me conscious of the educational system we were in, although not at the time.

Indian Education

The Cheyenne and Arapaho people had systems of teaching and learning prior to European contact. "Each was educated to be a good Arapaho or a good Cheyenne—and they stood in stark contrast to the white American schooled in the formal education system" (Mann, 1997, pp. 15–16). How do you define Indian Education? The meaning of Indian Education varies from family to family, and has been in my family since my grandparents worked at Concho Indian School in the 1960s. My mother has worked for a local education agency (LEA) in western Oklahoma since I was in 1st grade. And now I serve Tribal families by supporting their education as an executive director for the Cheyenne and Arapaho Department of Education. Our commitment to Indian Education and to our community happened within a 5-mile radius.

Telling stories about my grandmother, mother, and I displays what survivance means in spaces such as Indian Education, despite colonialism (Sabzalian, 2019). Also, to demonstrate the "ongoing struggles for Indigenous communities in settler-designed school systems" (Pewewardy et al., 2018, p. 38), specifically the predominantly white communities that surround the Cheyenne and Arapaho Tribes. I am certain my grandmother and mother were conscious of settler-designed school systems and how it affected their experience as students, as well as how the experiences affected the way they raised their children and grandchildren.

In the process of becoming leaders, we became conscious of the effect of settler colonialism, and we began to persist as we asserted our teachings and identities in our Tribal communities. The experiences that are shared throughout this chapter recognize the systemic racism that is embedded in school structures in western Oklahoma (Pewewardy et al., 2018). Additionally, once we became more conscious of settler-colonial education we chose to change our trajectory through Cheyenne and Arapaho teachings we passed on from one generation to another. What is important to us as Cheyenne and Arapaho women is exemplified through our stories and lived experiences. Through the stories of my grandmother, mother, and myself you will be able to identify the different stages of critical consciousness in settler-colonial educational systems.

THEORETICAL FRAMEWORKS

Transformational Indigenous Praxis Model (TIPM)

The Transformational Indigenous Praxis Model (TIPM) is described by Pewewardy et al. (2018) as a model to "promote critical awareness and cultural consciousness among educators" (p. 38). TIPM prioritizes the process of decolonizing curriculum, teaching practices, but most importantly the importance of critical thinking skills. This chapter will tell the stories and experiences of an intergenerational connection of a grandmother, mother, and daughter as Cheyenne and Arapaho female educators in the Concho and El Reno communities of Oklahoma. Informed by TIPM, the stories and experiences shared will help provide terminologies that support educators to transform their practices and their experiences, the dimensions of the model they embody, and the obstacles that actualize their collective hopes (Pewewardy et al., 2018). Additionally, the experiences shared are framed from my perspective as a Cheyenne and Arapaho woman, which inherently also emphasizes a community-based perspective of Indigenous feminism.

Furthermore, the chapter will tell the stories and experiences of a grandmother, mother, and daughter through female leadership experiences in education within the Cheyenne and Arapaho Tribal community. From a dorm matron/teacher aide to a Director of Indian Education to an Executive Director for the Cheyenne and Arapaho Department of Education, our stories have gained power through our educational leadership experiences. Also, this chapter will highlight the many forms of education we have encountered, i.e., boarding schools, Catholic school, public schools, and Tribal colleges and universities (TCUs). Each system of education has had a profound impact on how we view leadership and how we choose to lead. I also want to acknowledge that works such as these are only made possible because my grandmother and mother have protected our identities as Cheyenne and Arapaho women, regardless of various spaces we traverse and occupy.

Finally, TIPM and many Indigenous approaches to scholarship prioritize the need for our own stories and emphasize healing through engagement with our own stories. Throughout the process of writing this chapter I began to ask more questions about my grandmother. I knew she worked for the Cheyenne and Arapaho Boarding School, also known as Concho School, but did not know in what position(s). My mother began to tell me more stories about my grandma and her commitment to education, while also sharing her own experiences in Indian Education throughout the years. This prompted deeper personal reflections about my own journey, helping me see the foundation they have laid for me to become a leader in Indian Education, as well. Generationally, our collective story moves from a dorm matron/teacher aide to a teacher aide/Indian Education Coordinator, and now an Executive Director of a Tribal Education Department (TED). Our journeys are connected and have come full circle, particularly as I work in the same building as my grandmother, but now under the authority of the Cheyenne and Arapaho Department of Education, and no longer a federal boarding school.

Indigenous Feminism

Feminism or the label feminist is considered a white woman's movement and is not for Indigenous women (Green, 2017). Lorelei Means states (as cited in Green, 2017), "We are *American Indian* women, in the order. We are oppressed, first and foremost, as American Indians, as peoples colonized by the United States of America, *not* as women" (p. 94). Although I see myself as a Cheyenne and Arapaho woman, I failed to see the intersectionality of my positionality. We are in fact Indigenous people first, but our issues as women are more unique than those of non-Native people. As I study Indigenous women's leadership and Indigenous Feminism, I am interested in women's stories and experiences.

I know my grandmother and mother would not identify as feminists, because I asked my mother and her response was, "I don't see myself like that." However, our lived experiences and stories are unique, and our definitions of leadership align with a community-based feminist framework applicable to Indigenous women. Mary Jo Tippeconnic Fox (2021) stated the difference between white women's feminism versus Indigenous feminism. Indigenous feminism is not the same because white women's feminism is about rights, whereas Indigenous feminism is about responsibilities (Fox, 2021). Our leadership is based on the need to serve and empower our Tribal communities, prioritizing Tribal sovereignty, empowering women, and addressing sexism. Through my grandmother, mother, and myself, education has been transformative in the way we see ourselves as leaders, how we give back, and carrying the responsibility of our families, communities, and tribes.

Indigenous women's leadership has evolved throughout history and their roles and responsibilities vary depending on their Native nation. For Cheyenne and Arapaho women, historically, their roles were divided by men and women. As described by Berthrong (1963), "and the women's share of the community's labor was care of the household and the welfare of the family" (p. 36). Women's role in leadership was to rule the camps, propel men to necessary duties, and check men when they lacked good judgment. Additionally, Killsback (2020) shares:

> Women's societies were also a part of the system, but they functioned as social and ceremonial organizations, rather than military. Today the society system remains with both the Northern and Southern Cheyenne Nations, but their roles have significantly diminished because of colonization, assimilation, and modernization. (p.141)

Although their roles and responsibilities can be misunderstood as not having much value compared to men, women have always influenced their Native nations and continue to do so.

Neiwoo (grandma). The TIPM framework lists an additive approach as Dimension 2 that deconstructs and changes structural colonial frameworks. In the additive stage the author explains, "practitioners try to decolonize themselves and make some progress in doing so, but these efforts and realizations are not yet followed by regular practice" (Pewewardy et al., 2018, p. 55). As a dorm matron and teacher aide, my grandmother began her journey in Indian Education as a practitioner at Riverside Indian School in Anadarko, Oklahoma, then again at Concho Indian School. My grandmother's role as a practitioner was to care for and protect the students and "begin to view children and communities through an asset-based perspective" (Pewewardy et al., 2018, p. 55).

My maternal grandmother lost her mother at the age of 12 to pneumonia. She also attended boarding school as a young girl but never spoke about her experiences with her children. She had made the declaration to her family, "I will never send my children to boarding school." This statement reflects the assertion by Pewewardy et al. (2018), "However, the American educational systems used varying tactics to destroy Indigenous cultures and languages while imposing new, primarily Eurocentric social structures" (p. 42). When she was a young woman, she attended Haskell in Lawrence, Kansas, when it was a vocational-technical institution. It was there that she learned to type, as were the duties of a secretary.

By the time she married my grandfather, my maternal grandmother began working for the Southern Ute Tribe in Towaoc, Colorado. They decided to return to Oklahoma where they found work at Riverside Indian School in Anadarko, Oklahoma. After some time, they transferred to the Concho Indian Agency where the Concho Indian School opened in 1908 (Mann, 1997). The Concho School was operated by the Bureau of Indian Affairs (BIA) and closed in 1983. My grandmother began as a dorm matron and eventually transitioned to become a teacher's aide.

During their time in Concho, Oklahoma, they raised four children: one daughter, Dara, and three sons, Virgil, Jr., Steven, and Paul. In addition to raising her family, she was also the wife of an Arapaho Chief. She was a strong and traditional woman who did not tell us how to be supportive—she showed us. How she spoke to people, how she prayed for others, how she prepared her food, how she prepared a giveaway, or how she honored others, there was a lesson every time. When we were at ceremonies, powwows, benefit dances, sweats, or family functions, she was always in charge and my grandpa, her children, and grandchildren followed suit.

My grandmother dedicated her adult life to serving American Indian/Alaska Native students, but primarily Cheyenne and Arapaho students who were unable to live with their families. Throughout the years she worked at Concho Indian School she opened her home to students who were unable to go home. She took them in, adopted them as her own, and served as a maternal figure for many. My grandmother was strong, wise, caring, and always put her family first. Reflecting on my time spent with her, I wish I had asked more questions, asked for more stories, and her life story. I am grateful for the impact she had on my life; she never failed to correct me and tell me how a young Cheyenne and Arapaho woman should conduct herself. Lastly, she would always say, "Never forget who you are and where you come from."

No'oo (mother). The TIPM framework provides Dimension 3, the transformative approach, which is defined as when "they have come to understand the need for decolonization and cultivate a hope for decolonizing the minds of others" (Pewewardy et al., 2018, p. 56). Most importantly, this stage sees the need for systemic change and ways to enact it. As a teacher aide who transitioned to a Director of Indian Education, my mother was instrumental in providing culturally responsive education in addition to acknowledging Cheyenne and Arapaho epistemologies.

Because my grandparents worked for the Concho Indian School, my mother was raised in Concho most of her life and attended Catholic school from kindergarten–6th grade. By the time she reached middle school she was integrated into the whitestream education system (Pewewardy et al., 2018) in El Reno, Oklahoma, where her parents realized that discrimination and racism were present. Also, my mother always says, "there was nothing for us to do in El Reno, girls couldn't play sports at the time, and I loved to play softball." A friend of hers attended Fort Sill Indian School in Lawton, Oklahoma, so she asked her parents if she could go to school there. Reluctantly, they said yes, but told her, "You won't last 2 weeks there."

After graduating from Fort Sill Indian School, several of her friends were planning on attending Haskell Junior College in Lawrence, Kansas. She did not graduate from Haskell but met some good people and enjoyed herself, which are reflected in the stories she shares with us. She received her associate's degree in Early Childhood Education from Redlands Community College years later. Shortly after, she began working for the Cheyenne and Arapaho Tribes Head Start Program in Concho.

When my mother had her own children, she decided to send them to a rural school that was near El Reno. Her experience reflects TIPM by Pewewardy et al. (2019), who state, "These community-based experiences made clear that school structures continue to uphold efforts of assimilation and exclude the knowledge and experiences of Indigenous children" (p. 41). As a result, my sister began at Riverside Public School and eventually my mother transferred her to Darlington Public School when she was in 2nd grade.

Darlington is a rural public school located between El Reno and Concho, about 5 miles north of El Reno. When I was in 1st grade my mother was offered a job by the Superintendent at Darlington as a teacher's aide. I used to think, *this is great, my mom works at my school!* Not so great when your mom knows everyone and everything. She began as an aide in my class and eventually transferred to the Director of Indian Education and has served in that position for the past 32 years. As an elementary and middle school student I was fortunate to attend a public school system that had a Director of Indian Education; even better, it was my mom. She would say, "You're just as good as the white kids," and she had high expectations for us to be good students and respectful to our teachers.

I was fortunate to have a parent who was engaged and committed to my growth as a student. It never occurred to me that some of my peers, the majority of whom were American Indian/Alaska Native (AI/AN), did not have that same guidance and support. For example, my basketball game days were always exciting days. All the girls in my grade liked to have their hair French braided. My mom would have all the girls come to her class and braid them all up. I would get stink and jealous because in those moments of her being a mother to my classmates, I wanted her all to myself. Or she would do the extra work and pick students up who did not have a ride to school, make sure they were fed, and would step in for a parent who was unable to make it to school activities.

The TIPM structure is meant to support educators in decolonizing and Indigenizing their practices as they develop their students' critical thinking skills (Pewewardy et al., 2018). Furthermore, TIPM asserts, "This in turn supports the collective engagement, critical thinking, healing, and cultural restoration in the improvement of school-based educational offerings in order to better serve all children, especially Indigenous children" (Pewewardy et al., 2018, p. 39). It was my mother's mission to provide equal opportunity for the Indigenous students who attended Darlington Public Schools. At the center of her teachings was her identity as a Cheyenne and Arapaho woman. At every opportunity she would assert our Tribal language, stories, history, and the importance of identity to her students. This was her way "to put something back into the community" (Pewewardy et al., 2018 p. 41).

Notoo (daughter). Tous (hello), my Arapaho name is Nanak'ate Hisea, which means Light or Yellow Hair Woman, and was given to me by my late maternal grandmother, Violet Berniece Franklin. I was named after my maternal great grandmothers, Carrie Youngbear and Frances Franklin. My daughter is named after her maternal great grandmother, Violet, and we are second-generation mother-daughter, Carrie and Violet. I am a proud citizen of the Cheyenne and Arapaho Tribes and am a descendent of the Kiowa and Creek Tribes as well. My late grandparents are Arapaho Chief Virgil Franklin, Sr., Geraldine Tallbull Morton, and William Whitlow. I am the daughter of Dara Franklin and Billy Whitlow and the younger sister of Stephanie Roman Nose and William Whitlow. My educational journey includes the Cheyenne and Arapaho Head Start, Darlington Public Schools, Calumet Public Schools, Haskell Indian Nations University (HINU), the University of Oklahoma (OU), and Kansas State University (K-State). I am currently a PhD student studying Educational Leadership and just completed my first year in the program. I currently serve as the Executive Director for the Cheyenne and Arapaho Department of Education (CADOE). It was never my intention to work in Indian Education or be an educator, but I believe this is where I am supposed to be.

My mother gives so much of herself to her students, families, and school district, yet I never understood the significance of her position in a public school system until I transferred to high school. Public school systems in Oklahoma are predominantly white as reflected in the student population, teachers, and administrators. Once I no longer had the comfort of being at a school district with all my cousins and my mother, my identity suffered. My white friends were liked and respected by the coaches, teachers, and administrators and I wanted to be like them. I wanted to be liked as well. Instead of asserting my identity and uniqueness, I began to conform to who my white friends were. I wore colored contacts, highlighted my hair very blonde, and wore clothes just like my friends. I also made it a point to never share about my Tribal identity and culture. What is extremely unfortunate in this situation is that my family did not raise me to be this way. My grandma always said, "Never forget who you are and where you come from." I did not realize it at the time, but I was suppressing my Cheyenne and Arapaho identity to be white, to be accepted, to be liked.

As an undergraduate student I chose to attend Haskell Indian Nations University (HINU) to pursue a degree in American Indian Studies (AIS). HINU is now a Tribal college and university (TCU). My grandmother, mother, and I have an HINU connection. For example, my grandmother attended Haskell Vocational-Technical Institution, my mother attended Haskell Junior College, and I attended Haskell Indian Nations University. Haskell is exactly what I needed as a student to further develop my intellectual, physical, and personal growth. To be immersed in an environment that counters every whitestream Eurocentric standard of education I was accustomed to was life changing. Haskell is an example of when "Indigenous peoples have attempted to rebuild their educational systems, which the U.S. government tried to destroy" (Pewewardy et al., 2018, p. 42).

Tribal Education Departments (TEDs)/Tribal Education Agencies (TEAs) are an important part of the Indigenous landscape, yet there is minimal literature on TEDs/TEAs beyond describing what they are, or outlining profiles of different departments, programs, or partnerships. In my position as a TED/TEA executive director it is my responsibility to assert our educational sovereignty for our Tribal students and families in "settler-design school systems" (Pewewardy et al., 2018, p. 38). Additionally, utilizing the TIPM framework, my work consists of Dimension 4: Cultural and Social Justice Action, which "represents critical consciousness followed by commitment and action" (Pewewardy et al., 2018, p. 57). It is my responsibility as a leader to actively transform our Tribal educational structures, pedagogy, and curriculum (Pewewardy et al., 2018) by remembering who we are and where we come from as Cheyenne and Arapaho people. By doing this, I am extending the collective story of the Cheyenne and Arapaho women who have created the conditions for me to be in this position of influence.

LESSONS OF INTERGENERATIONAL CONNECTIONS

All the lessons my grandmother and mother taught me over the years were about preparing me to be exactly where I am now. I know my grandmother and mother have set a path for me to follow as a Cheyenne and Arapaho woman leader as we continue to navigate mainstream social structures within our Tribal communities. Pewewardy, Lees, and Shim (2018) share the following:

> To decolonize and liberate Indigenous education, we need to move away from imperial narratives based on colonial framework and find ways for healing and rebuilding Indigenous education by restoring Indigenous consciousness and languages so that we can create bridges between Indigenous and European knowledge bases. (p. 51)

As Cheyenne and Arapaho women leaders we continue to be critically conscious of our own experiences while being a bridge between Eurocentric and Tribal communities by serving as educators, advocates, and leaders.

How do you measure the impact or outcome your leadership had on students and families? Respect. I remember my grandmother receiving endless visits to her home by Tribal members or family members passing through. They often request-ed prayer, support, guidance, or sometimes they just wanted to visit. I see the same form of respect being displayed in my mother's home, family members now re-questing prayers and support from my mom. *Sometimes even at our local Walmart.*

CONCLUSION

This chapter has required the process shared by Pewewardy et al. (2018): "As we re-flect within ourselves and invest more into our Tribal communities, we increasing-ly use decolonizing analytical frameworks to help us tell our Tribal stories of who we are on our own terms as cultural beings" (p. 49). What has been transformative in our collective intergenerational narrative is our jobs, duties, and titles; but what has remained constant is who we are as Cheyenne and Arapaho women and our responsibility to our community. We continue, as women, to be centered in our traditional way of life and our intent to serve our Tribal communities, students, and families. Throughout the years, systems of education have tried to assimi-late American Indian and Alaska Native students and ultimately steal our identity. Through our cultural learning systems and traditions found outside of Eurocentric schools, we have been able to maintain our Tribal identities while growing as edu-cators, leaders, and scholars.

REFERENCES

Berthrong, D. J. (1963). *The southern Cheyennes.* University of Oklahoma Press.

Fox, M. J. (2021). *Native American women: Political leaders of the 21st century* [Webinar]. Amer-ind Online Programs. https://youtu.be/NUY0uREeXZo

Grande, S. (2015). *Red pedagogy: Native American social and political thought.* Rowman & Littlefield.

Green, J. (2007). *Making space for Indigenous feminism.* Fernwood Publishing.

Killsback, L. K. (2020). *A sacred people: Indigenous governance, traditional leadership, and the warriors of the Cheyenne nation.* Texas Tech University Press.

Mann, H. (1997). *Cheyenne-Arapaho education 1871–1982.* University of Colorado Press.

Pewewardy, C. D., Lees, A., & Clark-Shim, H. (2018). The Transformational Indigenous Praxis Model: Stages for developing critical consciousness in Indigenous education. *Wičazo Ša Review, 33*(1), 38–69. https://doi.org/10.5749/wicazosareview.33.1.0038

Sabzalian, L. (2019). *Indigenous children's survivance in public schools.* Routledge.

Our Collective Closing

As is tradition in book formats, we understand that a closing of it must take place. When we dreamed of how this could unfold, we wanted to hold true to our Indigenous values and have a collective conversation about Unsettling Settler-Colonial Education and how we can enact and dream of our Indigenous futures for our children, grandchildren, and future generations. Below, we present the process for our collective conversation, the message and voices, and present a song that brings the people together.

THE PROCESS OF OUR COLLECTIVE CONVERSATION

In an effort to bring everyone together for a collective closing of this book we organized a collective conversation in June 2021. We invited all collaborators to join us in this Zoom gathering in which we held a conversation with each other to dream the future of what TIPM can hold for us and for our future relatives and Indigenous education. What is presented below are pieces of these conversations presented in themes that center our collective voices and conversation.

OUR COLLECTIVE MESSAGE AND VOICES

In our collective conversation, themes arose within the sentiments shared by collaborators. Throughout the discussion, we heard commitments to (1) acts of decolonization and Indigenous reclamation, (2) land recognition and relationships with land, and (3) intentional movement toward healing. We forward the voices of contributors here and close this book with song to share our collective message as editors and collaborators. Opening our time together, we shared these thoughts as editors to begin the dialogue:

> "I think we wanted to have an open opportunity to discuss and dialogue about how we can dream about our future."
> "It's just really powerful having everybody together. To make those connections across our work feels like that's good work in and of itself."

ACTS OF DECOLONIZATION AND
INDIGENOUS RECLAMATION

Throughout our collective conversation, discussion of decolonization and reclamation threaded through the voices of collaborators. As the discussion was framed around the varying ways collaborators took up the TIPM in their chapters, decolonization and reclamation were shared efforts toward Indigenous futures. The quotes below are representative of the discussion:

"In some ways, this book is the antidote, you know, education was used as a weapon against Indigenous children and against us. In some ways we flip that script. So now we're weaponizing education, but to strengthen our community."

"I've always thought about the metaphorically and how Indigenous education has been a double-edged sword. Looking at that sharp side, how is the United States or the settler-colonial systems trying to destroy our culture and our language using school systems? Here we are on the other side of that sharp blade, using Indigenous resurgence theory made coming back and using the same sword for that edge, that purpose."

"It's interesting the way people have different versions and relationships to the state and what that means. People we'd see as the most vulnerable, as the most impacted by the state are actually the most resilient, because their hopes and dreams and desires aren't defined by that state."

"Settler colonialism is so entrenched."

"One of the things that really struck out to me was this concept of enduring indigeneity."

"I just think that that is something that could be a movement among our Tribal colleges to move in that direction, to then be able to fully realize the type of institution they want to be outside of that settler-colonial perspective. But to be able to do that too, they have to internally decolonize themselves."

"It's all about decolonization."

"How can we think about the long game and how we need to influence so many?"

"We must decolonize ourselves on our own terms, without the sanction and permission of the settler state . . . I might not know them all consciously, but they're in there."

"It wasn't just, you were putting the stories out there. We were also providing a context for how we want the stories read and that invitation I found really powerful."

"Like my mom says, take it own it and claim it. We know how to teach our people. We know how to pass down teachings. So how do we incrementally reclaim space in our institutions?"

"One of the things that jumped out at me was how we lift each other up and
we are lifted by others as well. Honoring our Elders and ensuring that we
focus on our Elders when we write and cite them as well."

"I call it the anti-trickster level to get to Dimension 4, but here we are people
that have already done that. They are genius. We are genius people, and
we can do this."

LAND RECOGNITION AND RELATIONS WITH LAND

As collaborators shared commitments to decolonizing and reclaiming Indigenous
education for thriving futures, they also shared the importance of land recognition
and reciprocal relations with land and more-than-human relatives. They discussed
the importance of this for themselves as mostly Indigenous scholars and the ways
that took form in their teaching and research:

"It's not how you recognize the land. It's how does the land recognize
you? . . . It's transforming that relationship to the land and the water, of
course, in all of those, all of those beings that we have relations to."

"Resurgence theory for me is really closely aligned with Stage 4. . . . I focus
so much in my work on everyday acts of resurgence. It's those everyday
things that we do, that we do in Stage 4."

"walking the land and I added it's walking the land in silence and inviting
people to walk the land in silence, and they have to share what they see,
what they hear, what they smell, what they taste . . . it's having them walk
in silence. And what are they seeing? What are those six senses telling
them about leadership? What's the land teaching now?"

"How will our Ancestors recognize us in terms of our actions, in terms of
our Indigeneity, and then also, how will future generations recognize us?"

"the land that, as part of our teachers, and we lift up the land as much as the
land lifts us up."

"They will actually be on Tribal lands taking their doctoral coursework . . .
thinking about how healing that is whenever you're able to have that. I
never took my doctoral classes on Tribal lands. And so I can imagine how
empowering that would be to be able to do that."

INTENTIONAL MOVEMENT TOWARD HEALING

Finally, and perhaps bringing the first two themes together, our collective conversation emphasized the importance of making intentional movement toward healing. Collaborators shared challenges faced in the work and the violence endured
through colonization, and strongly asserted that we must find ways to heal as a
responsibility to the generations before and those to come:

"There's that intergenerational grief that you're dealing with."

"I just close my eyes and I travel backwards and try to heal that time and just sit with, you know, my grandpas and grandmas and just, and listen to their words in Kiowa, Comanche, and just, and be with them at that time."

"not lose sight of what it is that we know should be our current realities and how we balance that in the everyday work"

"That Dimension 4 is an active resistance of what the settler state expects of us every single day. But everything my grandma protected is thousands of years old. And that's just as present. I've just been so conditioned to not pay attention to it."

"There's these things in that ceremony that have been in front of me my entire life that I see on a routine basis annually year after year, and then I'm 36 years old and I go, oh, that's actually deeper than I thought."

"So as we come together where we're doing the Elonshka, the wave jumping, we're doing the Ton-Kon-Gah, we're doing the rabbit, we're doing all the ceremonies that we are, because we're doing it together. We're teaching each other."

"Our people have always been wave jumpers. All we have to do is look at the resiliency and strength of our Ancestors. And when you think about the future, we also have to bring with us the work that our Ancestors laid for us. They didn't just leave us here, just for us to have our way, they had intentions for us. So we have to go back and listen to our hearts, listen to our Elders. What were those intentions that they wanted us to carry forward? And they have intentions for their grandchildren's grandchildren."

"We could all come together and we can dance together. We can parade in together. Processional just be, just be as one. I would love to see that day happen. I would like that way we could share not only your voice or stories, but with the people that are close to us."

"The medicine is in the song, it's the medicine in the book. And I think that we try to carry that out inside."

THE SONG HOLDS THE PEOPLE TOGETHER

Foundation of the Song (QR Code)

This book reclaims Indigenous ways of knowing, expands Indigenous voice and vision, and affirms Indigenous educational praxis and relationship-based pedagogy by presenting a model for decolonizing educational structures and individuals. The examples of pathway-making depict opportunities for creating space for Indigenous self-determination and sovereignty in public schools and higher education institutions. One cultural marker identified for including in our collective closing was a traditional song, especially a personal, traditional song. It was decided to develop a QR code for listening to the song as well as providing an explanatory text to describe the story of the song. Indigenous music and songs hold our people together.

We offer this song to the readers and to honor the spirit of this book, its collaborators, our communities, and Ancestors.

Interpretation of the Comanche Beloved Song
(Composed and translated by Dr. Cornel Pewewardy)

Beloved, beautiful and courageous people
You are so resilient given a difficult pathway
We raise our voice and call in an awakening of
  collaboration and unity of our people
We have to remain who we are.

Afterword
Decolonizing Futurities North of the 49th Parallel

Michael Yellow Bird (Mandan, Hidatsa, Arikara Nation)

I want to begin by offering my congratulations to the authors and editors of this volume for this impressive and generative body of critical essays. Each, in different ways, embraces the Transformational Indigenous Praxis Model (Pewewardy et al., 2018) as an analytical guide to gauge the efforts necessary to Indigenize and decolonize settler intellectual spaces in the systems of western education. A quote from Frantz Fanon's book, *A Dying Colonialism* (1994), appears to be an appropriate aphorism for what is happening in the academy due to a resurgent Indigenous intellectualism that continues to escalate through the incorporation of Indigenous ways of being, knowing, doing, and relationality: "It is the white man who creates the Negro. But the Negro who creates Negritude." To the same degree, it is westernism that created the Indian. But the Indigenous scholar who is creating a post-western world.

I have been in my present position as dean and professor of the Faculty of Social Work at the University of Manitoba since July 2019 and have felt very privileged to be here at this remarkable yet unsettling time in history. My experience has given me hope and the confidence that a decolonized futurity in western education is possible. A number of amazing initiatives and actions are being carried out every day on our campus that reflect our university's commitment and willingness to engage in the processes of institutional decolonization and Indigenization. What is occurring at my institution did not happen overnight; a number of key events had to be set in motion before our university was prepared to engage in this challenging work.

What does it take to decolonize and Indigenize western systems of education? My own academic journey has helped me understand how this came about in my present institution. In 1992, as I was completing my PhD at the University of Wisconsin–Madison, I was fortunate to be hired and appointed to the faculty in the School of Social Work at the University of British Columbia (UBC), Vancouver, Canada. During my time at UBC (1992–1994), important social and political changes were occurring in Canada that formed the bases of decolonization and Indigenization. In 1991, following the Oka Crisis, a land dispute between the Mohawk and the town of Oka, Quebec, Canada, The Royal Commission on

Aboriginal Peoples was established "to investigate and propose solutions to the challenges affecting the relationship between Aboriginal peoples (First Nations, Inuit, Métis Nation), the Canadian government and Canadian society as a whole" (Royal Commission on Aboriginal Peoples, n.d.). Around the same time the first Women's Memorial March was held in Vancouver, BC, to bring attention to missing and murdered women and to create awareness and build support for a national inquiry and response. This annual consciousness raising was one of the early precursors to the present-day Missing and Murdered Indigenous Women's (MMIW) movement. The early 1990s was also a time when a national dialogue was taking off regarding the appalling and shameful effects that government and religious sponsored residential schools had had on Indigenous Peoples.

Important events and national dialogues about Canada's sordid past treatment of Indigenous Peoples continued over the years. By 2006, the *Indian Residential Schools Settlement Agreement,* the largest class action in Canadian history, was drafted to recognize that "Canada and certain religious organizations operated Indian Residential Schools for the education of aboriginal children and certain harms and abuses were committed against those children" (*Indian Residential Schools Settlement Agreement,* 2006, p. 6). One of the major achievements of The Indian Residential Schools Agreement was the establishment of the Truth and Reconciliation Commission (TRC) in 2007, which "provided those directly or indirectly affected by the legacy of the Indian Residential Schools system with an opportunity to share their stories and experiences" (*Truth and Reconciliation Commission of Canada,* n.d., p. 1).[1] In 2008, Prime Minister Stephen Harper offered a formal apology on behalf of Canada over residential schools. In 2010, Canada signed onto the United Nations Declaration on the Rights of Indigenous Peoples. In 2017, Prime Minister Justin Trudeau offered an apology to survivors of five residential schools who were left out in the 2008 national apology. In 2021, the Prime Minister again offered an apology for the "incredibly harmful" government policies after hundreds of unmarked graves were discovered at the former Marieval Indian Residential School in Saskatchewan.

By 2015, the Government of Canada had spent $72 million to support the work of the TRC, which collected stories from more than 6,500 witnesses. It hosted seven national events to "engage the Canadian public, educate people about the history and legacy of residential schools, and honour the experiences of former students and their families" (*Truth and Reconciliation Commission of Canada,* n.d.). The TRC report identified 94 calls to action to "redress the legacy of residential schools and advance the process of Canadian reconciliation."

I believe the above events and actions were crucial for providing a means for my institution to engage in strategic priorities to include decolonization and Indigenization in our university's 2015–2020 strategic plan and goals. In the opening statement of our strategic plan, the president declared that our university will be "the national centre of excellence in Indigenous education, and in particular to allow Indigenous students to be prepared for and to achieve educational success in the full range of academic programs we provide." There are a number of strategic priorities that specifically target goals for Indigenous students, staff, and faculty, but I will only point out a few due to limits on the length of my afterword.[2] One priority compels us to "Identify options to ensure that Indigenous content is included in academic programs." Another stipulates that we "Provide educational opportunities for academic staff members to ensure they can incorporate Indigenous knowledge in their areas." Still another priority orders us to "Foster the inclusion of Indigenous perspectives in research, scholarly work, and other creative activities."

Since my arrival at the University of Manitoba, I have been involved in numerous working groups that have been involved with finding ways to fulfill the priorities of our strategic plan by implementing many of the TRC calls to action. Commitment to the work has happened at all levels including the participation of students, staff, community members, Elders, faculty, and the senior executive leadership (president, vice-presidents, provost and vice-provosts, deans, and directors). A major accomplishment has been the hiring of a Vice-President (Indigenous) at our university. This office "leads the development and implementation of a university-wide strategy that promotes reconciliation, advances UM's commitment to Indigenous engagement and achievement through initiatives, programs, curriculum, and research and addresses anti-Indigenous racism." The Vice-President (Indigenous) position was approved by the Board of Governors as a first step in implementing our commitment to Indigenous engagement and reconciliation, with an expectation that a Vice-President (Indigenous) would be appointed as soon as possible to begin the implementation process. Priority One of the office calls for increasing Indigenous representation in university governance and executive and senior leadership in our university.

In my own role as dean of the Faculty of Social Work, I have been working with our faculty, staff, students, Elders, knowledge holders, and community members, to completely revise our Bachelor of Social Work curriculum. One of our major course domains focuses on Indigenous decolonization and reconciliation and includes courses in Indigenous relationality, Indigenization and decolonization in social work, methods for reconciliation, land-based practices, treaties, and Indigenous knowledges. At the university level, I am a member of Faculty Partners for Reconciliation that was convened by the Vice-President (Indigenous) as Priority Three of the office. Our role is to work with all university faculties to (1) assist them to create their own Reconciliation Action Plan to address the TRC Calls to Action, (2) ensure that all deans and faculty committees have Indigenous representation, (3) work with deans so that they meet regularly with Indigenous faculty leaders who guide the TRC implementation in our institution, (4) help faculties to establish their own Indigenous Elder-in-residence, and (5) assist in the development of required faculty-specific Indigenous training for all staff and faculty. In the meetings and working group sessions that I have attended, I have been fascinated and encouraged as I have listened to my non-Indigenous colleagues regularly engage in discussions and analyses about settler colonialism, white supremacy, the TRC's calls to action, and the futurities of reconciliation, decolonization, and Indigenization.

A decolonized and Indigenized futurity in western education does not have to be a dream. Canada had to go through its own critical self-examination and accept the truth of what has happened to Indigenous Peoples due to the policies of the Church and Canadian government. There have been open, public, national apologies that acknowledge the harms done and an acceptance of responsibility by political leaders. But make no mistake, many past and present events have helped contribute to the changes that are happening. The major drivers of change are Indigenous leaders, communities, and settler allies who continue to remind Canada that reconciliation requires truth, accountability, and action. How can decolonized futurities in education happen in the United States? The United States has to go through its own self-examination and accept responsibility for its atrocities against Indigenous Peoples. Making land acknowledgments, as has become very popular these days, will do very little to change the consciousness of Americans. The establishment of a national Truth and Reconciliation Commission (TRC) in the United States is critical if there is to be any chance of a decolonized futurity. To the authors of this book, I say keep writing, keep resisting, keep creating, keep speaking out, and keep singing. Your work in Indigenization and decolonization waters the seeds of transformation, making possible a futurity of truth, justice, and reconciliation in U.S. western settler education.

NOTES

1. To understand the full scope of the TRC and its calls to action, it's important to read the entire report, especially the Terms of Reference and goals in Schedule "N": https://www.residentialschoolsettlement.ca/SCHEDULE_N.pdf

2. The complete document, *Taking Our Place: University of Manitoba Strategic Plan, 2015–2020*, can be found at https://umanitoba.ca/sites/default/files/2020-06/um-strategic-plan-2015-2020.pdf.

REFERENCES

Fanon, F. (1994). *A dying colonialism*. Grove Press.

Indian Residential Schools Agreement. (2006). https://www.residentialschoolsettlement.ca/IRS%20Settlement%20Agreement%20ENGLISH.pdf

Pewewardy, C. D., Lees, A., & Clark-Shim, H. (2018). The Transformational Indigenous Praxis Model: Stages for developing critical consciousness in Indigenous education. *Wíčazo Ša Review*, *33*(1), 38–69. https://doi.org/10.5749/wicazosareview.33.1.0038

Royal Commission on Aboriginal Peoples. (n.d.). *Report of the Royal Commission on Aboriginal Peoples*. Library and Archives Canada. https://www.bac-lac.gc.ca/eng/discover/aboriginal-heritage/royal-commission-aboriginal-peoples/Pages/final-report.aspx

Truth and Reconciliation Commission of Canada. (n.d.). Government of Canada. https://rcaanc-cirnac.gc.ca/eng/1450124405592/1529106060525#chp1

About the Contributors

Brandon Join Alik (Marshallese/Rilujennamu clan) is the eldest son of Eldon Alik (from Jaluit atoll) and Anita Jatios (from Elip atoll) of Marshall Islands, Rilujennamu clan. Born in Portland and raised in Tigard, Oregon, he is a first-generation Marshallese American. Brandon has anthropology and psychology degrees from PSU, and is an MSW student.

Geneva Becenti (Diné) is a citizen of the Diné Nation. Her scholarship focuses on policies related to K–12 Native American languages in public schools. She is an advocate for Native American language and cultural teachers and serves communities. Geneva continues to mentor her former students and assist her relatives in higher education.

Dolores Calderón (Mexican/Tigua) is an associate professor at Fairhaven College of Interdisciplinary Studies at Western Washington University. As a researcher who embodies the complicated subjectivities of the U.S./Mexico border—Mexican (arrivant/immigrant), Indigenous (Pueblo), and U.S. citizen—she is interested in researching and participating in work that untangles and unpacks the complicated way multiple colonialisms impact decolonial practices in education.

Hyuny Clark-Shim (Korean citizen) was born and raised in Paju-Si, South Korea, and arrived on the Indigenous Land of the United States in 2007. She is currently a doctoral student at Portland State University. Her research interest is an intersection of epistemologies and equity for Indigenous and immigrant populations.

Jeff Corntassel (citizen of the Cherokee Nation) is an associate professor of Indigenous studies at the University of Victoria. His research and teaching interests focus on "Everyday Acts of Resurgence," Indigenous self-determination, and community well-being. Jeff is currently completing work for his forthcoming book on sustainable self-determination, which examines Indigenous climate justice, food security, and gender-based resurgence.

Melissa Cournia (Settler) is an instructional coach at Bismarck High School and serves on school, district, and state leadership teams. She is Nationally Board Certified and has a master's degree in middle level education; her teaching experience ranges across math and literacy grades 6–12.

Anthony B. Craig (Yakama Nation) is a professor of practice and director of the Leadership for Learning (EdD) Program at the University of Washington. His main interests center on the expansive power of what happens when leaders and school systems transform when Indigenous communities and Indigenous knowledges are centered.

Chelsea M. Craig (Tulalip Tribes) is a cultural specialist and school administrator in her community of Tulalip Tribes. She has served her community as an educator and mentor for over 2 decades. Her passion is in shaping learning spaces that are liberating for our Ancestors and for young people yet to come. Anthony and Chelsea live in Tulalip surrounded by their four children and grandson.

Brenda Cruz Jaimes (Latina/Mexican) was born in Guanajuato, Mexico, and migrated to the United States. Brenda became a DACA recipient and is the first in her family to attend college. With BSW and MSW degrees, Brenda is currently the associate director of diversity, equity, and inclusion (DEI) at a private Catholic high school.

Austin Delos Santos (Chamorro; Pacific Islander/Commonwealth of the Northern Mariana Islands) is a Portland State University graduate in community development. As a Chamorro, he understands the need to de-escalate situations through gentle personalism and acknowledging the hidden issues so we can heal from all forms of trauma. In his free time, Austin enjoys spending time with family and barbecuing.

Virginia Drywater-Whitekiller (enrolled member of the United Keetoowah Band of Cherokee Indians) is a professor of social work whose research interests are situated around the strengths-based cultural resilience of Indigenous peoples, particularly as pertaining to higher education retention and child welfare.

Sherry Gobaleza (Pinay/Buhay clan in the Philippines) is a graduate of transpersonal psychology at Naropa Graduate School of Psychology. Living in Michigan with her spouse, Erica, and their dogs, she has devoted her life to working with marginalized communities. She considers it a sacred duty to answer the call of the Ancestors; that is kapwa in action.

Dawn Hardison-Stevens, PhD (Omushkeg Cree-Métis, Ojibway, Cowlitz descendant, enrolled Steilacoom, and council member), is a teaching associate at the University of Washington's K–12 teacher education program, American Indian Studies Department, and Native Education Certificate Program and also program manager. She focuses leadership, professional development, and educational pathways promoting Indigenous knowledge representation, plus cultivates Native people's academic success advocating intergenerational teaching and learning.

Jeanette Haynes Writer (Tsalagi, Cherokee Nation citizen) is professor of curriculum and instruction and an affiliated faculty member with Borderlands and Ethnic Studies at New Mexico State University. Her areas of scholarship include Tribal Critical Race Theory; critical multicultural and social justice education; Indigenous education; Native American identity; and teacher education.

Anna Lees (Waganakasing Odawa, descendant) is an associate professor of early childhood education. Anna works to sustain reciprocal relationships with Indigenous communities, opening spaces for Indigenous values and ways of knowing and being in early childhood and higher education. She engages research around land education and curriculum development with Indigenous early learning programs.

Hollie J. Mackey (Northern Cheyenne) is an enrolled member of the Northern Cheyenne Nation and associate professor at North Dakota State University. Her scholarship empirically examines structural inequity of Indigenous and other marginalized populations in educational leadership and public policy through multiple critical frameworks and methodologies.

Ann Jeline Manabat (Asian with Filipino roots; Pacific Islander/Commonwealth of the Northern Mariana Islands) is from Saipan, Commonwealth of the Northern Mariana Islands. She has a bachelor's degree in public health studies in pre-clinical health sciences from PSU, and will start the master of public health in health promotion to address public health concerns in Asian and Pacific Islander populations.

Robin Zape-tah-hol-ah Minthorn (Kiowa citizen and descendant of the Apache/Umatilla/Nez Perce/Assiniboine Nations) is an associate professor, director of the educational leadership doctoral program, and director of Indigenous education initiatives for the School of Education at the University of Washington Tacoma. Her research interests include Indigenous leadership, Indigenous based doctoral experiences, Native American sororities, and Indigenous motherhood in the academy.

yahnesuarʉ mohatsi (Comanche and Kiowa) is a citizen of the Comanche Nation and works in K–12 education with Tribal, state, and nonprofit leadership experience. His areas of scholarship include Tribal–state consultation policy with a special emphasis on meaningful collaboration. He facilitates work around state academic standards, curriculum development, and instructional design.

Tahlia Natachu (Zuni) is the youth development coordinator for Zuni Youth Enrichment Project, a 501(c)(3) in Zuni, New Mexico, where she helps to promote resilience among Zuni youth so they can grow into strong and healthy adults who are connected to their culture.

Cornel Pewewardy (Comanche/Kiowa) is the vice-chairman of the Comanche Nation and professor emeritus, Indigenous Nations studies, at Portland State University. His research explores the theoretical and philosophical foundations of postcolonial Indigenous research paradigms that focus on historical and political insight into the lingering impact of colonization faced by Indigenous peoples today.

Alex RedCorn (ꟄꞧꝛꞏꟅ/Osage) serves as an assistant professor of educational leadership at Kansas State University. His scholarship and service are focused on Indigenous research methodologies and building capacities for Native Nations to take on a more prominent role in the education of their citizens.

Sashay Schettler (Mandan, Hidatsa, and Arikara Nation) is a citizen of the MHA Nation and the Indigenous education director at Bismarck Public Schools. She is a McNair scholar, and is pursuing her master's degree in educational leadership. Her work explores the contemporary construction of Indigenous identity, Indigenous education, and advocating for the seven generations behind and ahead of us.

Shawn Secatero (Canoncito Band of Navajo) is a member of the Canoncito Band of Navajo and serves as an associate professor at the University of New Mexico. His scholarship focuses on holistic-based Indigenous leadership, dual enrollment, wellness, and higher education.

Alma M. Ouanesisouk Trinidad (Pinay/Paoay, Ilocos Norte, Philippines; Molokai, Kingdom of Hawai'i) is an associate professor and the Bachelor of Social Work program director/chair at PSU, School of Social Work. Her areas of scholarship, teaching, practice, and service include critical pedagogues of place, anti-oppressive and liberatory social work, social movements, and macro social work (e.g., organizations, policies, and community).

Carrie F. Whitlow (Cheyenne and Arapaho, Kiowa, Creek) is a citizen of the Cheyenne and Arapaho Tribes. Her Arapaho name is Nanak'ate Hisea, Light or Yellowhair Woman, passed on from her grandmother Violet Berniece Franklin. Carrie is a doctoral student at Kansas State University pursuing a PhD in educational leadership.

Verónica Nelly Vélez (Mexican/Panamanian) is an associate professor of secondary education and education and social justice at Western Washington University. Her research focuses on Latinx im/migrant mother activism, community-based participatory action research in grassroots contexts, popular education, and (re)imagining cartographic tools for movement building and critical inquiry.

Natalie Rose Youngbull (Cheyenne & Arapaho/Assiniboine & Sioux) is an assistant professor of adult and higher education. She engages in research around experiences of American Indian Gates Millennium Scholars (AIGMS), Native/Indigenous student success, Native Nation building, and intellectual leadership and capacity building within TCUs.

Index

Brower, B. C., 124
Brown, S., 50
Bucceri, J. M., 105
Burant, T., 64
Bureau of Indian Education (BIE), 150, 168
Burnette, C. E., 100

Cajete, G., 57, 78, 100, 104, 137, 139, 163, 182
Calderón, D., 49, 50, 51, 52, 138
Canada, Indigenous Peoples in, 103–105
  decolonial futurities for, 207–208
  residential schools for, 1–2, 125, 208, 210n1
Capodilupo, C. M., 105
Cappello, M., 50
Cardinal, S. W., 100
Carey, M. P., 129
Carroll, K. K., 127
Carver-Thomas, D., 78
Castagno, A. E., 90, 93
Champagne, D., 106
Chandler, D., 77
Chang, H., 161
Chiarotto, L., 64
"Chief Wahoo" incident, 68–70
  TIPM in handling of, 71, 72–74
Christian identity, white privilege and, 71–72
Christman, D., 182
Civilization Fund Act, 15
Clark, C. B., 100
Clark, F., 17
Clark-Shim, H., 3, 5, 16, 47, 61, 74, 91, 94, 98,
    99, 102, 136, 146, 150, 151, 152, 157, 167,
    169–170, 174, 193, 194, 195, 196, 197, 198,
    199, 200, 207
Clayton, K., 51
Coast Salish traditional teachings, 26, 27–35
Cognitive imperialism, 157, 173
Coleman, C. L., 126–127
Coley, J. D., 127
Collaboration
  across Indigenous educational communities,
    7–9
  culturally responsive/relationship-based, 42–43
  for decolonial future, 7–9, 65
  lack of, policymakers/administrators and, 39
  process/themes in, 201–205
  Title VI funding and, 41–42
Collectives, developing and working in, 32–33
Comay, J., 64
Community
  consciousness-building in, 184–185
  land-based pedagogies/learning and, 101–102,
    184–185
  microaggressions and, 105–106, 108
  needs and strengths assessment, 185–186

participation in policy arena, 38–39, 188
  reciprocity and, 184–185, 188–189
  values and pride in, instilling, 137, 138–140
  ways of being, 181–182
Community-wide learners, 137, 138–140
Concho Indian School, 191, 193, 194, 196
Consciousness
  community, 184–185
  critical, 2, 3, 7, 20–24, 125–126
  dysconsciousness and, 124, 131n1, 158
  land-based, 106–107
Content, Indigenous-informed, 48–53, 135–136,
    151
Contributions approach (TIPM dimension), 2,
    4–5
  in Corn Pollen model, 170–172
  Eurocentrism and, unlearning, 79, 82
  in faculty/teacher development, 48–49,
    122–123
Cook-Lynn, E., 70–71
Corn Pollen model, 170–174, 177–178
Corntassel, J., 99, 100, 101, 104
Costantino, M., 50
Coulthard, G., 58, 100, 101, 128
Council for the Accreditation of Educator
    Preparation, 72
Craig, A., 30
Creation stories, 182–183, 189
Critical consciousness, 2, 3, 7, 20–24
  study groups, 2, 7, 125–126
Critical Indigenous Pedagogy of Place (CIPP),
    114
Critical Indigenous Research Methodologies
    (CIRM), 48, 58–59
Critical self-reflexivity, 115
"Critically conscious collective efficacy," 53
Cross, T. L., 127, 170
Cultural and social justice action (TIPM
    dimension), 6, 7
  in Corn Pollen model, 174–177
  Diné Paradigm and, 21, 22
  in doctoral programs, 189
  kincentricity, 128–130
  in TCU faculty development, 90–91
  in teacher education programs, 52–53
Cultural resilience
  focus group/interview findings, 103–104
  isolation and, 106–107
  microaggressions and, 105–106, 108
  theory of, 100–101, 103
  U.S. and Canada similarities, 104–105
Culture(s)
  navigating, 137, 140–142
  protection/restoration of, 3, 78, 164
Curammeng, E., 52